THE CHILDREN OF LOVERS

The Children of Lovers

A memoir of William Golding
by his daughter

JUDY GOLDING

faber and faber

First published in 2011
by Faber and Faber Ltd
Bloomsbury House
74–77 Great Russell Street
London WC1B 3DA

Typeset by Faber and Faber Ltd
Printed in England by CPI Mackays, Chatham

A CIP record for this book
is available from the British Library

ISBN 978-0-571-27340-9

2 4 6 8 10 9 7 5 3 1

For Viggo

The children of lovers, says the proverb, are orphans

Contents

The Way We Were

Annoyingly, for a family as superstitious as the Goldings, it was Friday the fourteenth.

We had set sail the day before from Shoreham in Sussex, my parents and me and three friends. But David, my elder brother, was not with us. He and my father had agreed that the two of them were not getting on well enough. Usually in a boat, both of them happy and absorbed, they could bury their differences. Not that time.

It was July 1967. I had just taken my degree at Sussex University. Among much else, our boat contained my degree certificate as well as the outfit my mother Ann had worn at the graduation ceremony (pale blue silk jersey; a dramatic, wide-brimmed hat). We also had with us the slim green Olivetti on which my father had typed *Lord of the Flies*. A year or so earlier, he had bought himself a new machine, and given me the old one so I could type my essays. And, as well, there was a notebook in which he had started writing something new, something promising.

They had bought *Tenace* a year earlier. Her name was French, as in 'audace', but she was Dutch, a racing barge, expensively varnished to a deep amber colour and with canvas sails of tawny red. Compared to our previous boats, she was comically luxurious, with a reliable diesel engine, a shower, three cabins, and lavish trimmings of wood, brass, and copper. She had an enormous pair of thick, varnished leeboards, and she went like anything to windward. My father was full of joy and guilt, a habitual mixture for him. Success, that supposedly hollow thing, had brought him the boat he really wanted.

But for both my parents *Tenace* was also something else. After a difficult time in the mid sixties, problems with their children and griefs about each other, they hoped they had turned the corner. They were going sailing again, another voyage in their personal tradition. This time, however, they were going first class.

Now, with hindsight, I see that all the ingredients were there for the day's events – at least, they were in a literary way. If I were making it up, that's how I would begin.

In spite of a morning mist, there was a breeze, and *Tenace* was nipping along. You could hear her rippling through the water. I even began to revise my long-held opinion that sailing was both boring *and* frightening. My father went below, leaving my mother at the tiller. He feared *Tenace*'s speed might make her take on water. He organised bailing.

But then my mother cried out in terror.

'Bill!'

He rushed back up on deck. Impossibly, the grey mist ahead was thickening. It became a sharp grey triangle. Then it became a cliff. It was the bow of an enormous ship, fifty, sixty, seventy feet above us. There was no time for fear – I remember my mind seemed washed clean of it. But it was not a simple situation. It was vital, truly a matter of life and death, to obey the rules. We were sailing, so we had right of way; but we would lose that right of way if we took avoiding action. Even worse, there would be confusion. If they gave way to us, as the law of the sea dictated, and changed course to avoid us, and at the same time we altered course as well, we might then again be heading for collision. We must decide. In that meagre handful of seconds, my father must decide. We did not even know if they had seen us, and the ship came on at appalling speed, unbelievably fast, inevitably, ruthlessly it seemed.

My friend from university, who knew nothing of ships or sailing, started to come on deck, to see what the fuss was about. I told her to stay below. I thought she would be less frightened there. But another friend, wiser than I, silently beckoned her up. Seconds later, when collision was imminent, my father put *Tenace* about, just in time, as the law of the sea permits. The great knife-like shape struck us a glancing blow, casually splitting *Tenace*'s fender-like wooden rubbing-strake, and tearing away the wire shrouds and rigging from the mast, like a hand brushing away a cobweb. We bumped and clanged messily along the sheer metal side. Then I saw a man run along the edge of the huge ship, screaming hysterically down at us. I saw that he was small and thin, with dark hair – Chinese or Japanese. I found I was on the cabin top. I had walked towards the approaching ship, as if I was curious.

The boom – the piece of timber along the bottom of the sail – began to swing loosely and menacingly, like a mad animal, but not from the wind. All the wind had vanished. We were in the lee of the ship that hit us. But once we were no longer shielded by her bulk, the wind would pull on the sail again, and without the starboard shrouds – the wire cables that run from the masthead to the sides of the boat to provide support – the mast, that forty, fifty feet of timber, would snap under the strain, possibly killing someone, almost certainly making a hole deep under water in *Tenace*'s hull. As it was, we could all see that the timbers of the hull were sprung. Already water must be pouring in. Once enough water was inside, the unthinkable would happen. Our timber shell would be outweighed by the water and the huge engine. The laws of physics, despite our incredulity, would send us to the bottom and we would drown.

There was hardly any time. Dream-like, a well-drilled crew, we set about lowering the mainsail, quickly and in silence. James launched the rubber dinghy and fetched flares, bottles of water and, I remember, Scotch.

Then the great cliff moved away in a padded silence, and was lost in the fog. We looked around. My mother had been hit on the head by the tiller, a piece of wood five inches in diameter. It had been swung by enormous force as the collision jerked the hull of *Tenace* through the water, and irresistibly made the rudder move as well. At first I thought her jaw was broken. Her face was grey and rigid.

My father moved towards her. They had identical blue sailing jackets, puffy ones, and as he sat down beside her in the cockpit the effect was of two small, bear-like children, holding on to each other desperately. He touched her face. But she was shocked, not injured.

James and Viv had lit one of the distress flares. We none of us knew how to hold them, and my father got slightly burnt, ironically since we were all afraid of drowning. We were beginning to wonder what to do, how soon to abandon our poor old boat, as the brown seawater rose up above the cabin floor. Then we saw through the fog, thinning a little now, the familiar solid greyness. The huge ship was moving in a stately circle. Soon she was bow on, and her silhouette relatively small. She came at us straight as a bullet.

My father muttered, 'Come back to finish the job.'

But this was unjust. With precision, the ship manoeuvred closer and closer. At last she seemed motionless but this was an illusion. Still carrying way, she was drifting towards *Tenace*. Someone began to hail us. My father cupped his hands around his mouth, but found he could make no sound. His throat was too dry.

My mother got to her feet and methodically descended the companionway, into the murk of seawater that already swirled thigh-deep in the cabin. She waded over to the galley, filled a glass with fresh water from the tap off the water tank, and came back. She passed it up to my father, and then climbed back on deck. I don't think I could have done that, and it was characteristic of her that she didn't ask anyone else to do it.

My father looked at the glass and drank. His mind, faithful servant of a sixty-year preoccupation, presented him unasked with a matching fragment of Shakespeare.

'Too much of water . . .' he said, smiling wryly at us.

Too much of water hast thou, poor Ophelia. It was too close for comfort and I saw his features contort strangely. In all twenty-two years of my life I had never seen him cry. He struggled. His face reverted to composure, another lifetime habit. Once more he cupped his hands. This time his voice obeyed. People from the ship waved at us. They made a rope ladder fast and threw it down to reach the waterline.

After minutes of agonisingly slow, engineless floating, we were alongside, and I began to think that perhaps, *perhaps*, we were safe. All at once I felt a sharp desire for life. Ordinary things seemed gorgeous – television, lipstick, dull Sunday mornings at home, books, Marmite sandwiches, a drink of water. I understood then that I had expected to die.

A small wiry man came down the ladder at frantic speed, and jumped on *Tenace*'s deck. His gesture was unequivocal. We must leave. My father and Viv beckoned my friend to the bottom of the ladder, and this was the only point in the whole affair at which she showed any sign of fear. I was also getting very jumpy. I could feel *Tenace* moving differently, settling lower. I could see that the stern with the heavy engine in it was lower than the bow, and I knew what that meant. I offered to show her how easy it was. I offered to climb underneath her if that would help. I could see we were running out of time.

Heroically, terrified yet understanding what was at stake, understanding we needed her to go first, Paulette reached out for the rung opposite her head. She swung on to it, over the thin, menacing gap of slopping water. People put her feet on the rungs below. They held the ladder so it didn't swing. And she climbed like a monkey up the side of the ship and was grabbed and brought safely inboard. Then they beckoned my mother. She refused to go before me and I didn't argue. I could see the thing was speed. I shot up the ladder as fast as I could, and on to the deck. Then my mother climbed, then James, then Viv. That just left the man from the freighter and my father. Maddeningly, formally, they bowed each other on to the ladder. After *you*; no, after *you*. *Tenace* began to rock erratically. Soon the stern would be level with the sea. Soon any small wave would fill the cockpit and *Tenace* would vanish. So would anyone left on board, helpless in the pull of that descent.

The sailor leapt for the ladder and scrambled up. And just at that moment, with my father on the starboard catwalk, looking up at the ladder calmly as if considering its aesthetic qualities, *Tenace* began to tip, up, up in the air, with her bow starting to lift clear of the water, showing the ungainly, ugly shape that you are never meant to see. Then at last my father did leap eagerly for the ladder. He missed his footing. I heard a child's shrill voice shriek 'Daddy!' Just as I realised the scream was mine, I also saw his big fists around the rung. I saw him swing away from *Tenace*, I saw him bang and twist against the metal side of the freighter. And then I saw that he had found his footing. He began to climb.

The skipper, once we were all safe through his efforts, shrewdly gave my father whisky and asked him to sign an admission of 50/50 liability. My father declined, and I believe no further attempt was made. The crew gave us green plastic slippers and wrapped my mother up carefully. They were very kind to us. We transferred to a coastguard launch, and landed at Bembridge. We were taken to a big, old-fashioned hotel, and we sat on the grass in the sun and had tea. Some of us slept. The instant I started to doze I saw that grey triangle coming towards me. I saw it many times.

We took a taxi to the hovercraft and by then there were journalists. My father was now in shock, my mother already ill, breathing badly. The journalists followed us on to the hovercraft. We surrounded him, trying to shield him from their questions and their poking lenses. But I had a coil of rope from *Tenace*, I have no idea why. In a moment of absolute stupidity, something I often had vis-à-vis my father, I handed it to him as we landed at Lymington. I should have known better. At long last, after all the dangers, he burst into tears. The journalists delightedly pressed closer, as if he were a holy relic. I protested. It's just a job, they said. 'Yes,' said my father, weeping openly over the beautiful lost *Tenace*, the drowned ship, gone for ever. 'And you chose it, didn't you?' They fell back, perhaps ashamed. But by then they'd got their pictures.

My parents spent the next few days recovering in bed. A large cardboard box arrived from the British Museum, addressed to my father. Listlessly, he forced himself to open it. Inside was a replica set of the walrus-ivory chessmen from the Isle of Lewis, traditionally – and appropriately for us – supposed to have survived from a shipwreck. My brother had ordered them some weeks earlier, as a surprise birthday present for my father, an avid, skilled chess-player. I cannot think of anything else that could have brought him pleasure at that time. One of the first things he did, outside the house, was to go and look for a chess table worthy of this wonderful gift. It was a marvellously imaginative thing to have done. I was rather jealous.

My parents fell in love the first time they met. Both were engaged to others. It was the spring of 1939, and they came face to face at a meeting of the Left Book Club in London. An hour or so later, they found themselves alone together, walking deliriously up the Strand, talking in rapid French. They slept together that night. For the rest of their lives, they were always by far the most important people in the world to each other, bar none, absolutely none: friends, lovers, children, grandchildren.

The earliest image I have of my father shows me the two of us walking together along the London Road, then on the outskirts of Salisbury. I am very small, three perhaps. It is raining and I complain, shrilly and with no fear of irritating him. Walk behind me, he says. He strides ahead, a huge grey slab, a huge man in a long grey mackintosh. He shields me from the rain. This means we are no longer having a conversation.

I have memories of touch rather than sight, which must be earlier than this. I remember when his enormous hands surrounded my chest completely. I remember the complex smell he had – of mulched-down tobacco and gorgeously masculine sweat. I remember touching the fissure along one fingernail. I asked him how he got that.

'I bit myself,' he said. 'I dreamt I was a dog.'

I completely believed him. Why would he say something that wasn't true? Was it funny, in some abstruse, adult way I didn't understand? There was a great deal about which I was supposed to be ignorant. The area of potential indecency stretched so widely around me that sometimes it was difficult to seem sentient, let alone intelligent.

In winter our flat was savagely cold. My brother and I would get dressed in the sitting room, in the small half-circle of warmth from the electric fire, with its smell of roasting dust. My father would help us in our daily fight to get dressed, David with his tie, me with all my clothes. They always seemed too tight and slightly damp, hard to get on and off.

When I was a young woman, home from Oxford with a new boyfriend admiring my thinness, I tried to get my father to bolster this new, elegant image.

'But Daddy – wasn't I always rather thin?'

He knew what I was doing. And he wouldn't play the game. He looked out of the window, leaving me behind, looking at pictures I never saw.

'No, no. You were always a lovely, roly-poly little thing.'

It has taken me forty years to accept the love in that remark.

When I was small, he brought me comfort and safety. He had a round solidity that my mother did not. She was unpredictable, a volatile mixture, with sharp elbows and a clear, definite voice. I loved my father's deep, furry voice that matched his beard. I loved the way I could disappear into him, bury myself in his comfortable embrace. Then, I was completely at ease with him. Once, when I was cross – he had refused me something – I pinched him, painfully, on his right thigh. He gave a hissing yelp.

'That's my scar. That hurt.'

It was about three inches across, exactly the shape and depth of a tea saucer. I knew it came from the war.

I felt complete, unquestioning love for him long before I knew the word love. I needed him like the most basic of food and drink. I copied him. I tried to be left-handed. I deepened my voice. I ran downstairs the way he did, lightly and with toes turned out. With my hands I made the same shapes he did on the piano. I tried to imitate his air of troubled, heavy patience, which appeared especially when he pushed the mower up and down our vast, ragged lawn, or struggled with our vegetable garden, with its sulky cabbages sunk in the clay soil. I bitterly regretted being a girl. I wanted to grow up like him, to have broad shoulders, to put my hands in my trouser pockets. But he liked me as the opposite. Plaits, hairslides, little ankle socks.

David, my brother, was born in 1940, so my father was away in the navy for much of his baby years – the equivalent of those years that for me were so memorable and full of him. I was born in the summer of 1945, sunlit at least in retrospect, when the war was nearly over, and my father at home, this time for good. Home then for us all was the creaky old house which overlooked the Green in the small Wiltshire town of Marlborough. It was already crammed with meaning and memories, the central, dark place of my father's childhood. But now it was full of our stuff, my cot, my bath, baby paraphernalia. My grandparents gave up their bedroom to their son and his wife, a kindness my mother never forgot.

Years later, a self-conscious teenager, I whisked my half-dressed body out of my father's sight. I was embarrassed, but also I had some feeling he might find it distasteful. His reaction was unexpected. He was mildly but visibly offended.

'I did bath you as a baby, you know.'

I couldn't say, for some reason, that I was not a baby now.

He often took me out with him, and I am told this started early, when I was still in my pram. A few months before, he had been captain of a rocket ship, a landing craft loaded with lines and lines of rocket shells, something that could obliterate a whole village. Now here he was, in an English country town, pushing my pram.

He took me down Marlborough High Street and stopped outside the bookshop, parking the pram by the bargain boxes. He was superb at sudden concentration. You could see him switch it on, like pressing the button of a lift. The world became inside his head. He left briskly, invigorated, and walked home to 29 The Green. He met my mother in the hall, and asked her,

'How's Judy?'

She stared at him.

'Ooh my God,' he said, and ran.

For her, it was a favourite story. And it always made her laugh. He would say nothing, do nothing, except perhaps smile reluctantly.

We left my grandparents' house in Marlborough during 1946, just after my first birthday. We moved into a flat in an ugly Victorian house, 21 Bourne Avenue, Salisbury. I wondered recently if my memory was distorted by the grimness of life there – perhaps in reality the house was mellow and gabled and attractive. So I went and looked, and found that it was just as I remembered – relentless cliffs of orangey-red brick, with a few harsh windows, unsoftened by age. Ugly as it was, we were lucky to have it. The council let us live there because my father was a schoolteacher and they needed him.

My room, over the front door, is now a kind of boiler cupboard, but it was perfect when I was about two, with a small bed and chest of drawers. I drew contentedly on the walls with fat wax crayons. I would have been completely happy had it not been for the night. This unmeasurable stretch of time was full of fear and boredom and I dreaded both. I screamed for my parents, night after night.

Eventually my father would appear, weary and lugubrious, in his old green dressing gown. He would calm me and tell me stories and jokes. I would gaze at him, trying to store up some of the safety he represented. But it was no good. After he left I would helplessly begin again.

One night became so ruined that he gave up, climbed into my little bed and turned his huge square back on me like a cliff. My mother often told me that if I had been their first child they would not have had another. 'We were too tired,' she said. Now I have a lot of sympathy with them, and even at the time I knew it was wicked of me, but I could not see any way out. During the day the room was fine, and I was happy in it. Darkness changed it into a different place, for which the only solution was company. It was a battleground.

My mother did not understand my fears. She thought them irrational and unnecessary, as if they were optional. And she was always a brave person – she saw a fear as something to be conquered. But my father's difficulty lay precisely in the fact that he did understand. His own childhood had been shot through with terrors of the dark. And he had still not conquered those fears, even as an adult. I barely understood this, but I knew I had no need to convince him of the invisible evils crouched around me, lying at the bottom of the bed, behind the door, or worst of all waiting in my sleep – of the caution one had to exercise, remembering something fascinating that was nevertheless a bringer of terror in the dark (my enigmatic, immobile face in the mirror, the strange men down the road, the dreadful plausibility of ghosts). Night after night, we struggled. He tried to give me a talisman against such fears, one he could have done with himself.

There were other struggles. I see them now as impressive, out of character. Later, I could not have carried them through. But then I was not so aware of the need to be accommodating. On the top of my head is a small bare patch, the size and shape of half an old sixpence. I did it aged two, jack-knifing in my father's arms, as my mother tried to tease the knots out of my hair. The top of my head met his front tooth, already loosened in that legendary time – during the war. My mother told me the tooth came out, and I picture it now, stuck in my head like a small tombstone.

This loss gave him a piratical air, though sometimes the tooth would grow back, especially when he went off to school. I thought the gap was splendid. I would probably have knocked out my own front teeth to match, if I hadn't lost both of them anyway, playing 'Ring-a-ring-a-rosy' at kindergarten. This made a convenient space for the two longest fingers of my right hand, and I stuffed them in my mouth and sucked them, day and night.

My parents tried hard to get me to give this up. I was told it was childish, which was I suppose true. But they didn't tell me their real objection – it looked awful. I have since wondered if it suggested to them that something might be wrong – with me, perhaps, or even worse with them. I was coaxed and bribed, and my fingers painted with bitter stuff used later to stop me biting my nails. In the end I was given a rigid gum shield that went all round my mouth and prevented me from sucking away at night. They got it from the dentist. He had alarmed my mother by suggesting that my new teeth would grow crooked and stick out, like the pink-and-white goofy teeth you could buy in the newsagent's.

When we went back to the dentist for him to check it after a week or two, he found my gums were neatly outlined in pearly pink blisters. He was horrified.

'Why didn't you say?' he asked.

I considered. Why didn't I?

'I thought it was meant to be like that.'

Nothing more was said, but it was the end of the gum shield. I carried on, unconscious of victory, with my fingers pushed up to the hilt. I was a small, sturdy child, with a big head, white-blonde hair, and a solemn expression. I was shy and preferred to listen in the background. This gave me a ludicrous, polysyllabic vocabulary. And my rare comments, in unusually deep tones, became a kind of party trick for my parents. Their favourite was surprising. ('Go on. Say it. Say it, *please*.') So I did, again, mutinously, and with decreasing conviction.

'You're threatening my sense of security.'

They would roll around with glee. Even my unrehearsed speech would often trigger a sharp, unexpected cascade of adult laughter, falling about my ears and turning me scarlet. I learnt how unpredictable adults were, how they might go either way, even my father.

Time with him was precious. He was teaching full time, doing adult-education classes, directing plays, acting, playing in the school orchestra, singing in the choir. And also he was trying to write.

I knew about writing, or thought I did. I used my crayons to do lines of squiggles on the walls of my room. People would ask me, humorously, what it said and I would make something up, perhaps about boats, or murders, or money. These were the topics that came to mind. Bankruptcy was a word I knew from adult conversation, though I didn't have a clear sense of its meaning, except as something very bad and very final. It was one among my collection of fears, along with burning to death when the house caught fire. I would imagine leaning desperately from my window – better to jump or better to burn? Or being stabbed at night while I slept. I used to lie on my side, hoping that the knife would pass harmlessly through me.

While in the daylight I knew these fears were ridiculous, at night my internal enemy would remember everything that could cleverly substantiate them. Many things read to me had precisely the right hint of horror – a phrase turned barely towards the uncanny, a brilliantly ambiguous picture, a shadow, an image in water, a hand round a door. My parents censored them, but they could not do so completely – stories had to be told.

So night after hopeless night, I would greet my exhausted father with the simple, factual explanation, 'I've had a nasty thought.'

He did not ask me to elaborate. He knew exactly what I meant. And, naturally, as I grew older there were real horrors to collect; murders, train crashes, tales told by my friends. There were apparently girls like me who just disappeared, to be found *decomposed months later* – terrible words – in a shallow grave in the forest. Even the shallowness was horrible in some way I didn't understand. So, of course, was the deep six-foot trench for a proper grave, cut precisely like a slice of ginger cake. Also, I half-believed there were witches. I often wondered if I was a witch myself. I was fearful of what I might do by accident to those I loved. After all, my mother had said she was a witch. Come up to the forest at midnight, she said, and I'll change your shoes into rabbits. I looked down at them. They were shiny and strapped. I could just imagine them starting to change shape, then all at once leaping away, vanishing . . . and I would be left there in the dark forest. Would my mother vanish too? Would my father come to look after me? I knew really – they were pulling my leg. But there were horrid stories – Rumpelstiltskin tearing himself in half, the Ugly Sisters cutting off bits of their feet, their shoes filling with blood, there were evil stepmothers. Of course the wolf killed Red Riding Hood. It was obvious.

My parents were kind as well as desperate, and they gave me a nightlight, in spite of the cost of the electricity. Even that didn't help much. They decided the thing to do was to get me so tired I would sleep anyway. They sought to turn the night into a time of oblivion, as it was for my mother, instead of fear and struggle as it could be for my father and me. So we went for enormous walks, or I had long rides in my pushchair. It was completely accepted that fresh air made children sleep. If I didn't sleep, that just meant I hadn't had enough.

However, my mother was often too busy to put this plan into action herself. One cold winter day it was Alec, my grandfather, who took me out. How do I know this? My mother told me.

Next day, I found there was a buzzing city behind my bed, and – very oddly – around my tongue as well. It was a foreign country. I tried to tell the grown-ups about it but they seemed preoccupied. Into my room came a tall dark man. He appeared twice a day to give me injections in alternate buttocks. I didn't mind the injections – can that be true? – but my mother was panicky and dragged my pyjama top painfully over my ears, pulling them. I was dosed with the new penicillin, which saved my life.

Gradually the buzzing city faded away. I hung on to it, but normal life closed over it like water. And while I recovered from double pneumonia aged two, my brother was in hospital for a mastoid operation. My poor mother dashed between her children by bus, only able to visit David, she told me later, if our upstairs neighbour would come and sit with me. I have no impression of my father's presence.

I never talked to Alec about what happened. Now I wonder how he felt, whether they got a message to my grandparents in Marlborough every night – neither my parents nor grandparents had a phone. Did they wait every night for bad news? Once, later, staying at Marlborough, one of the many times I was ill there, I looked up from my bed at Alec's face, seeing through my tears an extraordinary expression on his face – dread, compunction, helplessness.

And then, all of a sudden, without warning, there was a boat in our garden, our boat *Seahorse*. My father, an impoverished schoolteacher, living in a flat owned by the council, arranged – and paid – for her to be brought up from Southampton on the back of a lorry. We even have a very small photo, a blurry image of him busy, happy, preoccupied, kneeling in *Seahorse*, as she sits already loaded on to the lorry. My brother remembers that she bent the council's metal fence as the crane swung her into the garden. She was a converted ship's lifeboat, brought up to Salisbury in the autumn of 1947, after our first summer in her.

While *Seahorse* was sitting in our garden, the school cadets helped convert her. Alec helped as well, arriving – my father said – with a bag of tools and a smug expression. But my father's characteristic approach triumphed nevertheless. At the end of the great task the new cabin top with its bizarre components was slightly out of true. Even Alec, that careful man, who worked slowly and accurately, couldn't make my father stick to straight lines.

But during our first summer she was hardly converted at all. My parents' – or my father's – defiant wish that they should do and have what they wanted, even a boat, in the post-war world of making do, made life a kaleidoscopic, perpetual struggle. It also meant that we became allies, the four of us, like birds building a nest, or – a favourite image of my father's – caddis flies, those small bugs living at the bottom of the bright chalk-streams of Wiltshire, contriving a shelter out of debris.

This was especially true of *Seahorse*. He improvised and scavenged. He took the wooden door off the coal-hole in our Bourne Avenue flat, incorporating it in the cabin top. There were other shifts and adaptations. But the trouble was *Seahorse* was not designed for sailing. As a lifeboat, she was shallow-draughted, her hull dipping only a little below the surface of the water. This had been sensible in her previous life. It meant she could be rowed away as fast as possible from a sinking ship. But she would only sail reasonably with the wind dead astern. Any other direction turned her into a paper boat, skimming helplessly downwind. To remedy this, my father made two wooden flaps that could be lowered, one either side – makeshift leeboards to substitute for a keel, the wooden spine at the bottom of a boat. The school's Combined Cadet Force had a school whaler, an open sailing boat used for healthy outings in the Solent, that narrow patch of sea between Southampton and the Isle of Wight. My father was their commanding officer, so we acquired a pair of the whaler's oars.

That first year, we had beginner's luck. The weather was perfect. It was 1947, the year the ground had been frozen for most of January, February and March, the year coal could not be moved because it was frozen solid at the depots, the year I have been told people forgot what green fields looked like and cried when they saw them again. It was something that year just to be warm and in the sun, however ramshackle our life spent under a draped tarpaulin, with a bucket for a loo.

My parents would find a sheltered anchorage for the night. They built a fire of driftwood on the beach, and my mother would cook over it. They also had a Primus stove, and apparently 'primus' was one of my first words, used – according to my proud father – metaphorically. But, however enriching its concept, the paraffin it required was too expensive. There was a perpetual, painful shortage of everything, not just money, but food, fuel, rope, tools, crockery. We were always on the lookout, and it made our lives a sort of poignant farce. One sunny day, in the Solent, my sharp-eyed mother spotted a likely piece of driftwood floating near. We sailed across to pick it up. It was one of our own leeboards.

Seahorse's rudder at one point became entangled in a rope just as we were crossing *Queen Mary*'s bows. My father, with a knife in his teeth, climbed over the stern to free it. To my parents' amusement, I became distraught, crying, 'Daddy! Daddy! Come back!'

David quickly became a very good sailor, and in that situation he and my father were allies, with respect for each other's courage and skill. It took a great deal to erode that. David soon became adept at pinching up to windward, keeping the boat just on the point before the sail flapped. He enjoyed testing things out. In this he was like my father, but of the two David was the more cautious.

Seahorse frequently ran aground. I assumed at the time that these were blows of malevolent fate. Later, when we had a car, I noticed that we were always running out of petrol. My father liked to edge as near as possible to mild disaster. In the boat, he would pinch up across the outer reaches of a shoal, daring the seabed to rise up against him. Again and again we felt that special, brutal jolt. If the tide was going out we were stuck.

He was always keen to experiment with sailing techniques – he had read a great deal, memoirs, handbooks, stories. So on one of these occasions he decided to kedge *Seahorse* off. This involves carrying the anchor and cable away from the boat, sticking the anchor in the ground in deeper water, and then hauling the boat up to it, off the shoal. Of course, we had no dinghy to carry the anchor far enough. So he jumped over the side, put the anchor on one shoulder, and strode off through the shallows. It was raining and, as he waded into deeper and deeper water, he was thinking – he told me later – of Odysseus carrying an oar inland from the sea coast in penance to the god Poseidon. Suddenly my father tasted salt. The sea was level with his mouth.

It was a time completely accepted by David and me. I remember little of it directly, except the brilliance of the light on the sea, and the cavernous dark of our makeshift cabin. I doubt that it occurred to me that the light came off the sea and I might drown in it. That came later, in our other boats. In *Seahorse* I felt completely safe, next to my parents day and night, warm, rather dirty, in a kind of five-week picnic. I took for granted my parents' unhabitual activities, only objecting to what looked like signs of their departure. Instead of a carrycot, I slept soundly in a wooden drawer taken from a chest at home. My mother said it always reminded her of something else, by which I assume she meant a coffin. On beach after beach David and I played all day with sand and water, the perfect toys. We were too happy to quarrel, which was particularly lucky for me.

We sailed to the Isle of Wight and moored near Alum Bay for a day on the beach. My brother said admiringly, 'Look at Judy. Isn't she clever? She's swimming.'

I am very grateful, and not just because of his undeserved praise. Actually, I was drowning. A wave had knocked me off my fat little legs, and my nappy kept me afloat, face down. They picked me up. Did I cry? I don't remember and neither does David.

But in the end there were no disasters, though my father, in his account of our trip, guiltily confesses to taking a dreadful risk as we sailed into Poole Harbour. Typically, this spurs him to imagine the worst, and he produces the best bit of writing in the whole account, a visualisation of our four white bodies turning over and over in the green swell.

I wish now I had asked my mother how she managed in that boat, with rationing, nappies, and practically no money. For years and years, if some evil beset me, love affairs, failures, the illnesses of my children, she would say, 'Never mind, darling. At least you're not in *Seahorse*.'

Finally, I asked her why she hadn't burnt that bloody boat at the end of the first summer. My father laughed but she looked astonished. It had never occurred to her to object. She would follow him anywhere.

'Only Bill', she declared, 'could get us out of the things that only Bill could get us into.'

After the Alum Bay episode, my father taught me to swim, in North Wales, in the chilly waters. He stood for hours, he said, thigh-deep, shivering, while he persuaded me to trust myself to the water – that it was magical; if you believed it enough it would happen. There was one single enormous hand under my ribs. Just pretend, he said. Just pretend it's still there. Suddenly I was set free, a tadpole, given the liberty of the water, unable not to swim, just as now I can't look at a page of print and not read it.

Life in our boats, sordid by many people's standards (including those of my grandparents), taught us other things as well. It became a staple of our family's experience, shared with a very few other people, and often – later – testing our endurance and courage and loyalty. It was a world with dangers, fierce necessities and obligations, which we all accepted. We would have been different without it. So, I suspect, would my father's books. And the *Seahorse* holidays were also the first of our family voyages, those bits of life and perhaps escape, outside normality, when – maybe through isolation and hence appreciating each other – we actually talked.

But my father's account of our first return home tells me that I uttered cries of joy at the sight of my cot. And my brother remarked, after his first bath for five weeks, that it was nice to be clean.

It was a good ending. They had been happy, had triumphantly voyaged around the Solent, from Marchwood Creek in Southampton Water to Poole Harbour and back again. They had seen the English sea coast, and from seaward, rather than from a repressive boarding-house. However uncomfortable *Seahorse* was, she was theirs, and they had lived bearably in her. Nothing awful had happened and a lot of it had actually been good.

In its vindication of my father's vision and strength of will, and the need for my mother's support, it was actually a model for his later success in writing. I suspect that the success of the *Seahorse* holidays, from 1947 to 1950, gave him some of the necessary confidence. In 1951 *Seahorse* mysteriously disappeared, apparently stolen, however hard that is to believe. She vanished, and a few months later my father started writing *Lord of the Flies*.

During these years, we still felt tremendously poor. We all believed this completely, though I can see now how skewed the picture was. My parents worried about money – I did too, though without the expertise necessary for genuine obsession. Nevertheless, David and I went to private schools, in his case at one stage by taxi. I had ballet lessons, as well as a proper Sylphide-like ballet dress for our dancing displays. This was made by my mother from white tarlatan she had more or less to fight for, in Style & Gerrish, Salisbury's biggest but still austere department store. David and I both had piano lessons, and David learnt the flute. He also had a magnificent archery set, complete with quiver, leather wrist guard and a dozen terribly precious arrows – we spent far more time looking for the arrows than he did shooting. We had a boat – a dreadful one but still a boat. I had a pearl necklace, with tiny spare pearls for when I grew. My father had a piano, a cello, an oboe. For some reason we had a clarinet no one played. My mother was beautifully dressed, though I learnt only later what ingenuity that took.

But the great luxury was books. My father bought masses of them. He never lost his hunger for them, nor his surprise and delight later at just being able to go and buy them. And he passed this on. When I was at university, both Sussex and Oxford, he set up an account for me in a bookshop, and told me I could put any book I wanted on it, English, Persian, hydrodynamics, anything, if that was what I wanted. And he never, ever, complained about the considerable size of the bill. Books were so desirable – almost any books. And bookshops were places, in their own way, as powerful and mysterious as banks. Far more pleasant, of course.

Our flat in Salisbury had no shelves, so he built a bookcase, badly, the length of the sitting-room wall. He loathed carpentry, his father's expertise, and botched the task on principle. The big old volumes, ribbed, gold-lettered, and leather-bound, which he bought from Beach's, the ancient, beamy shop in Salisbury High Street, are now on the posh shelves in the library at Tullimaar, but then, in the forties and fifties, they were on pieces of wood that sagged like a washing line.

He spent many hours in Beach's. It was a duel – at least he thought it was. He knew the stock well, especially things he cared about. One day someone made a mistake, and volume one of the *Odyssey* appeared in the sixpenny box. My father knew perfectly well that the matching second volume was inside, on the shelves. He paid the sixpence, and waited. About a year later volume two appeared, in the twopenny box. He bought it with real glee. Another time he bought two Japanese prints (Hiroshige, no less) for a fiver each. The frames alone, he claimed, were worth more than that. How he did this, and paid the school fees, and converted the boat, I have no idea, especially since he and my mother smoked about forty cigarettes a day each.

The struggle at the bookshop extended to the rest of us. When I sold my Enid Blyton books to old Mr Beach, my father was thrilled that I got a good price. He said it was because of my pigtails – a steadfast belief of his being that no man of more than sixty could withstand them. I knew perfectly well it was because they were lovely books, with parrots and mountains and ships stamped on the covers in relief as well as colour. But I knew my father was (a) in some ways unsophisticated (b) too delighted with my victory to allow any other explanation. I was sorry to sell them. I needed the money for the Arthur Ransome books. My brother had refused to lend me his copies, for some trivial reason such as my having broken his bow.

Beach's had lots of children's books. They smelt wonderful, quite different from the gluey whiff you got from modern stuff. But the shop's real if esoteric glory was its collection of classics and theology. It was only a few yards to the Cathedral Close and I suspect old Mr Beach appeared, mournful but prompt, on the doorstep of each newly deceased canon. My father liked theology and found it soothing – William Law, Bunyan's *Grace Abounding*, even C. S. Lewis – partly out of real interest, partly I think in rebellion against his father, a convinced rationalist. But his real appetite was for poetry. He sought out the Greek poets – Sappho, Theocritus, Hesiod – and the tragedians, especially Euripides. He would even buy an occasional Latin poet if the binding were handsome enough. But most of all, it was terribly hard for him to leave a copy of Homer in any shop, especially a second-hand shop. It felt to him like an act of desertion, as if the books were comrades abandoned on some alien shore. I believe the *Odyssey* was his favourite book in any language. When I was a child I would hear him reading it. He would mutter the Greek to himself, sotto voce, breathily, in a rustling whisper like the rattle of frosty leaves. I hated it. I was embarrassed. It sounded dreadfully as if he was praying.

He would have been horrified if I had told him that. Prayer – if it took place – would have been an intensely private, hidden activity, embarrassing both because it was a matter of shame, and confusingly because one might thereby have been claiming virtue.

At this stage he still talked companionably to me, while he got on with other things. However, if the subject required an effort, he would fix you with a straight, ostensibly candid stare that was really its opposite. God, death, the lavatory, anything emotional, anything personal – these were difficult for him and thereby for me too. Later, sex was included as well, but at this stage I had no idea the subject even existed. When an older, more sophisticated girl (about seven, I should think) told me the facts of life, I laughed at her with buoyant confidence and refused to believe such a ridiculous story. And of course my parents never mentioned it. It was too important.

Once, in their bedroom, I opened a drawer. There on the top of the clothes lay a tidy stack of rubbery things. What are those? I asked my father. Finger-stalls, he replied, in a special, 'that is the end of the discussion' voice. I was much ashamed of my curiosity, which had clearly overstepped some mark or other – I had evidently ignored a signal.

On Sunday mornings my parents would get me up, give me a Marmite sandwich, and put me in David's bed, a situation that neither of us liked. Not surprisingly, we would quarrel and fight. Often we fought so much we broke things. Sometimes my brother threatened to fetch our parents, so mysteriously preoccupied in their own bed. But he never did. We settled things ourselves, resentfully.

Sundays at home in Salisbury were generally challenging, though one could be discreetly idle with care. Staying at Marlborough, with my affectionate but also rather tired grandparents, I could do what I liked. At home, I obediently trotted off to the dreadfully boring Sunday school in the nearby church hall. This was child-minding, not religion. Nothing of interest happened there at all, not even singing, except one year on my birthday they gave me a card with a lovely picture of Jesus on it. He was young and beautiful, with long Titian-red hair and a sombre expression. The caption read 'The Lord looked on Peter . . . and Peter remembered.' I was especially impressed by the dots, thinking they represented something awful I was not allowed to read.

The threat of religion became more oppressive when we got a flat across the road in St Mark's House, the former vicarage next to the church. Then one day, briskly, David told me that at a comparable stage he had just told our parents he wasn't going to Sunday school any more. It was a revelation. Unfortunately, I was not as tough as him. My parents put up a fight and eventually made a bargain. I could give up Sunday school, but I had to go to church. I would hear all the hymns and liturgy my parents found so unnecessary. So I marched off on my own, sanctimoniously incredulous, into the church next door, a small person in a beret from an apparently heathen family. When eventually the vicar called, my brother proudly showed him the Buddhist temple he had built in our garden.

I was touched by David's advice, touched that he bothered to help me. Church was far better than the awful Sunday school, shorter for one thing, and also you could daydream unpersecuted, no longer surrounded by kindly, tweed-skirted bullies.

Out of a similar – and unexpected – sibling loyalty, I once protested fiercely at my parents' declaration that David would have to buy himself three new pocket handkerchiefs. He had used one of a set of three as a parachute for a wooden toy. Meticulous as always, he carefully cut a circular hole in the middle of it. I said indignantly that they were being unfair – maybe he should buy one new one, but not three. I must have been about seven. I remember the look on my father's face. It was rueful, amused, and even perhaps faintly admiring.

But such alliances between David and me were exceptional. Mostly, we contradicted, argued, fought, wept, and raged. It must have been utterly exhausting. My father's parents, who loved us both, refused to have us to stay together with them unless my parents were there to keep order. My mother told me this reproachfully. It meant they always had to have one child with them at home. They would have liked to send us off to Marlborough, together.

2

Two Small Children

It is 1950 and I am five. Far above me, my mother's perfect face is revealed to the startled bus conductor. She puts my bag in the luggage space, then jumps off the giant double-decker, the red number 9 to Marlborough. She waves goodbye. She doesn't usually smile at me like that, but the other passengers think, *what a nice young woman*.

Marlborough is an hour and a half away. I hope no one will talk to me. The conductor is bound to, so I clutch my paper strip giving me the right to travel the twenty-seven miles. I can show it wordlessly, discouraging any well-intentioned reassurance which would actually not reassure me.

The sun is setting. It will be dark when we get to Marlborough. Alec will meet me – Alec, my grandfather. It never occurs to me to doubt that he will be there, peering at the bus.

Just before Marlborough, the bus shoots along the edge of Savernake Forest, with its fast straight road, its tall beech and oak. The top of the bus rattles the branches. Then we hurtle down the big hill towards the clustered roofs, we slow down over the bridges, we trundle along the south side of the High Street. By St Peter's Church we do a rocking swerve round the corner. We regain our balance and come to rest at the bus stop near the Castle and Ball hotel. Alec gruffly kisses me. His cheek is a bit like sandpaper. He shaves in the morning and by now the stubble has grown again. I recall the sound of his cut-throat razor, rasping over his cheek.

We walk home, past the shops, carefully crossing Kingsbury Street on the corner where Alec once saw a man knocked down. We dive under the tunnel that goes past Calvert's, the store with the faded raincoats and old-fashioned hats. Now, on either side of us, are the two sections of the graveyard. I don't give a thought to the bodies in the earth, even when I glimpse their gravestones. Alec completely removes the uncanny.

We arrive at the green wooden porch on the south wall of 29 The Green. Nowadays there is no door, no porch, only bricks. The little porch vanished in the 1960s, when the house was gutted and became an ordinary place. In the hall is the shadowy figure of my grandmother. She bends down and kisses me. Her face is cool and wrinkled, ancient beyond imagination. She says little. I am shy of her. Now I realise she was shy of me.

Later, when I was seven, my mother would take me out to the bus stop and leave me there. The first time she did this, I assumed that she had arranged things, had perhaps told the bus driver in some magical way. It was clear to me that there was a vast league of grown-ups who knew everything, whose loyalty to each other was absolute. So I watched the enormous double-decker go by, not understanding that I ought to stick out my arm. But I learnt to do it, and if the bus was late I would see her come and look over our tall garden fence, see me and go away again.

When I came home to Salisbury on Sunday, Alec would come too. He would shepherd me into the flat, and turn straight back to the bus stop, catching the bus on its return journey to Marlborough. He said this was because the bus route didn't terminate at our stop, as it did at Marlborough. It might have swept me on down into the town where there were perils like drunken soldiers. Actually, I think he declined to be responsible for putting me on the bus on my own.

My mother often said how brave it was of me to travel on my own, perhaps hoping that if she said it often enough, it would become true. In reality I felt there was no choice. She wanted me to be adventurous, as she was. No doubt she believed the solitary journeys to Marlborough would make this happen. Sadly, I think it did the opposite. It made me distrustful of strangers, and fearful of solitude, as I still am. I have had to learn that independence is a pleasure. What it did teach me was a love of travelling, and a practised absorption in fantasy. I didn't need a book on these journeys – indeed I didn't like having one. I preferred to launch myself into thought – I could examine things in detail when they were non-existent or miles away. I could travel in sunlight, while the bus rattled on in darkness.

She did what she could with me, I expect, but she was not motherly by nature. Perhaps nobody is. She fed me herself till I was a year and a half. I have a very ancient memory of an oblong pinkish-brown object, three-cornered and large. I recognised it when I was feeding my first child. It is a human nipple, moulded by a baby's mouth. She made me lovely dresses, tried to deal with my agonising ear infections, my colds and coughs, my – to her – alien fears. She tried to ensure that my mediocre looks would not be further eroded. But I could always tell. It was a bit like having a stepmother – not a wicked one, just someone who was naturally more interested in her relationship with her husband than she was in the connection she had with his children – or, at any rate, with his daughter. I think she really was fond of David.

And it never occurred to me at that stage, when I was small, to wonder if my father felt the same way. He was sometimes abrupt, even cold, sometimes inexplicably hostile. But palpable affection rose off him rather like steam, and it made me love him with passion, as I did Alec, and for much the same reason. My feelings extended to everything about the two of them: voice, smell, hair, hands, face – and their clothes, which I thought expressed their nature so strongly, their ancient sports jackets, flannels, shirt and tie, their worn brown shoes.

My father and Alec mostly wore the same set of clothes every day. Neither of them considered clothes important. Both hated new ones. Grandma, despite my mother's encouragement and persuasion, felt the same way. But they all accepted my mother's delight in the whole business, her skill and taste. They felt people were entitled to scope if they were good at something. Of course, sometimes there *was* competition and that was not good. But clothes were not a matter for rivalry. If you had seen my mother surrounded by Goldings, you might have thought of a butterfly on a pile of dead leaves.

In the post-war years, my parents were so poor that my father still wore his naval clothes. We have a photo of him in 1951; it was taken during the Festival of Britain, and he is holding up a Union Flag tied on to a boat hook, which he is going to fix in a tree – he was always profoundly patriotic. He is wearing a flapping pair of white knee-length shorts – they were for tropical use and my father had been issued with them for his brief stay off Port Said in 1943. I expect he pictured the naval officer from the final scene of *Lord of the Flies* wearing them. In the photograph he is cheerfully oblivious, wearing what looks like a badly cut skirt.

I admired his disregard for the whole business of clothes, and I imitated him, unsuccessfully, since in my heart of hearts I rather liked them. But I wished passionately to be a part of that world, the warm, exciting world of tweed jackets and tobacco, deep voices and excitement. I did not so much want to be a boy as long to be a man, to be among them. I still catch myself now, more than half a century later, adopting a pose that I think of as masculine. From somewhere I acquired the unfounded belief that my pseudo-masculinity would be likeable. Since I wanted men to like me – my father in particular – I should have learnt to be like my mother, with her weekly hair appointments, her clothes, her striking make-up. But I knew – without articulating the thought to myself – that this would be no good either. It would merely provide my father with another problem – how to notice my appearance without offending my mother. Instead, I developed a sort of travesty identity, a pageboy persona, like Viola in *Twelfth Night*. I acquired the proper clothes diligently, in a parody of my mother, among my brother's cast-offs or from jumble sales. No one ever told me I should do this. But I knew it was the way.

As I grew older it became difficult to unlearn the habit. I found it impossible to believe that looking like a girl would be welcomed. And yet my mother made me pink dresses with puff sleeves, or very short velvet dresses with blond lace collars, outfits that I can see now had a kind of lollipop suggestiveness. It was all very puzzling. My father silently disapproved. My mother dressed me up as a dolly – an obedient one.

Secretly, wickedly, I found her frustrating and irritating. When I was about eight, I had a dream. There she was, talking away brightly, when, suddenly, her head fell off – to one side, I remember, and with rather a thump. This is so embarrassingly Freudian that I have never mentioned it before. I didn't hate her. I simply knew I couldn't rely on her because she wasn't very interested. Clothes interested her, and so I was beautifully dressed. But one day, catching the bus to my little school in the Close (I was probably seven – I can't have been older), I had a quarrel with another small girl at the bus stop and her mother shouted at me. I went home in tears and rang our doorbell. My mother leaned out of our upstairs window, and told me to stop crying at once and go off to school. Once I got to school, the tears became a cascade, and the teachers gathered round. Their questions were solicitous, so much so that I had to pretend I was crying because I'd forgotten my pinafore, another much-admired garment made by my gifted mother. I was ashamed of the real reason.

Now, when I look back, I see that most of the mothers I knew were a slightly uncomfortable experience: sharp voices, sharp elbows, an abrupt, self-satisfied censoriousness. Their life in post-war Britain was restricted and frustrating, especially in small-town Salisbury. It may be that some of them missed the independence the war had given them. They tended to be critical and teasing, even Grandma, my father's mother, who loved me, I know, and showed that love, if shyly. But nevertheless, towards us, their daughters and granddaughters, the army of women who surrounded us were full of a knowing reproof, as if they knew we were after their privileges – sex, money, make-up, rustling skirts, the interest of men.

By contrast, my friends' fathers were often irritable, but they were straightforward for the most part, and easy to avoid. They usually found conversation difficult, but then our distance was tacitly agreed on both sides. They exemplified a kind of benign neglect – mostly benign, at any rate. Also – like my own father – they were comparatively unsophisticated. People's mothers, alas, were the opposite, deftly creating unease. I suspect now that I was parked on them, rather as I was parked on my grandparents. But, in one of the great strokes of luck in my life, Alec appeared to welcome my presence, as I believe he did David's.

My brother took after my mother, inheriting her dark, vivid good looks, her blue eyes and symmetrical features. She was very protective of him, because he had been born with an undeveloped foot – at birth it had no heel. In earlier times this would have become a club foot, like Byron's. But in the 1940s there was treatment for it – hours of manipulation, special splints, plaster casts and eventually special shoes. By the time he was ten his feet were normal, in fact rather beautiful, with long straight toes.

When he was a teenager he would sometimes break into a kind of abstracted running or hopping, down the garden or round the room, in a circle. It never went anywhere. It was a memory, a celebration of a hard-won freedom, won for him by my mother. During the war she took him round on buses, trailing across the countryside to various hospitals, faithfully doing the manipulations, faithfully carrying out the treatment as instructed. My father said she had given David a foot.

To her, David was a frail figure. To me, he was interesting, large, strong, and slightly frightening. He roamed more freely than I did, knew much more, and had fascinating friends. Sometimes he shared those friends with me, as well as his things – bows and arrows, bicycles, books, model boats, Meccano. Sometimes we fought chivalrously, with wooden swords made by Alec. We would fight on our bikes. We had huge, staged battles where we were whole armies. If I did well, he would knight me on the field of battle. Arise, Sir Judith Golding.

I liked fighting, though I suppose in common with everyone I hated losing. I usually lost, since I was smaller and weaker. Occasionally I won, and would be accused of wickedly using some dirty trick. Often I had.

My father watched us with calm neutrality, intervening only if we were at risk of real injury. He forbade us, for example, to joust on our bikes. There is a photograph of my brother bicycling towards a tower of cardboard boxes, with a spear couched correctly under one arm. War was good fun to us then.

But I loathed our quarrels. They were frantic, hot, uncontrollable verbal encounters, filled with pain on both sides. They gave me (him, too, no doubt) a despairing sense of how impossible it was to *explain* – to make the grown-ups understand why I felt it was so unfair, a phrase that even now I expect to be followed by some adult dismissal of its importance. I felt bullied by David. Maybe David felt bullied by me.

My mother wouldn't intervene, blandly declaring that she didn't care who started it – we must both stop it. Privately, I felt she favoured David, and I was pretty sure my father favoured me.

There was, for example, a shameful episode involving the fair, which came to Salisbury every year, as it had done for centuries. David's school, as mine did later, forbade its pupils to go, claiming that it was a breeding ground for awful diseases, the sort for which in those days there were health certificates to be signed at the start of term.

Really, I suspect our schools didn't want us getting up to that much tawdry, lower-class fun. Since David couldn't go, my parents decided that I shouldn't either – quite reasonably. But I wheedled my father – with a skill I have not retained – till he finally gave in and took me, one evening when David was somewhere else. My father said I wasn't to tell him, and I promised not to. But then, in some way, the prohibition ceased to mean anything, and I told him anyway. He burst into angry tears, which astonished me, though I see now with an adult grief why he did so. My father looked at me. I had committed a great family sin – revealing something we all knew but never mentioned.

My parents went out together on many evenings, often taking part in amateur dramatics. My mother was particularly keen, and rather good, I think. She took the lead in several productions, and I remember her well in them – beautiful, dramatic, very effective. Sometimes I would come home to hear her talking in what I think of as her theatre voice, while my father or brother heard her lines. My father acted occasionally, though he more often directed.

But he also went out on his own, to take adult-education classes in outlying villages, of which Wiltshire seemed to have an inordinate number. He gave courses in modern literature and, on one occasion, music appreciation. He said the fee hardly kept him in cigarettes on the long bus journeys. I hated him going out at night. If he was there in the flat I felt comforted, even if I couldn't see him.

Before he went out, I used to ask him, as a last-ditch ritual, 'Will I have a nightmare?'

For a long time, or so it seemed to me, he would reply soothingly that I would not. But one day he said irritably, 'How on earth should I know?'

Then he left to catch the bus. I knew better than to ask him again. But I still called for him in the night, ruthlessly, helplessly. And he still came.

Some evenings he was at home, busy writing, while my mother went off into her brilliant outside world. He told me later how failure preyed on him at that time – how he despised himself for staying at home, scribbling away pathetically, while his beautiful wife went out. Eventually, he told me, he came round to the belief that it would be better if he died – better for her.

I find this astonishing. How could it have been better? They had been married little more than a decade, they had two small children, the war was over, they were in love. What on earth was he thinking of? Surely this was self-centred, egotistical, of him? My mother appeared to care for him deeply, found him attractive, found life good with him. And she really, truly believed in him as a writer. This was a major factor in his achieving that ambition.

However, I do think his account was a truthful picture of the way he felt. He told me this in 1962, when I was seventeen and having a nervous breakdown. He used it as evidence of how one could achieve objectivity – not, I think, a very good example. Unfortunately, at the time, it made me think I was free to voice my own wish to die – to kill myself – and this created a terrible furore. Locked in my own egotistical misery, heavily drugged, I failed to notice – or maybe to care – that I said this in front of my maternal grandmother, whose youngest child John had killed himself a few years previously. This dreadful event had created a kind of shock wave around the idea of suicide, and mentioning it was seen as a terrible act of violence in itself. My father shepherded me out of the room, with an appearance of gentleness. Outside the room his whole demeanour changed. His face filled with disgust and hatred.

'I know you're *sick*.'

'Sick' was a euphemism, and he spat it at me as if it were poison.

'But really—' he added.

Words, his *métier*, ostentatiously seemed to fail him in the face of his appalling daughter – as if I was so wicked that I had actually murdered that ability as well.

My grandmother uttered no reproach. Perhaps she was too shocked to speak. As far as I could tell, though, she continued to treat me with her customary distant affection. But then she disliked my father. My mother too was silent. We never talked about it again. It became one of the many submerged rocks in the choppy sea of our family life. Sometimes you saw the waves breaking over them. More often they were completely invisible, disastrous to those without local knowledge.

A particularly destructive hazard concerned my father's writing. A hapless visitor would innocently, politely as they thought, enquire if my father was writing anything at the moment. The temperature would drop drastically, and one or other of us would rush into the dreadful silence, trying to repair the damage.

When I was a small child these situations didn't arise, because he wasn't such a venerable figure. Later, people sometimes took me to task for treating him like an ordinary person. Alastair Sim's wife once upbraided me for saying my father wasn't very good at tennis – which he certainly wasn't – as if I was committing sacrilege. The irony was that I believed he *was* far more important, more extraordinary, than anyone else.

At last, and sadly, he too began to be a little shocked at opposition. But that was later. When I was very young, he liked a little rebelliousness, if it was sufficiently attractive. I apparently emerged from under a table, aged four, announcing in deep accents, 'Bill's being *rude* to me.'

This was regarded as tremendously good.

Before the war, in his twenties, my father had played the cello in local amateur orchestras, wreaking havoc all over, he said. One performance of Mozart's *Eine kleine Nachtmusik*, conducted by the young Adrian Boult, seems to have featured my father botching a final low G, top G, the bass note of the chords concluding the movement. He played low G, top F, which provided an apparent dominant seventh lurching horribly towards a new, nonexistent section in C major. He told this often, perhaps to exorcise the shame he felt. It's very dreadful for the performers when a musical performance goes haywire. And the memory stays with you, ready to supply food for self-contempt whenever needed.

A year or so after the war he gave up the cello, putting to one side the awful old instrument that our musical friends the Browns nicknamed *Taté-Lylé* because of its uniquely cardboard qualities. He took up the oboe again, his third or fourth instrument. The school orchestra needed one.

I have no memory of him playing but I used apparently to cover my ears when he put the oboe up to his lips. He doesn't seem to have felt this was unfair criticism. Indeed, he said it led to my first joke. One day when I was in my high chair watching him, he put a cigarette in his mouth. I covered my ears, shrieking with laughter. I have an uneasy feeling I may have repeated this, since he certainly smoked a great deal, and children see no reason why repetition should give diminishing returns.

As I grew older, three or four perhaps, and if anything more demanding, I would still call out for him in the middle of the night. When he appeared, often very cross, I am told I would say encouragingly, 'Be funny, Daddy,' or even with appalling, little-girl coaxing, 'Be jokey, Daddy.'

I don't remember being like that. I remember being troubled, angry, frightened. But in *his* memory I was small, round, a bit flirty and – at that time – harmlessly direct.

3

Life in a Fog

Last Year in Marienbad, a film made by Alain Resnais in 1961, is a classic of French cinema, and some have unkindly suggested that it won such status because it's so baffling. When I was in my first year at Sussex University, a whole troop of us obediently trotted off to watch it at the Continental, the local art cinema. My companions emerged puzzled almost to the point of rage. I was puzzled about their puzzlement. Apart from the chic black dresses and the long corridors, I thought it was just like life.

Even now, much of my life is passed in confusion, and the acceptance of it. As a child I lived in an eternal social fog. 'Why doesn't Auntie Theo sleep with Uncle Jose?' I said one day at Marlborough. By sleeping I of course meant sleeping. This was before they married, and many there must have thought it an interesting question. The watchful, held-in silence (no laughter) which followed my remark showed me I had made an error. However hard one tried, it was impossible to avoid all the pitfalls. Occasionally people would make things clear for me, some out of kindness, some out of spite.

So, one day at supper I asked my father, 'Was it dark *all* the time in the war?'

My parents looked at each other. When I was older, and tired of the story, I said that I had been muddled – I was really asking about the blackout. By then, though, it was too late. It had become part of the war, part of its role as the great event of their lives. It reassured them. And it's true that I dimly remember an idea of the war as a time of constant darkness, and that must have come from them.

My father's answer reflected a policy decision. No, no, on the contrary, he assured me. He produced a whole bunch of stories designed to bring the daylight back. There was the one about HMS *Queen Elizabeth* passing the Cunarder *Queen Elizabeth* and signalling 'Snap'. There was the jovial cry of the petty officer, rousing the ratings on the mess deck, 'Wakey, wakey, rise and shine. The sun's burning your eyes out.' (Others have told me since that this was the sanitised version. The real one was 'Hands off cocks'.) When my father was drinking in a bar in Reykjavik with his shipmates, one of the rough-and-ready ratings asked where the Gents was. His companion pointed to a door with a jagged, consonant-stuffed word in Icelandic. 'Can't you read?' he said. There was some long story about mops and buckets that had my brother and me weeping with laughter so that our stomachs hurt. There was the bizarrely practical request to grow a beard – 'Permission to cease shaving, sir!' There was the apocryphal telegram greeted with joy: 'Send lorry. Rommel captured,' a mistake for 'Send lorry. Camel ruptured.' There were many more.

Of course, it didn't quite work. I suspect my father didn't really want it to work. While he sheltered me diligently from the grimness of war, he also needed to tell me about horrors that preoccupied him. He once described to me in horrifying detail – when I was about twenty-two – the vindictively misogynist atrocities and mutilations committed by a nationalist leader whom I had carelessly mentioned with some slight approval. He spoke aggressively to me, and with passion. I burst into hysterical tears. He took me on his knee, and said – this is word for word – 'Don't you see? I *am* you.' I still have no idea what he meant.

For him, in fact for all of us, the war felt very near. It lay behind us, just out of sight, during the whole of my childhood, and it came up all the time in conversation. Children really did ask men – not women – what they did in the war. It was considered a natural question, not impertinent, unlike almost any other question one might want to ask.

The Second World War was always just 'the war' – as if there had never been any other. Any unusual circumstance was generally attributed to 'the war', accurately or not. One writer my father knew had sent back every income tax demand he received with 'Killed in the blitz' written on it. And our surroundings were sprinkled with evidence of it, even in Salisbury. Sometime in the mid fifties I went to a friend's birthday party at her home, an ex-army Nissen hut – a half-cylinder of corrugated metal with makeshift doors and windows. If you touched the inside of the wall in winter, it felt icy cold. Yet my friend's mother was posh – county, in fact – and her father a senior officer in the air force. They were richer, I am sure, than my parents, but the housing shortage was still so acute that the RAF had to put him and his family in a tin hut.

The war had devoured so much – people, buildings, money. Even colour. It seemed to be leached out of things. I remember – or imagine that I do – ugly heaps of discarded war stuff left lying around, picked bone-clean by scavengers, while any usable objects – motor torpedo boats, compasses, corrugated iron, timber, wheels, chassis – were avidly digested into peacetime life. In allotments today, it is a matter of pride that useful things should be rescued and reused – baby baths, broom handles, CDs, saucepans – and I imagine that after the war the whole of Britain looked rather like that. Our school thriftily used old ARP wardens' helmets for bases in rounders – I was astonished later when I found you could use wooden sticks. Men would show each other the guns they had secretly kept. Almost every large building bore the signs of institutional, war-related occupation, a casual grimness that now you might see in the disused sections of old hospitals – a relentless bashing about of anything beautiful. And no wonder.

But my parents were survivors in every sense. If you had met my father then, in the fifties, I suspect you would have been struck by his qualities of energy and strength of will, though perhaps you would first have noted his unsmart clothes and straggly beard. An early photo of him, taken for *Vogue* at the publishers' persuasion, shows this by unpleasant contrast. He looks shockingly, disagreeably dapper, very unlike himself, Faustian and frightening. I should be sorry if that endured as a portrait of him – a glimpse of his dangerous side, mostly though not entirely hidden from his daughter. The trouble was it held some of his strength, along with the danger.

Usually I saw in him determination but carelessness, and this was no affectation. He organised the dull bits of life around what he saw as simplicity. Complexities, and perhaps contradiction, were reserved for the things that interested him. Sailing manoeuvres were often elaborate. The intricacy of chess fascinated him. He would attempt the most difficult piano music. But he wished to be able to forget about mundanities. I noticed he always kept his shoelaces ridiculously short – I remember the fumbles of his huge fingers as he tied them. When I asked him why he didn't have longer laces, he explained it was because they would trip him up when he left them undone.

One of the important things, in his eyes, was worry. I think he believed in worrying as a way of warding off misfortune, so he – logically – took care to worry about the absolute worst case, believing that in fairness fate could not then bring such a case into being. This was tiring for the rest of us, especially my mother, whose optimism was as occupational as my father's anxiety. Ironically, once my father's worst fears proved groundless, he became happy-go-lucky, something that seemed to annoy my mother even more.

But pre-eminent among important things was music. It was always a large part of his life, a matter for all his strength of will. Unusually, my mother took hardly any direct part in it, though she was always a good listener. She loved his playing, and encouraged him, as I must say she did me, far more than my father ever did. She was wonderfully conscious of the good qualities of a performance, even one as inadequate as mine – my father was the opposite, possibly because he cared more. But it was generous of her – she too had learnt the piano as a child. She chose to be a benign audience.

My father spent thousands of hours – he calculated that it

added up to many months if not years – playing the piano. Since we had no gramophone till I was about ten, the music I did hear was mostly him pounding away at our small upright. It was so old and ill-used that I learnt where middle C was because its yellowed key had the largest notch in the worn ivory, black like a dirty thumbnail.

Music aroused mixed feelings in him. He loved it and played it energetically. But he was ashamed about it. Because he was so fascinated, he made friends with people who were better musicians than him, two in particular, John Milne and Tony Brown, both colleagues at Bishop Wordsworth's, the school where he taught. Comparison with their playing brought him grief, not at all too strong a word. 'I have joined the room-emptiers,' he once remarked.

When I was a teenager, he said to me sadly, 'John and Tony would say – of course, Bill's not a *musician*. Nice chap, lovely wife, but not . . .'

Actually, he was a very effective musician, exciting, committed, capable, persistent, passionate. He was a brilliant, inexorable sight-reader. He simply would not let a piece defeat him, possessing – like a great general, perhaps – the capacity for jettisoning the less essential. But he practised obsessively, as well: Schubert, Beethoven (especially his most challenging sonatas), Chopin studies, Brahms, Liszt's great sonata in B minor, Bach. A little Mozart, but not much.

He once said, 'In Mozart you have nowhere to hide.'

It's true that his playing was often not accurate. He prized verve and achievement, and besides I think he wanted to hear immediately what a piece sounded like. You could sometimes hear him just sketching it in. At other times, with Bach's Italian Concerto, for example, he would work until he got it right.

For years, when I was very young, I thought these great sweeps of sound were one long piece. Before I could read music, or much else, I would stand on his left, watching for the unconscious tensing of his body that meant he was near the end of a page. This would ensure I was ready for the crisp nod telling me to turn it. During my birthday parties he would play for musical chairs, or just for us to dance around. As a bravura finale, after tea, he would play Grieg's *March of the Trolls* – I remember the stiff, ugly shape of his left hand leaping back and forth in the octave passage. We sat around on the floor, a circle of excited little girls in party frocks, and we clapped like anything.

My father, David and I sang round the piano. David had the nicest voice in the family, unfortunately not high praise. We had an old copy of Schubert's songs, with the note-heads drawn at a slant, the shape of ants' eggs. I blundered my way through many of the songs, always hoping that the next one would be slower or lower. My father seemed never to have heard of female altos, and continually pointed me at top Gs or even As, like a horse at an impossible fence. Even though he said he was pleased I was a girl, I suspect now that part of him would have liked me to be a boy soprano.

He himself had a nice baritone, which he dragged up into the tenor range by sheer force of will. He was an accurate singer, surprised and perhaps irritated by the difficulties of pitch or rhythm that beset his children. David and I sang the sweet and easy duet from Handel's *Acis and Galatea* – 'The flocks shall leave the mountains . . .'. My father, this time as a bass, interjected Polyphemus' protests – 'Torture! . . .', adapting effortlessly if one of us hesitated. He would find a spare finger to play the requisite note, a musical life raft. But we never really learnt things – our singing had all the disadvantages of sight-reading, with none of the excuse.

We had a book of Elizabethan love songs, full of classical names and flower-studded gardens. I thought of them as sounds, and it was a shock later to find many of the poems naked on a page. We loved 'The Lost Chord', and Tosti's 'Goodbye', which transferred to the boat as a source of appalling jokes about being seasick ('Goodbye, leek soup! . . .'). We tried to sing 'Come into the Garden, Maud', but David and I could never manage the middle section, a trap for the unwary, who know only the famous bit. My father sang it, stepping agilely from one testing interval to another. He seemed able to do anything musical, from the top A in the Tosti ('Good*bye* for ever! Good*bye* for ever!') to the tenor solo at the beginning of *Messiah*.

When David and I had given up (my mother never sang), my father would turn back to the Schubert volume. We would hear the menacing rumble of 'The Erl King'. He sang the boy's phrases in the adult range – 'My *father*, my *father* . . .' – but I remember them now as the voice of a child. I could see him, half under his father's coat, gazing backwards, terrified yet fascinated by the dark figure in pursuit. It was always our last song. He would get up from the piano, moved and exhausted. He would vanish; perhaps to write or just to think. After all, the death of children occurs many times in his work, and a child's vulnerability was something that fascinated him but pained him intensely too. Sometimes, with actual children, even his own, he just couldn't bear it. He would ensure that the child kept it hidden.

He and my mother spent a lot of time with us, which is to their credit, given how much else they wanted to do. And, apart from music, most of the family activities involved them both.

We often went to Salisbury Cathedral. My father would tell us about the discarded glass from the windows, the blue and red lying around in the city sewers, the colours that used to fall on the stone. But the inside of the cathedral was now a delicate grey, though sometimes cut through with the solid bars of sunshine my father describes in *The Spire*.

Its silvery coolness held some awkward sights. Death was indecent, one of the subjects I knew better than to ask about. There were bodies in stone boxes, held decorously in place by stone lids. My parents must have distracted us as we passed the cadaver tomb, with its collapsed, decaying body. My father uses it for Jocelin's monument in *The Spire* but I never saw it as a child. We looked at the ostensibly jollier ones, where people were dressed up for a party. We looked at the elegant effigy of William Longspée, the stone carved to show the weighty chain mail sinking in a fold below his arm. It looks soft, as if you could press your thumb into it. I pleased my parents by saying it seemed modern. ('Yes, *yes*,' they said, with delighted approval, and I still feel a warmth when I look at it.) We felt inside the big round holes in the tomb of St Osmund. He was our local saint, loyally supported like the home team but not quite believed in. Sanctity vanished somewhere in the English Channel, rather like the ability to make wine.

I had very little sense of the cathedral being connected with God. God was mentioned by us reluctantly, in a proper context, school, perhaps, where he was clearly present, or Christmas, where the subject was made safe by practicalities and pressing material concerns. Curiously, the cathedral itself did not qualify.

Having no car, we went round to all these places on bicycles, all of us. Until I was old enough to ride one myself, I sat in a little square seat behind my father's huge square back. We rode round through the empty countryside to Clarendon Palace, to Stonehenge, and to a number of strange, grass-covered humps. We picked up stones, teeth, pottery, had picnics, and went blackberrying. We paddled in the cold rivers. We stopped and looked at things closely – the river-weed moving like hair, and the water lilies, small flowers on stalks above the water. And we walked as well. It seemed to me that we did so for miles and miles.

Our nearest walk was along the path towards Old Sarum, a path white from the chalk soil, and bordered with scraggy hawthorn trees yanked to one side by the incessant wind. Near to Old Sarum there was a special tree, which our parents called the howling tree. If we were being stroppy, quarrelling, or aggressively dawdling, they would stand beneath this wretched tree and wail and weep and sob, very realistically. They never minded being looked at. Eventually, after our muttered promises took effect, they would suddenly stop their behaviour and carry on as normal.

My father's talking, given half a chance, would develop naturally into story-telling, something of which his pupils probably made good use. And if he did tell us a story, the walk would roll itself up and vanish. At Old Sarum he told us about the man who wished to build a new cathedral. The Virgin Mary appeared to him and told him how to choose the site. There was no description, no wonderful lady in blue and white, just the briefest account of her clear, practical directive: 'Take a bow and shoot an arrow.'

Old Sarum had its good points. Even to a small child, the wind-scoured view it commanded was remarkable. But it was also a little dispiriting. We did better when we investigated the unkempt places. David always knew things, knew what we should play. The King and Thomas of Canterbury . . . we played their game, highly suitable since it was about quarrelling. When David stabbed me with his wooden sword, he always thoughtfully provided my death-groans, though I protested that I could do them myself.

My mother sometimes tried to tell us stories, but we were clear that this was not her job. However, she was adept at providing small, colourful details, often rather risqué ones. At such moments my father would silently raise the hairless ridges where his eyebrows used to be before they were blown off in the war.

His knowledge seemed inexhaustible and I took him for granted as a source of information. Only after his death forty years later did I realise how accustomed I was to stretching out my hand for that fund of knowledge. It was like pulling a book off the shelf except far easier. And often he was wise, broad-minded and learned. He carefully explained to me, when I was about fourteen, that Antonio's remark in the opening scene of *The Merchant of Venice* – 'In sooth, I know not why I am so sad' – was because Antonio was homosexual, and – as my father put it – 'The boys are growing away from him.' I knowledgeably repeated this judgement in an English lesson at Godolphin. It was met by embarrassed silence and the heavy implication that I should be ignorant about such matters. My father disagreed, to his credit.

But sometimes he was ludicrously wrong. He would improvise. After all, he had a reputation to keep up, and if the subject awoke his imagination he would happily deliver an answer. He always had an air of authority. He could bluff for England.

Over the years I regretfully learnt caution. When we first

went to Greece, in 1961, and gazed at the open-air theatres that hummed with crickets and had heat rising visibly off them, he told me that the small, neat channels, bridged with something that looked like a couple of inches of marble ribbon – 'you see, useful *and* beautiful' – in the front of each white marble seat, were to allow people to empty their bladders in the middle of the day-long performances. Now I can see that actually these channels were to allow the rain to empty off the marble surface, rather than eroding the stone by staying in the precisely carved, buttock-shaped depression in the seat. But this had not occurred to him. So he made something up. And as he did so he built a truth for himself, and it stuck much harder than mere information would have done.

When I was small, before I could read, he sometimes told me bible stories, but these were handicapped, and not merely by religious reticence. He told me once how the disciples were sailing on the Sea of Galilee, just like us in *Seahorse*. Something shining came towards them on the water. 'And what do you think it was?' he asked indulgently, waiting for me to utter a childishly sweet reference to Jesus, a name he was shy of articulating himself. 'A whale?' I suggested. That was the end of the bible stories, a relief to us both. He was best on stories where people did things. It would have been tremendous if he'd described how the Apostles rigged their boat, or mended their nets. He would tell you methodically about some process, and it would be fascinating.

There is a small grey-and-white photograph of the three of us – David, my father, me. We are laughing. My mother is the photographer, and she has waited for the punch line. We are in the ruins of a hill fort on a Welsh mountain. I am seven. I have fair hair in pigtails, and I wear shorts, white socks and little leather sandals. David is nearly twelve, dark-eyed and handsome. He has a neat woollen blazer – it is a British summer. My father, raffish and bearded, but with sketchy hair, is wearing an old linen jacket pulled out of shape, probably by books. He leans back against the stone wall. He tells us how the fort was built long ago by elephants. He has described how they put the big stones one on top of each other, planned the round buildings so that they could sit down, and lived there very comfortably with all their belongings. Finally, he points to a large round hole.

'And that,' he says, 'is the place where they kept their trunks.'

We all laughed. At the time I didn't see what we were laughing at, and I still have a puzzled, surreal vision of the elephants neatly coiling their trunks, rather like snakes in a basket. Many ideas had a grey hinterland of possibilities, just out of sight. I usually decided to leave them, stored in a special part of my mind, for later examination. But I laughed anyway. The laughter was part of the warmth that wrapped round us all, a feeling hard to describe because it was so taken for granted. Only in our worst days as a family, later and temporarily, did it disappear completely.

My parents were very unlike their children. My friends were slightly shocked by my mother's good looks, her frankness and occasional swearing, and far more so by the fact that she shopped at the Co-op and actually had a divvy number. I once mentioned that she thought highly of communism. The sky darkened around me. Nevertheless they liked her, and more important so did their parents.

My friends' fathers were in the army, or lawyers, or farmers. Sometimes they just had money. They drove cars and wore suits. They did not sail ramshackle boats. Above all, they did not spend their evenings writing – not then the harmless, popular activity it is now. In the Wiltshire of my childhood it was a bizarre pastime, even an unhealthy one. The epithet 'intellectual' was not a compliment. This had nothing to do with actual morals. Some respectable people, I learnt later, were serial adulterers, bullies, financial opportunists. My parents were actually rather straitlaced. But they were guilty of a number of social sins. Their leftwing views could just about be tolerated, as could their living in a rented flat, my father's straggly beard and careless clothing, even our frightful boat. However, when writing was added to this dubious bundle, the Goldings became troubling.

Success did not alter this, rather it accentuated the subversiveness. When the early novels were published, many of my friends' parents were patronising – sneering – about them. I would see them smile, as if it was all trivial and contemptible. Perhaps it was to them. Or maybe in some obscure way it was a threat.

My mother did her careful best to provide camouflage. Her voice, uniquely in her family, lacked any regional quality, Kentish (she grew up in Maidstone) or otherwise. It was perfect BBC. With her talent for clothes, her charm and her often well-disguised intelligence, she was very acceptable, if slightly too attractive for perfect assimilation. Some wives must, I think, have been wary of her. But she had a miraculous capacity for becoming Boy-Scout-like, instead of dazzling, if she saw she was alienating another woman. It was extraordinary to watch.

My father, on the other hand, always stood out – and he liked it that way. I doubt that authority ever really warmed to him, which is to his credit. When he became famous and successful – wealthy, even – there was a way for the suspicious establishment to tolerate him. The grit had become a pearl, if a rather baroque one. Before – at school, at Oxford, in the navy, and as a teacher – I think he always annoyed the people in charge. This was often deliberate, and yet curiously he was both proud and resentful of the result.

He became prone to see any reversal as directed at him personally. After the publication of *Lord of the Flies*, my parents decided we should have a larger, nicer home than our flat in Bourne Avenue, or its successor – also owned by the council – across the London Road and next to St Mark's Church. They applied to become tenants of 17 The Close, a creaking, ancient house opposite part of Bishop Wordsworth's School. It had moulded plaster ceilings, gables, and many other attractions, though the finer points were lost on me once David revealed, as he had been forbidden to do, that a bishop had died in it. My parents correctly understood how this would add to my repertoire of fears, and hence their difficulties. I duly pictured an oval, patrician face sunk beneath the flagstones.

We didn't get it, and there are many possible reasons. But my father was convinced for the rest of his life that the Dean and Chapter had refused his application because of his portrayal of choirboys in *Lord of the Flies*. Nothing could shake his conviction – no other possibility was ever entertained, and this was long before the publication of his novel *The Spire*, which really did offend a Dean of Salisbury. What's more, despite the occasional inconvenience, he rather liked to believe he had offended people – it fired him up.

But I was deeply ashamed that we had been thought unworthy of a house in the Close. I would have hated living there, with the dead bishop, the Close gates shut at night, the relentless bells, the sanctimonious pecking order, the ever-watchful Dean and Chapter. Nevertheless, the thought that all these people were cross with my father was anguish to me.

When I was older, an adolescent just beginning to recognise that he was occasionally rude, especially when he had drunk too much, I tried to suggest to him that people might not like what he was saying. He swung towards me, his eyes ferocious.

'*Your* trouble is you want everything to be *smooth*.'

Actually, that was disingenuous. He really didn't like me to upset people – especially him. He taught me to revere establishment rules, while he could show contempt for them. In that way we would always differ. It was not something I was brave enough to emulate. He had taught me too well.

4

The Old House at Marlborough

When, in the 1960s, my mother's daily help said she was going on a coach trip to Marlborough, we laughed at her. By then, even I had accepted the family attitude towards the town where my grandparents used to live. But as a child I felt very differently.

Salisbury was my home, so I despised it. I thought it totally lacking in glamour – despite the cathedral, Stonehenge, the old houses, the bridges and views, the strange names – Penny-Farthing Street, Gigant Street, the Canal (where perversely there was no water whatsoever). But I loved Marlborough, even the dreary parts, even in the rain. I thought it the richest, most colourful place I knew, and I was often astonished by the indifference shown by others. Even David was not as besotted. Its houses, with their red, fish-scale tiles coating their uneven walls, the wide High Street, all the secret passages and cool, narrow chasms between the buildings, the astonishing forest, with its towering trees, the hotel with its wonderful golden globe with a castle on top – all of this seemed to me prodigal and brilliant, perfectly expressing the rich character of the town itself.

I have dragged numerous friends round it and been puzzled when they said, as if pushed, yes it was pretty. Pretty? That was not the point. It was triumphantly unique; it was itself to the power of n. But my parents' view of the place was very different. For my father it was a place feared and disliked, that he had escaped from. For my mother, it represented baby-sitting.

I knew by the time I was eight or so that my parents sent me to Marlborough to be out of the way. Understandably. They were busy. They wanted to get on with things, lots of things. My memory is that I didn't care. The time I spent at Marlborough was by far the happiest of my childhood. Every room in my grandparents' house had mysteries and richness in it. Even when we had given the house up, the memories themselves became like a big bunch of grapes that I could hold in my hands and squeeze. But I was often ill there, the earliest example I know where my body forced my insensitive self to recognise what I was feeling.

Not that Marlborough was comfortable. It was brutally cold. I once lay in bed there in the Easter holidays, and watched my fingers turn blue. My grandparents' house had many dark corners, with looming strange spaces that had their own mysterious purpose, lost ages ago. It was sparsely lit, with few and badly placed light switches. The stone-flagged kitchen had no need of a fridge – the coolness of its three wells, hidden beneath the flags, permeated the room. The wire-mesh meat safe that stood in one corner added to the particular smell of the place – gas, damp, and old food. There was an enormous table, the top scrubbed white and velvety soft. There was an old dresser with three blue-and-white jugs, and a tall jar for the milk with a crocheted cover on it, weighted with blue glass beads. There was a white sink with a wooden draining board, scrubbed like the table. There was a gas stove, and next to it the old solid-fuel stove, now disused but still carefully blacked.

The beds, many carved and made by Alec, had lumpy mattresses, with feathers that poked you. They had flannelette sheets, and always felt clammy. Every evening, except in high summer, my grandfather would fill the black swan-neck kettle and push it into the coals of the dining-room fire. It would hiss and hum for about two hours, and then he would fill the old stone water bottles. He and I would solemnly distribute them among all the beds to be slept in.

When I knew the house, in the 1940s and 50s, it was still an Edwardian set piece. It had servants' bells. Until 1918, and the end of the Great War, if you were too poor to have servants you were probably one yourself. I was shocked to learn that my socialist grandparents had servants – two, a maid and cook, both live-in – but they would not have seen it that way at all. It was normal, and regarded as benevolently supplying employment. Eventually those servants had been 'let go' during the late 1920s, with much regret and I imagine some guilt, probably so that my grandparents could support their two sons at Oxford. I remember in my childhood, twenty years after this, that dust blurred the outline of the bells. But the sliding bell-pulls were still on the walls.

Next to my grandparents' brass bedstead was a curvy marble washstand. It was crowded with ornate china: an enormous bowl, a big-bellied jug for hot water, soap dishes, a shaving mug, even tooth mugs. On a low shelf, with two resilient-looking chamber pots, was a china bucket with a lid and bamboo handle. All the china matched, with gaudy, full-blown roses and a thin rim of gilding. This incongruous, almost vulgar wedding present had stood at their bedside for the fifty years of their marriage. No one used it – there was a spartan bathroom and a tall copper geyser, which erupted monstrously with a roar and a burst of flame like purple irises. But the washstand remained. On the other side of the bed, on my grandmother's dressing table, were silver button-hooks for the boots she had given up in about 1918. There were silver brushes for her silvery hair, and a pot with a silver lid in which to stuff the hair from her hairbrushes, used half a century earlier to pad out the structure she had worn as a young woman, piled on her head like the ice cream in a cone. She was thirty when Queen Victoria died. She and Alec married in 1906.

Their married life was one of wholesome thrift, and a necessity became a pleasure. My grandmother served up leftovers with ruthless persistence, until the last scrap was finished – or until some desperate family member surreptitiously threw it away. Lists were written on old pieces of card, then these were crossed out and the reverse side used. Sweaters, gloves, scarfs were unravelled and re-knitted, their wool squiggly, even after washing. Pencils were sharpened down to the last inch, and the sharpened bit was sometimes longer than the rest, so you could hardly hold it. My grandfather kept a pocket-knife for this purpose with him perpetually. Also in his pocket were small bundles of coiled string, various India rubbers, and a neatly folded and laundered but ink-stained handkerchief. Since his twenties he had had the same pocket-watch, steel-cased with a white enamel face and thin Roman numbers. It cost him two guineas in the 1890s and lasted more than sixty years. It hung on a small stand every night by his bed and never needed mending.

Things were bought to last. Plain and serviceable, they were nevertheless sometimes incidentally beautiful, and then giving pleasure. But I doubt that my grandparents sought such pleasure out. Perhaps they didn't know how. And this stemmed from morality as well as economy. From it, my father inherited two things – a permanent anxiety about money, liable to flare up suddenly like toothache, and a rebelliously contradictory desire to spend.

When I was off to university, he said to me, 'David has always been very good with money. I hope you won't be as good as he is.'

I wasn't. But I kept calm about it, which I think rather disappointed him. He felt the question of money required panic, as a kind of religious observance. Of course I was averagely extravagant, but not extreme, and I filled in counterfoils and checked bank statements, which was a further blow to him since he thought it unfeminine (though my mother did the same). For us, money was rational – it never was for him, however rich or hard-up he was. To him it was as uncontrollable as the weather, and never temperate.

At Marlborough, my grandparents' thrift had allowed the modest purchase of necessities. But it also permitted expense on objects others might have ignored. There were slides for Alec's two microscopes, glass plates for his old concertina camera, pads of thick paper for water colours, several metal paintboxes full of little tablets of colour, some still wrapped up like sweets, and with exotic names. Each box had a small white porcelain tray for mixing. There were camel-hair brushes in about twenty sizes, there was proper Indian mapping ink – I remember its smell. And musical instruments and books. In the mid 1930s my grandparents bought a car – a new one. They sent both their sons to Oxford for four years each. They paid for my father to do a fifth year, a DipEd.

It was a family article of faith that they were poor. But, as with my parents, their poverty was of rather a special kind. Soon after they were married, my grandmother was left a very little money, perhaps a couple of hundred pounds. It was from her father, a Cornish mining engineer called Thomas Curnoe. He had roamed the world – partly, it was said, to avoid murdering his wife. In California, Australia and Africa he found several small fortunes in gold, which he promptly lost again in Cornish tin. During her last years, Grandma told Theo, my uncle Jose's wife, that a little gold ring she had was 'Judy's ring'. It was small and bright, almost red, with triangular facets engraved with strange designs, possibly Masonic ones. Thomas Curnoe was a Freemason – I found his prayer book and regalia in the attic at Marlborough. And after Grandma's death, Theo faithfully gave the little ring to me. It was the last of Thomas Curnoe's gold, and appropriately – given the role of Cornwall in its making – it was lost in that shipwreck of 1967, when our yacht *Tenace*, almost the same colour as my ring, was run down and sunk.

Grandma was a taciturn woman, superficially quiescent with occasional bursts of stubbornness. Having sampled a savoury snack and liked it, she invested her Curnoe money in it, against all advice. The snack was Smith's Crisps, an absolute winner. I have wondered since if she liked them because they were so noisy to eat.

The success of her revolutionary investment put my grandfather in a quandary. A lifelong socialist, he believed it was wrong to make money from money in such a way. He told me when I was about nine that you should only earn money through your own labour, a simple statement I completely understood then but have since allowed to elude me. Luckily he also believed in the independence of women, and declared it was Mil's money, and she could therefore do what she liked with it. When she died in 1960, there was £1,900 in her estate, in cash and shares (the house itself was rented), a good sum in the circumstances. Sadly, she spent little on herself, buying few clothes, few books and as far as I can remember absolutely no luxuries at all. The only time I ever saw her handle money was when she gave me a three-penny bit to put in the collection plate. Even that may have been because my grandfather did not really approve of churchgoing.

But there were blazing contradictions, just like the washstand china. In the attic they kept extraordinary things. Going through it was rather like ransacking Tutankhamen's tomb. My grandmother had a wonderful little parasol of olive-green silk, with a slender folding handle of ivory and wood, and a three-inch fringe. She allowed my cousin Lizzie and me to play with it, carefully, and we took it in turns to be Cleopatra. My grandfather had a silk opera hat, which was collapsible and could be unfolded by a flick of the wrist. Rummaging shamelessly in the attic cupboard, I found two blocks of engraved calling cards, in flowing copperplate:

A. A. Golding

Mrs. A. A. Golding

There was a mauve cape of heavy silk, a copy of *Magnall's Questions*, crocheted collars, edgings for sheets and tablecloths. There was a bundle of lace, the piece bought by Alec for his dearest Mil before their marriage. He recounts in his journal how he ventured nervously into a shop in Brussels ('where there were only females'), and asked for it in what I imagine was very halting French. I keep it still, although it's very yellow, because his love for my grandmother made him brave enough – and extravagant enough – to buy it.

When I was eight or nine, I found a little white embroidered suit, for a boy of about six (my uncle's age when my father was a year old). I squeezed into it and went downstairs, to show off to my indulgent grandparents. If they minded me poking around among their old stuff, they never said. I expect they were grateful for peace and quiet. Usually, at Marlborough, I would be doing things with Alec, or even sometimes with Grandma. It must have been exhausting, and I am glad now to think that we all enjoyed my treasure hunts.

While my grandparents were alive, Marlborough with all its riches was just a place I loved to visit. It never occurred to me that it might vanish. After our family gave up the house in 1959, it naturally became something different. Painfully unbreakable associations from it litter my experience even now. Early on, with bloody-minded love, I chose to misinterpret the lines from 'O Little Town of Bethlehem':

> Yet in thy dark streets shineth
> The everlasting light . . .

They still, more than fifty years later, make me see the special blue-white street lamps of Marlborough, sparkling faintly in the winter fog.

There are other pictures, mostly of my grandfather – Alec in his seventies, bringing me my breakfast in bed; my absorption watching him at his workbench in the cellar, with the smell of the newly planed wood, and the plane itself, metal and high-stepped, like a dance slipper; the rhythmic, patient sound of Alec sawing wood in the cellar; Alec, his glasses reflecting the setting sun, playing patball tennis with me on the cool and dewy lawn, with the old racquets, one with a fishtail handle; Alec escorting me up to the dark lavatory in the evenings, because I was frightened of the overhanging shadows and open doors; Alec waiting for me on the landing, his vast old head on his arms, leaning on the banisters while, I now realise, he gathered back his breath.

When I was little, we would get up together so early that it seemed like the middle of the night. My earliest Christmas memory is of the dark dining room at Marlborough full of shadows, while I lit the white candles on the tree – with Alec patiently standing guard. I remember his age-spotted hands, their long fingers moving over the piano keys, finding the sounds he wanted. Notes for him were as if written out – he told me he could see a tune in his mind.

My grandmother must have realised early on that she could not compete with him. She was an indistinct figure, amiable but somehow in the distance. Did she mind this? Perhaps it suited her lifelong habit of living, like my father, mainly inside her head. But she too played the piano. I remember her playing a long, silvery piece – did the silver come from the name or was it already in the sounds I heard? – the opening of the Moonlight Sonata. And even she could sometimes emerge from the deep well of her reveries to tell me brilliant fragments about herself as a little girl. One of these – running home along the cliff top in Cornwall, bringing back a covered jug of cream, and stumbling so that it was all spilled – was so vividly poignant that for a while I remembered it as something I had seen on television.

But to my father the memories of 29 The Green were dark and troubling. After my grandparents died, I tried to explain how much was lost for me and how much I missed it. He said calmly, ruthlessly, that the house was really no more than the people who lived in it. Since they were dead, there was no point to the house. It hardly existed.

Vengefully, it continued to haunt his dreams for the rest of his life, sometimes with odd, discordant images, more often with nightmares. These, he told me, were literally hair-raising – it started, he said, with an unwilled tightening of the skin at the nape of the neck. Then you felt the hair slowly rising, lifting itself against gravity.

I used to feel the character of the house against my cheeks as I came in the door, even in sunshine. We were assured it was no older than the time of Charles II, built after the fire of 1653 almost consumed the town. My father thought this was rubbish. He believed the cellars were Saxon, with reused Roman tiles in the floor and walls. The age of the house became rather like my grandparents' poverty – a thing to believe in.

Alec himself would move through it in the dark, walking expertly round the place he had lived in for nearly half a century. He would work alone in the cellar, immune to its dark corners, its heaps of evil-looking coal and strange, humanoid shadows. He pushed away its effect by sheer force of belief. To him it was a place without atmosphere.

And the house itself is appealing, with two roof-gables and a projecting upper storey to the front porch (it held a very small bedroom that David and I used each to call 'my room'). It used to have a wavy, red-tiled roof, mossed and settled with age. It has a patch of back garden, carved out of the old burying ground. And the garden comes right up against the graveyard. The wall between these brilliant green spaces seemed to my father an entirely insufficient barrier against the dead bodies buried there. Even now, the tombstones confront the wall of the garden in a purposeful way, rather as if they are marching towards it.

But all of Marlborough was settled into the buried past, sunk in it, like someone up to their ankles. The roads near the Green have pictorial names – Silverless Street, Barn Street, St Martins, Tinpit, Kingsbury Street, Blowhorn Street, Coldharbour, Stoneybridges. Even Herd Street, which sounds prosaic, recalls the time when the locals drove their cattle up to the Common, while someone sounded a horn. The path through St Mary's churchyard, where Alec and I walked back from the bus, has a covering of stone flags, but it is still called Patten Lane, because in earlier times ladies had to use pattens – shoes with raised soles – to get to church through the unpaved mud.

Many of the Marlborough names are scattered through my father's novels. Place names delighted him. He collected them, much as his own father did mosses or flowers, fossils, or glass slides for the microscope. Coldharbour, he believed, meant the Romans had a camp there. Silverless Street had been the Jewish quarter, the 'less' reflecting their eventual eviction under a medieval monarch. My father may well have been mistaken, but as so often with him, accuracy was not the point. He even liked the way names had grown distorted – a pub in Ramsgate called 'The Case is Altered' was really, he told me, a reference to a causeway altar. He planned a story called 'The Goat and Compasses', which he said was a corruption, a smoothing down, of 'God encompasses us'.

Embedded in the old south wall of my grandparents' cellars, about eight feet below Patten Lane, was a piece of rotting wood. My father said it was an old window sill, a relic of an earlier time before the crumbled dirt accumulated on the path and rose up to bury the old window that used to look out into the daylight of the lane. Certainly the level of the graveyard has risen – for obvious and to my father disturbing reasons. He saw the earth thudding down on the coffins, the ground rising above the sleeping dead. But had it really risen on the path, year after year, gradually and inexorably? Had there really come a time when its slow rise had forced the old window to be finally abandoned and bricked up, earth-filled and useless? For my father there was no question. It was a sign that centuries had passed, and the piece of wood told that story.

Later, after Alec's death, and our departure from Marlborough, it became difficult to talk about the house, and the people who had once lived in it. The subject became indecent, not just with the indecency of death but for another reason – it struck against a barrier my father had built around matters he would sooner not discuss. Any allusion to them would trigger in him a special, hostile impassivity, an unapproachable, threatening silence. The subject would be frozen out. For many years the only way he and I could meet in conversation about the time at Marlborough was to remind each other of our shared sense of the uncanny. A discussion along these lines would generally finish with him retelling me with relish that Alec had discovered . . .

He would pause here on *discovered*, and he would look at me, opening his eyes in pretend horror, tensing his body as if recoiling. I would obediently feel fear. Alec, he would declare, discovered *human bones* in the garden. To my father this was absolutely the worst thing, the source of many terrors, in real life and in his novels. It's possible there were lawfully buried bones in their cheerful little garden, but that is a picture lighter than some. Or am I just being brave in daylight?

In any case, one does get used to such ideas. My look of surprise and horror eventually became over-rehearsed, and one day he suddenly said, 'Did *you* ever see anything?'

It was a challenge, a curiously hostile one. I scanned my memories. These were far more about feeling than seeing. However, I did remember one sight, inexplicable but not uncanny. One Christmas holiday, with all the family filling the house, I had been sleeping on a camp bed in my grandparents' bedroom, just under the window. One morning, looking curiously round the room in the early darkness, I saw a brown, friendly looking creature beside the fire, gazing back at me calmly with shiny dark eyes. We looked at each other, acknowledged each other, then, as the cold light grew, the creature changed, altered shape, lost colour and became a small bookcase. In rather the same way, when I described the experience my father's voice, usually warm, became non-committal – a voice from which all emotion was subtracted. He often used it for reading aloud.

'But it didn't frighten you, did it?'

'No – it was just there, that was all. And then not.'

He turned back to his book.

I felt, as I often did, that I was boring him. I had always tried to avoided reading his novels so that I could truthfully plead ignorance when asked to comment on them by teachers, scholars, university lecturers, vicars, etc. So I hadn't read the scrap of a reference in *Free Fall* to the little white creature Sammy Mountjoy sees on the top of the window – the creature that radiates friendliness. After my father's death – before I came across the *Free Fall* account – I read his two longer descriptions of his own experience that had inspired it, one in his journal, one in the account he calls 'Scenes From A Life'. As a child, in his cot in his parents' bedroom, that room where I had been, he too had seen something. I was shocked, but more at his reaction than about the possibility of this mysterious creature's existence. Perhaps what I had seen as boredom was chagrin at our shared experience? Or fear that a story he had told, and perhaps embellished, was true? And why, for both of us, was the creature friendly, though the house itself often felt so threatening? I never answered these questions, and I certainly never asked him. The whole matter became another awkward aspect of that house he hated in a town he disliked.

My father's resentment against Marlborough had set for ever in the winter of 1958–9, when it seemed to him that its inhabitants failed to express adequate sorrow over Alec's death. I don't think it occurred to him that people might have written to his brother Jose, as the elder of the two. Nor would this have been a good suggestion to make. I think he had always associated the town with unfulfilled desires, not just sexual ones (though there were plenty of those), but also his early ambitions – to be a poet, a musician, a success. In his years growing up in Marlborough, constrained and fretted by his parents' restrictive code of conduct – hard work, socialism, celibacy till marriage (and quite possibly after it as well), the worthy consolations of art, music and science – he had nursed a distaste for the small-town confinement which he thought Oxford would dissolve.

Also, Marlborough exemplified something he loathed all his life, even though he was fascinated by it and often carefully obeyed its rules. His novel *The Pyramid* examines with a kind of mesmerised contempt the tenacity of the English class structure. It was the only one of the non-*Flies* novels that was sold in Egypt, and must have puzzled many of its purchasers. His pyramid is an English one, illustrated through the medium of Marlborough, named Stillbourne in the book – a stagnant river, a still water that runs deep, a stillbirth of many lives. But the Bourne is also one of Salisbury's rivers, and runs into the Avon just south of the city. The first flat we rented there was in the road named after it, Bourne Avenue. One of my father's unpublished novels, which portrays a school rather like Bishop Wordsworth's, was written while we lived in that road, and it too is set in a town called Stillbourne.

So Stillbourne doesn't just stand for Marlborough, it stands for any English town, stratified and deadened by convention and class. He may not have calculated all this – he was often amused by the complex interpretations critics applied to the names he chose, names that he said had usually come to him by accident, or by a trivial process of association. Dawlish for Salisbury, Ifor instead of Evans. Actually, I think the process was far from trivial – rather, it was instinctive and sometimes poetic – but he thought of it as private, and did not wish to load it with literary significance.

Marlborough was also the place where he had struggled with Alec, father and son, teacher and pupil, ruler and ruled. When I eventually found the courage to tell my father how Alec's death had affected me, how I had loved him, how I still felt a painful lack of the affection he had shown me – my father replied levelly, almost threateningly, 'He had mellowed by the time you knew him.'

No doubt this is true. My father mellowed greatly as a grandfather, and I recognised then how he must have felt, watching Alec's care of David and me, how Alec had all the time in the world for us, how gentle he was, how his teaching went step by step so we never felt inadequate. I saw the same change in my father.

But he also had a steely reticence about Alec. When, after Alec's death, I asked what he had died of, my father looked up from his book, took off his spectacles, and said, in a voice full of distaste and disapproval, 'Let's just let that be Alec's secret, shall we?'

There was no question of a reply.

Alec and Grandma, stuck for ways of entertaining their children, especially in winter, took them for long healthy walks, as my parents did us. They would take Jose and Billy round Marlborough and its outskirts, and up to the forest, sometimes several miles. My father describes one of these occasions, when he was perhaps five or so, lagging behind and whining (his word) to be carried. Then, all at once he was terrified to see his parents had disappeared into the winter twilight. Looking around him, he saw the enormous head of a stag, peering at him with a 'terrible indifference' over a thorn-brake.

So I trundled as fast as I could down the path . . . and then my parents stepped out from behind a tree where they had hidden from me in a small family jest to see how Billy would behave, lost on his own in the dark forest.

Can it have been a joke? A child's misinterpretation? A disinterested scientific experiment? My grandmother – who had many fears of the uncanny herself – certainly had harshness in her, and temper, learnt by example from her own mother, of whom I was told she was terrified. Maybe that is the explanation. But my father included Alec in his condemnation, and never forgot or forgave that moment in the forest.

Not long before Alec died, I stood one day, an uncritical twelve-year-old, watching him in the kitchen at 29 The Green. Alec was boiling bones to make glue, a bizarre but habitual activity of his. The glue would be used to help Jose make models of battlefields for his pupils at the school in Grantham where he taught history.

And Alec said to me, as the pot steamed on the gas stove, that Jose had worked hard all his life but Bill had had all the success. I found that extraordinary, even at the time. Did he really not know of the hours writing novels that didn't work? The concentration? The undoubted sacrifices? I should have said – since I knew it – that my father worked very hard indeed. But I didn't. Worse still, after Alec's death I faithfully conveyed the gist of it to my father. I expect it was intended that I should. All he said was 'Really?' with an upward inflection, but not so much that I was obliged to reply. The conversation was halted. By that point, of course, Alec could no longer be challenged; my father could never be victorious.

During the Marlborough years, for those of us who were prepared to assimilate the reassurances of my grandfather, conveyed via his picture of the gloriously material world, the shadow quality of 29 The Green could be made tolerable – with Alec's qualities, not only his knowledge and skill but also his affection. But my father refused to impoverish or reduce the ambiguity that the rest of us ignored when we could. He would not accept Alec's assurances or his world, and so he was left with the fears of the one he preferred. No wonder Marlborough was not rich for him. It was a battlefield.

Many aspects of my father's life after Alec were versions of escape. The daily round at home sometimes had too much of Marlborough in it. His most spectacular and successful leap for freedom was his defiant purchase in 1985 of a lovely, really rather posh Georgian house in Cornwall, a house that was above all *light*, a house where the cellars were quite without threat, where there were no dead bodies. But such fears were not only uncomfortable, they were food for his imagination. Now I wonder, were the novels an escape from Marlborough too? Perhaps, when he really had escaped, the novels were not as easy to find.

When I was ten or eleven or so, I made an attempt to cure my fears of the long night. By then I was old enough for the future to spoil the present, and I needed freedom from the approaching dark. I went to my grandfather and told him how frightened I was. Alec, loving and calm, drew on his own great strength.

'Look,' he said, 'it's quite simple. You see, nothing can be visible or make a sound or move, unless it has the physical means. There has to be energy, and energy has to be produced by something physical. Ghosts cannot exist because they have no means of existing. It's as simple as that.'

Later, in an experimental spirit, impressive in its way, I put to my father the same plea for help. He took me on his knee, his large and flat hands round me, a warm bulwark against anything. Unusually, he put aside his religious reticence.

'Look,' he said, 'it's quite simple. You see, each one of us has a guardian angel standing behind us. It never sleeps and its job is to watch over you. God has sent it there although you can't see it. And it follows you wherever you go and keeps watch over you all night. It's as simple as that.'

5

A School for Gentlewomen

We were walking round Laverstoke, a long, river-edged village below Bourne Avenue, on the outskirts of Salisbury. I was seven. My father pointed up the hill. I saw a high wire fence. Beyond it were girls – women, they seemed to me. They were running around, waving sticks.

'That's your school.'

I went there a year later, in September 1953, two months after my eighth birthday, to Godolphin School, Salisbury. The three hundred pupils wore stiff straw boaters – our special Godolphin name for them was 'boards'. Our school badge was a double-headed eagle similar to that borne by Holy Roman Emperors and for some years I believed that the Hapsburgs were a branch of the Godolphins. We carried our books in brown canvas bags but poshly we called them sacs. Bags would not have done at all. During the day at school we wore blue cotton smocks or pinnies over skirts and ties and jerseys. Some girls had a full-length cloak, a navy-blue semicircle of wool, lined with scarlet, often worn with a corner flung toga-like over one shoulder. My father adored these, and would have loved to buy me one, but only boarders had them. For my first eight years at Godolphin I was a day-girl, an inferior sub-species. When in 1961 I did become a boarder I was too angry at the whole business to gratify my poor old dad by dressing up. Especially since he would not be there. He would be in America, teaching rich American girls, which I minded rather a lot.

Of course, there were no boys.

'Oh God, the giver of all good gifts,' we intoned, at least once a week, 'Who didst put into the heart of Elizabeth our foundress the will to care for Thy children . . . Grant, we humbly beseech Thee, that we, beholding her good works, may by the truthfulness of our speech, by the loyalty of our work and the gladness of our lives, show forth our thankfulness for these Thy mercies, and by Thy grace leave a goodly heritage for those that shall come after . . .'

This elegant prayer, which could pass for seventeenth-century prose, set the school in the sedate, comfortable world of the Church of England, *and* the Tory Party, *and* the Establishment. We knew where we were. The prayer itself was a beautiful piece of work. I was lucky that it became so familiar to me. In many respects Godolphin was a very good school.

It was founded in 1726 by Elizabeth Godolphin and her husband (and cousin) Charles. At her death Elizabeth left money to be used for 'the education of eight young gentlewomen'. Not young ladies. Never, ever, were we told to be ladylike, heavens no. Even in the 1950s, we were still young gentlewomen, and this distinction is brutally drawn in Jane Austen's *Emma*, where the social-climbing Mrs Elton expresses her surprise at discovering Emma's former governess, Mrs Weston, to be 'ladylike'. Emma's comment to herself is savagely precise: 'Astonished that the person who had brought me up should be a gentlewoman!'

This was a game we all learnt – the precise weighing of social nuance – and we were often better at it than our teachers. A member of staff once instructed a pupil to pick up her serviette. Calmly, cruelly, the girl replied that she had already picked up her napkin. We were appreciative. She had definitely won that round. When I told my father, he buried his head in his hands. But he continued to send me there.

By contrast, my brother was sent to Bishop Wordsworth's School, which was free, and effectively the local boys' grammar. He hated my school and declared we were all snobs, which at the time I thought outrageous and untrue.

The money it cost to send me there was a problem virtually up to my last year at school. I was very aware of my parents' heroism in coping. They had not only to pay the fees but also buy the extensive, esoteric uniform. There were many garments which had to be ordered from a special, ruinously expensive out-fitters in Bournemouth. There was a navy serge divided skirt for games, possibly the ugliest garment I have ever worn; two ties, a plain red school one (I wore it illegally on election days) and a flimsy striped house one; two blue pinafores; a blue beret as well as the loathsome and painful board; house sweaters for games; a navy-blue cardigan; four pairs of navy knickers which we wore for gym; three ordinary and three sports Aertex shirts; two sum-mer dresses. There were white tennis dresses too, if you were any good, which luckily I wasn't.

There was the brown canvas sac printed to order with its own-er's name, though it was decreed that 'girls whose mothers are Old Godolphins may use their mother's sac'. This meant some girls had a sort of shadow identity, a glimpse into their mothers' past, and – even weirder – into a time when their mothers were *girls*. There was a navy winter coat, a navy raincoat, a navy suit. If you did music you had to have a brown leather music bag, expensive and extremely heavy, and – like the sac – printed with your name.

We had gym shoes, netball shoes, tennis shoes, lacrosse boots, indoor shoes, outdoor shoes, boots. Uncharacteristically, the tennis shoes also did for cricket. There was a shoe *bag*, on which my mother rebelliously economised, dyeing my old ballet one the regulation red. There was the amazing lacrosse stick, wood-en and leather – the leather had to be oiled. I wore special wide navy-blue hair-ribbons on the ends of my plaits.

When I became a boarder, I had to have two dozen small and one dozen large white handkerchiefs, as well as a few non-controversial non-uniform clothes, known as 'mufti'. That word, with its hinterland of masculinity, the army and the empire, brings back the life of a boarder to me as precisely as the smell of school soap. None of this was trivial – it was designed to set us apart. It was rather like being a member of a secret society. It was all expensive and almost all exceptionally ugly, a good example of how much money you need in order to be really badly dressed. When – usually to the sound of my father hissing and sighing with anxiety – a new batch of clothes was bought, I would feel angry and guilty, both about the cost and the horror of it all. I would unpick the old name tapes – J. D. GOLDING in red capitals, a person I felt was not me – then iron them and sew them in a rage on to the ghastly new stuff.

I hated it – and I always felt ugly at school, not just because I was a rather pudding-faced child by that time, but because my brother loathed the fact I went there, and fiercely resented the money it cost. I believe my mother did too. Worse, the school's special subject – social status – sometimes pierced her careful camouflage. In 1953, when I was in my first year, and inscribing the envelope for my report, I wrote '21 Bourne Ave', as my parents did. My teacher reprovingly told me using 'Ave' was 'lower-class', and I took this piece of information back to my mother. Her rage was blistering.

When David and I cooked up a scheme for me to go to the girls' grammar, thus freeing my parents to spend more money on our latest boat, my father was indignant.

'It's her school. It's a very good school.'

I tried to explain that I felt it was unfair. I waited for support from my brother, but he had mysteriously absented himself. A better strategist, he recognised a fruitless argument. He saw, as I did not, that the real debate was not about education. It was about class.

My father told me many times that when he went up to Oxford in 1930 he didn't even know which knife and fork to use. I believed he was exaggerating, as he often did. I was also surprised at his use of such a hoary old cliché. I didn't understand. It took me decades to realise that he had gone out and paid good money for my failure to comprehend.

The uncomfortable truth is that, however much I disliked Godolphin, however much I felt the contempt of many – though not all – of my teachers, the decade I spent there did give me the capacity to slip comparatively unnoticed into the snootier reaches of middle-class life. I became practised in the subtleties of the class system, and acquired feelings both in support of it, sadly, and against. My father had to scramble himself into this knowledge unaided. He knew it took time and effort. In 1970, when Terrell came to stay for Christmas as my actual – paid-up, as it were – fiancé, we went to a party where Lord David Cecil and his wife were also guests. My father was impressed by the relaxed way in which Terrell addressed Rachel Cecil as Lady David, a bizarre but correct formula.

He muttered to me, 'I *say*. Terrell *has* got the title business weighed off, hasn't he?'

His admiration was quite unselfconscious, quite without irony or (heavens) reproach. He might have been talking about a good shot at tennis. And there was relief as well, because it *mattered*. Terrell's graduation *summa cum laude* from Columbia and his scholarship to Balliol, his Phi Beta Kappa membership, his confident independence, none of this made nearly as good an impression as that half-minute of conversation. Class for my father was a real source of fear, a sort of bear pit in the drawing room.

It was quite clear that he had been unhappy at Oxford, yet he equally clearly wanted both David and me to go there. After his death, I decided to see for myself what information the university still retained about him. I went to Oxford and met two archivists: one from his college, Brasenose, and the other from the university. Both were extremely helpful (as they were subsequently to John Carey, my father's biographer). The college archivist showed me letters from my father that revealed how much of a dreary financial struggle the whole thing had been – not just for him, but for his parents. The university archivist provided a further, sharper revelation. The University Appointments Committee – an early form of careers service – had carefully noted on their index card their considered judgement of my father as 'not quite a gent'. The jaunty, Wodehousean tone doesn't mean it's a joke, and it's certainly not a compliment. The judgement was precise and professionally significant.

I wish I could learn to be pleased about this. I could believe, for example, that he had more vigour in him for not being the younger son of an earl or the grandson of a general. But his own bitterness about Oxford came through very clearly in his journal, and in novels such as *Pincher Martin*. Other details are very positive – he has passed his exams, knows several languages, can play the piano well, the cello, the violin and the oboe, and, they say, 'may get a first', though he didn't. His tutors are distantly favourable, though perhaps not enthusiastic. On a later card, from his DipEd studies in 1937–8, they describe him as 'a decent, sincere man', and they mention his book of poems published by Macmillan in 1934 – a considerable feat for a grammar-school boy of twenty-three. But in the coded initials of his entry (interpreted for me once more by the scrupulous university archivist), he was N.T.S. Not Top Shelf.

It's too late now to apologise to my father for being shallow and unsympathetic. I should have realised. When he repeated stories it was usually because they were vital to him, like Alec's discovery of human bones in the garden at Marlborough. He wasn't reshaping or polishing. Instead, he was reminding himself of a truth that might otherwise vanish – in the case of Oxford, into sentimentality or nostalgia. Oxford in the 1930s was still a place of outrageous privilege, of rigid and effective class divisions, which both subtly and unsubtly apportioned opportunity by rank, and permanently shaped people's careers and lives, so reinforcing privilege for the next generation.

With all my father's talent and energy, with all his gifts and readiness to apply them, Oxford somehow managed to keep from him and a possible employer a sense of his particular value, as well as any sense of that institution's approval. One might say that the University Appointments Board had to safeguard the currency of its recommendations, given the expectations of future employers. After all, otherwise someone like my father, on the basis of his many good qualities, might have ended up quite unsuitably in charge of some top-shelf children. But the board makes sure this will not happen. It carefully notes that he is 'fit only for day schools'. So he sent his daughter to a place he hoped would fix that.

Why not his son?

The obvious answer is that he knew Bishop Wordsworth's was a good school. While he disliked the headmaster, Freddie Happold, and laughed at him behind his back – as many of the staff did – he also recognised that the school was exceptional. There was no fee-paying boys' school in Salisbury remotely comparable either to Bishop Wordsworth's or Godolphin. But that was not all. It was favouritism towards his little daughter, as well as the product of a complicated desire – to see her protected from the humiliations which beset him, to see her transformed into a successfully feminine creature, to see her within reach of the freedoms, however much he despised them, of the English upper middle classes. Also, I believe he wanted her – me – to be well trained. Obedient. And I must say, I am.

So he paid his money and to a certain extent got the result he wanted. 'Vive Godolphin!' he writes in his journal in 1972. He is showing us slides of their holiday – sixty-six in number, most genuinely beautiful, and half of them taken underwater.

I was amused and grateful to notice that Judy managed to make sixty-six different noises of approval and admiration – no mean feat in social behaviour. Vive Godolphin!

Also, much as I fight against acknowledging this, it *was* a good school and taught me many good things – the virtue of loyalty, the value and something of the cost of truthfulness, a belief in justice even if it was called fair play, an admiration for female strength and individuality, a sense of honour. Unsurprisingly, it made no attempt to teach open-mindedness, or the desirability of questioning the status quo. I am still, half a century later, appallingly docile in the face of authority.

But what about David? Didn't he require the same disguise, the same opportunity?

By the time I was old enough to notice – perhaps seven or so – our family already had a pronounced diagonal structure. David and my mother, Daddy and me. Of course it wasn't always clear, but that shape was the foundation, the default. My father's feelings about David, in particular, were full of contradiction and things unsaid. He believed that David was stronger than I was, more assertive, more capable of dealing with the outside world. This was understandable. But there were less generous elements, and as David became a teenager, and would soon be a man who might challenge my father, these grew obtrusive. The bond (a very strong one) between them grew more anxious and irritated. As every contact became fraught and competitive, their conversation stilted, their mutual but stifled anger more densely apparent, my mother and I would find ourselves holding our breath. If David entered a room where his father sat alone, he would turn round and go out again. My father did the same, though he tried to disguise it. There was too much memory, too much history.

What did that history contain? I first noticed trouble when I was about ten, and David fifteen, in 1955. I would often find him miserable on mornings before school. He would of course tell me nothing. I still don't know what was behind it all. But this was followed by a long build-up to storms, unwillingness to go to school, and arguments with my father. Then there was trouble with schoolwork, though of the two of us David had always seemed far brighter. Now it looked as if he might not do well at O level. A specific, vertiginous fear swamped our home. Failure in exams was a terrible thing. It was like death – it just mustn't happen. And if it did – then that was the end of everything.

I suspect the real problem started much earlier, when David was small. Born at the beginning of the war, he spent his first five years with his father an occasional and puzzling visitor. And his father, an affectionate, warm-hearted man who loved his own father deeply, despite their differences, was driven all his life, up until his final decade, by a searing competitiveness. He was strong, full of self-will, full of the need to succeed, to be different from and better than his peers. It was that need which helped him become a writer. He told me privately once, with shame, but also with a kind of bravado, that he wrote *Lord of the Flies* partly to prove he wasn't 'just an ordinary schoolteacher'.

It was hard for him to let any rival win. The difficulty would appear, subtly, even in his role as host, one that he regarded (I don't exaggerate) as sacred. Some managed to defeat him even so. But David found this increasingly difficult. His father was better than him at everything he tried – sport, sailing, science, chess, music, languages. The one area where David achieved and his father did not was mathematics. If my brother had been able to excel at school in a subject not already claimed by his distinguished, charismatic father, who was also one of his teachers, perhaps he would have been able to leave that particular sphere of conflict, and move out from the family. Sad to say, his interest in the subject evaporated. Is it possible he didn't value something unless his father was good at it? Is it possible that his father subtly belittled such achievements? Either way, it was a missed opportunity.

There were other problems. For several years my mother had been anxious about David's lack of height. She said to me on many occasions how sad it must have been for him to realise he would never grow taller than five foot five. Actually, I believe it upset her more than him, but her feelings were clear to all of us. Above all, she was his favourite parent, as my father was mine. Though she was protective and affectionate towards him, he knew she was in love with my father.

As things grew more strained between them, I would see my father make conscious efforts to put David first. Sometimes when we were sailing, for example, he would praise David to other people. But the tone of his voice would always take back much of the effect. Love and a cough cannot be hid, and certainly the particular sort of love – fierce, possessive, grudging and contained – that my father felt for his son could not be ignored. For one thing, it embraced something which looked like its opposite, perhaps because he so often hated himself. On rare occasions I actually saw him use some excuse – an urgent errand for my mother, for example – to knock against my brother, to push him out of the way. I saw he was glad to do this. He was giving in to a powerful feeling. And I saw David's bewilderment.

As time wore on, my father understood this himself. In 1975, a parent for thirty-five years, he writes with sad self-knowledge:

> I only say that the trouble with parents is that they cannot give their children freedom even if they want to. Each generation tries and fails, with a sense of mixed good will and duty.

In our family this difficulty had a particular edge. Despite my early awareness of the fault lines in the family, I hardly ever managed to protect David or help him. Partly, this was mere cowardice. But I found it difficult to think ill of my father. I admired and loved him. And he was fun. He made life exciting. It's taken me fifteen years since his death to arrive at what I think of as a balanced view – to hold the two aspects of him together in my mind. While he was alive I think it was impossible.

During the years I've spent writing this memoir, I've had at the back of my mind an event from my childhood, something I wanted to include, without understanding why. But it did not involve my father.

When I was about seven or eight, in 1953 or thereabouts, I belonged to a little gang of girls. We were allowed to roam very freely, and consequently had many adventures, some scary.

One of our risky pastimes was ringing the bell of a neighbouring house where two men lived. Mostly, the nice one would answer the door and give us glasses of rather weak orange squash. I remember it had bits floating in it. Still, we drank it and thanked him politely. Where was the risk? Well, sometimes the other man answered the door. He looked quite similar but he was completely different. He would snarl and shout and threaten to set the dogs on us. Then we would shriek and run down the path, gathering out of breath in the nearest of our hideouts to enjoy our fear.

It was about thirty years before I realised that the two men were one person.

Samuel Johnson said, 'In lapidary inscriptions a man is not upon oath.' Daughterly memories might well have the same dispensation. But I believe I must reject it. I need to make these two men one – the warm, embracing man I adored, and the indifferent, sometimes self-centred, occasionally cruel man, who could drink too much, could be crushing, contemptuous, defeating, deadening. This is hard. It has taken me a decade and a half to write it down. But it is part of my family's story and especially part of David's.

I need to stress that he was often generous and self-deprecating. He was hugely funny. He let me boss him around – send him to the doctor, tell him some (though only some) difficult truths. We shared many private jokes, many companionable times. I was delighted when I pleased him, when I made him laugh. I never saw quite the same between him and David.

I now realise that for years I tacitly assumed that fathers do not love their sons. When, in 1989, David was recovering from his second psychotic episode, we all met at the hospital in Salisbury where he was being treated. My parents had not seen him for some weeks. My mother embraced him. My father and he awkwardly shook hands.

I knew that my father loved me, of course. But I carefully hid from myself the idea that he didn't always want to be bothered with me – that I was in the way. After Alec, and after Alec's death, he was the most important person in my world, the one – until I had a family – whom I loved the most. His affection, challenging but warm, had been there all my life. Hadn't it? On the rare occasions when that warmth withdrew, to be replaced by a cold and deliberate rage, I felt shrivelled, obliterated. I imagine that was how my brother felt quite often.

There were practical barriers for David too. Families allocate roles to individuals. My parents and I were quicker of speech than David, and were often able (and willing) to deny him the opportunity of answering back. As we three showed off, our words neat and fast as the slip-catching we would practise in the garden or on the beach (David, by contrast, was very good at that), he became conversationally more and more uncertain. It was hard for him to find a way in. Very rarely, I allowed myself to see how unfair this was. I intervened once in a discussion, quite an amiable one.

'Come off it, Daddy. You can't tell David what he thinks, and then criticise him for it!'

David, startled, thanked me. This alone showed me how little he expected support. But my father was skittishly amused, giggly, as if he'd been caught out. He had known what he was doing.

My mother was protective towards David, but there were times when she was unable to intervene. And perhaps there were times when she thought she might make matters worse. She told me this had been so when David was a small child. She would feel she had to tell him off before my father did, because she would do it more gently. And different things mattered to her. She didn't understand what was really painful for him.

Above all, I think both my parents saw their children as a kind of extension of themselves. A friend of the family once told me how my father had confided in her, describing David's mental illness as the tragedy of my father's life. That seemed wrong to me. If it was anybody's tragedy, it was David's. Though also, perhaps, my mother's.

When I was a child, my mother's life was very full. She ran the family, shopped and cooked, looked after us if we were ill. But she was also helping my father with his writing, pursuing her interests in acting, making clothes for herself and me, and after about 1957 teaching part-time. She had little opportunity to give us practical help, though she often gave me good advice. She told me that it is always more effective to give one excuse rather than several; also, that the more socially poised you are the briefer your farewells.

I think that in many ways she wished me well, unless I actually got in her way. As a child, I was no sort of rival to her with people outside the family. Occasionally, though, I would see that my closeness to my father irritated her, and sometimes she was furiously angry with the pair of us. Naturally, her energies were limited. She was very focused on my father, and after that on David. When I was about eleven, my dentist ticked her off in the waiting room for failing to bring me for a couple of years. She excused this by saying we had had 'family problems'. After she had left, he asked me what she had meant. I was appalled by this invitation to disloyalty, and said I had no idea. So he asked if it was trouble about my brother. I probably agreed, out of cowardice apart from anything else. As so often, I hadn't recognised what was going on. It was a shock to find myself part of a situation with a name – 'family problems'.

She always, I believe, saw herself as a good mother. In some ways she was right. We were well fed. We were given many opportunities though, as I suspect is often true, our seizing of those opportunities was much affected by our parents' fears and preoccupations, as well as our own. They tried to give us freedom through money and education. They told us about their own experiences, hoping to prevent us from making similar mistakes. But we lacked confidence, and this sabotaged the good things. Of course there were exceptions. David's sailing was a freedom for him. Godolphin gave me a better camouflage in some ways than my mother's. And we both knew we were clever. But something seemed to stop us. It was as if we accepted that we could not make a go of things.

Also, they did make mistakes. My mother was very determined, and once she had decided to do something she carried it through regardless. So it sometimes happened that her example got me into real trouble. I didn't understand that a form of behaviour people appreciated from her was not acceptable for me.

She carried things off with a combination of charm and personal theatre.

When I was about nine, she told me to kill any wasps I saw, because they would damage the strawberries she grew. I hate to think of the number of harmless creatures I slaughtered. I now find it puzzling that I didn't see her instruction as wrong, but she was very clear about it. All round our garden there were dreadful jam jars with drowned wasps floating in them. There was even one on the kitchen windowsill that smelt of jam with a whiff of decay. And she would tread on the wasps, squash them against the windowpane. So I copied her, obeying orders. One day I did so at school and there was uproar. She was no help at all in the resultant row. She had the survivor's capacity for just not being there.

On this occasion I think the storm was accidental. Later, there were times when I'm sure it was deliberate.

After my father won the Nobel Prize in 1983, many film crews descended on my parents' cottage, heaping cameras and cables in my mother's sitting room. The place filled up with casual groups of strangers, nipping through the flower beds or into bedrooms in search of a better angle. I was staying there with my two children during one such invasion, heavily pregnant with my third child. My mother, famously hospitable, was making sandwiches. After a while, however, she grew irritated at her kitchen role. The celebrated author was being interviewed elsewhere, behind a closed door. She told me to go and knock, and tell them lunch was ready. Naively, I did as I was told, thereby interrupting the perfect take. The director could barely contain his rage. It was smoothed over by the luckless girl whose job it was to be nice to everybody. In some distress, I told my mother about it. She smiled grimly.

'It's *my* house.'

I was thirty-eight at the time – even at that age I didn't see what she was doing. For years afterwards I couldn't connect her instructions with her remark. I assumed the whole thing was co-incidence.

Of course, she was a mixture. She was very generous to me once they had money. She told me that she was sorry that I had so few toys during my childhood (though actually I had as many as I wanted). Sometime in the late 1980s she offered to give me Tullimaar, their beautiful Cornish house that my father put in her name. But her feelings were ambivalent – I can see that now. Incredible as it would have seemed to me at the time, I think she envied me – I have no idea why. Perhaps just because I was young. None the less, I often felt her contempt, usually amused and utterly patronising. In my childhood she and my father quarrelled about things they did for me. She was angry with us on one of my birthdays, and spoilt the day. When I was quite small, I was sent over to Marlborough as usual one weekend, and when I came back my bedroom had been beautifully wallpapered, covered in lines of pink rosebuds, diagonally, like trellis. My mother, pretending to laugh above an erupting resentment, subtracted much of my pleasure by telling me that she and my father had quarrelled so badly over it that they stopped speaking.

Occasionally she simply took things from me – a purse I had bought which matched her handbag; a blue bath towel that my father had said brought out the colour of her eyes. The way she looked was supremely important to her, and she assumed the rest of us accepted this necessity. But such events brought me a bitter sense of my unimportance. I feel anger about them even now.

She tried hard to do better than her own mother, of whose shortcomings she was very aware. I imagine that she feared, as I have in my turn, that her mother's characteristics affected her own capacity to raise her children. She often told me, self-consciously and out of the blue, that she *did* love me, as if we both needed convincing.

She liked us to seem close as mother and daughter. In front of others, especially men, her manner towards me became far more affectionate. I suspect this happens quite often – a parent in public puts on a bit of a show. No doubt I do myself. But with her it was a sharp contrast and a bravura performance, and I played along. I didn't want to embarrass people. Maybe I hoped the affection would become real. But I despised myself as I did it.

She tried gingerly to prepare me for change, though she had many inhibitions – especially about my body, something she approached with a hesitation, both verbal and physical, that I thought remarkably like distaste. She told me in the autumn of 1957, when I was twelve, that it looked to her as if I would soon begin menstruation. I nodded diligently. I thought it was probably a new kind of maths, my mother's best subject – at school we had just started geometry and algebra.

One day the following January, I woke up with a searing pain in my stomach. I went to the bathroom. When I took down my pyjamas, I saw streaks of thick brownish blood. I felt faint with terror and shock. What had I done? Then I heard my mother's voice outside the door.

'Darling, can you unlock it?'

I opened the door, and for the first and last time flung myself into her arms, weeping.

My mother changed my bloodstained sheets and put me and my new pink sanitary belt to bed. Then, without another word, she rushed out of the house. She came back three hours later, explaining that we had needed more sanitary towels.

That evening, my father sat on my bed and told me that I was a woman now, and (interestingly though perhaps untruthfully) that he believed this to be an honour and a privilege. He said it meant I was like the Queen, whom he thought of as a glamorous young woman. It depressed me, since I saw her as middle-aged (she was just over thirty). After that, inspiration failed him, and there was a silence between us, though a kindly one. I was besotted with ballet at the time, and shyly suggested that this also meant I was like Alicia Markova. Born in 1910, she had probably by then embarked on the other end of the process, but my father prudently decided the menopause could wait for another day, and agreed that yes, indeed, I was like Alicia Markova.

I suspect he had also been detailed to instruct me, at a high level of generality, on the complex responsibilities of being a woman, such as not answering back and not getting pregnant, responsibilities that could in a prettier girl have come into conflict. But by then his lack of embarrassment had been overwhelmed by a more customary reticence. Poor man, he did not attempt to explain any of it in biological terms. However, his practical knowledge was considerable. I often became extremely tetchy before a period, and I must say he was patient to a fault on these occasions, greeting my tearful apologies with the resigned remark that it was 'just nature, darling'.

But the theory of the whole business was another matter. It was not a neutral subject, perhaps coloured by what he terms his horror, as an adolescent, at the imagined physiology of women. He once told me that 'primitive people' believed that menstruation was killing a baby. I did not like to ask him what he believed – I thought I knew, but it would have been rude to suggest he was 'primitive'. However, I developed the inconvenient habit of fainting, bang on schedule, every twenty-six days, partly because I so hated and loathed the eruption of blood, and knew that I must hide it at all costs. Ironically, it was when I became a boarder – aged sixteen – at Godolphin, that I learnt what it was all about. I had the good luck to share a dormitory with a cheerful girl called Vicky, who was doing A-level biology. The fainting stopped. Later, she became a paediatrician.

But all this was far ahead. My arrival at Godolphin in September 1953, aged eight, had coincided with my father sending the dog-eared and much travelled typescript of his novel, 'Strangers From Within', to the tenth publisher to receive it. The publisher's reader succinctly and famously rejected it, but it so happened that a new editor, a young barrister called Charles Monteith, picked the typescript off the slush pile and read it. A year later, in September 1954, an edited version was published, with a new title – *Lord of the Flies*. (This confused me greatly; I had thought the novel was going to be called Faber and Faber.)

Almost immediately our lives began to change. My father no

longer dispatched parcels in hope or received them with mourning. He frequently caught the train up to London from the centre of Salisbury. I asked my mother why he didn't go down to the bottom of our road and get on a train there. I had heard the train passing in the night, hooting and roaring. I visualised him standing there with his arm out. My mother gravely explained that one had to go to the railway station, a place of great mystery and excitement to me since we went everywhere by bus.

Other mysteries appeared. For the first time I observed alcohol and its transformative effects in the adults around me. Strange people came and went with great suddenness. My father became even more preoccupied, and had long discussions with my mother. Was he happier? It is often assumed that people who achieve their heart's desire are doomed to disappointment. Happier or not, he was certainly busier. Oddly, he thought of himself as a lazy person. That's quite wrong. Activity delighted him; he just wanted to be able to choose the activity. In 1954 it began to seem as if he could.

6

Summer and the Sea

Seahorse disappeared in 1951, lamented by some of us and not others. We spent the next four summers – blissfully in my case – with my father's parents, in Cornwall, Devon or North Wales, in genteel hired houses found by Grandma in the classified pages of *The Lady*.

My father would catch the bus to Marlborough the night before we left. I watched at the garden fence in the early pinkish light, and eventually my grandparents' black Morris 10, with the big canvas bag for luggage on the back, came chugging sedately into view down the London Road, my father stoically at the wheel, thoroughly supervised by his father as navigator and his mother as general advisor.

Our holiday, begun excitingly at 4.30 a.m., would continue with us leaving Salisbury around 7, stopping about two hours later to eat hard-boiled eggs with salt and limp slices of white bread. This was lunch, a meal my grandmother pushed earlier and earlier. Everything after it was declared to be tea, and therefore trivial. One year we had a fourth or fifth tea of choc ices in a traffic jam in Honiton. Some years my mother would decide there was no room for her in the car, so she would catch the train. It was a long time before I realised this was not the great sacrifice I thought it.

During the summer of 1954 we went to Devon and stayed in a house in Paignton. Sometimes we went with my grandparents to the town beach, below the promenade with its paths and flower beds. My grandparents sat in deckchairs obediently facing the sea but it was not really their idea of a beach. It was too domestic, too southerly, too full of things for holidaymakers. They missed the rolling breakers of Newquay. In their view, if you didn't have to wrap up, you weren't at the seaside.

My parents discovered another beach, small, very pretty, and deserted. We often bathed naked there, though I remember my brother refused to do this. But the remaining three of us jumped in and out of the water, in my case quite unselfconsciously. My naked father ran up and down the beach as well, and I think it is just possible that he was trying out what it was like to do that, as research for the naked Neanderthals in *The Inheritors*. The dates on his first draft for that book suggest he didn't start it until several months later, but he could have been planning it. Or the action itself might have provoked him to wonder about the precursors of *Homo sapiens*. He writes in *The Inheritors*: 'Lok's feet were clever.'

At the time I wondered bitterly why my parents always had to be so bloody unusual. They compounded this by asking, in a deferentially liberal way, if they could take my photo. We still have a rather arty pic of me gazing soulfully out to sea, naked and shiny with damp, while a long plait streams tastefully over one shoulder. There is no sign at all of my fury.

It was during the holiday in Paignton that my father gave my grandparents their copy of *Lord of the Flies*. It was dedicated to them, and my father signed it below the dedication – 'For Mam and Dad from Bill'. When I first looked at it, after my father's death, I found it still contained several reviews, neatly clipped out and annotated in careful ink – 'Bill's book' – by my grandmother. Also a recipe.

The following summer, 1955, my grandparents hired a house in the small Cornish village of Polruan, across the river from the town of Fowey. At the bottom of our steep garden was our own small private bit of quay, with steps down to the water. We borrowed a sailing dinghy and pottered around the estuary.

As the holiday progressed, my father began to suffer from terrible toothache. Preoccupied and unreachable, he took the little ferry straight over to Fowey, and the nearest dentist.

Much later, he recalls that time in his journal, his memory jogged by more toothache:

Tuesday 10 July 1973
I can't understand it – . . . both the wisdoms are gone on that side – one extracted by an exhibitionist in Fowey . . .

That tooth, or rather the memory of it, erupts in my father's third novel *Pincher Martin*, published in October 1956. Pincher, an unsympathetic character, is a naval officer on a destroyer, and is thrown into the sea when the ship is torpedoed, ironically just as he is faking a torpedo attack as a means of killing his old friend Nathaniel. But the drowning Pincher finds a rock which is achingly familiar, with its crests and crevices. It owes much to the troublesome wisdom extracted at Fowey.

I suspect that Pincher himself acquired some of the Fowey dentist as a form of revenge. My father's describing him as an exhibitionist is heavy criticism, since he always condemned 'putting oneself forward'. As children we felt ashamed of seeking the limelight, though it must be said that he and my mother were hardly shrinking violets. And I have another example of such secret payback. Around the time my father was writing *Lord of the Flies*, a friend of my brother's made an illicit bonfire in our garden. He included in it my nice new dolls' pram, lovingly made for me by Alec. My father was darkly furious, all the more because little could be done. They bought me another, inferior one. I think he brooded over memories of that bonfire, with its shouting, fire-lit boys and exuberant destruction. He used the boy's name in *Lord of the Flies*, giving it a very special role. My brother's friend was called Roger.

By 1955, aged forty-four, my father was amused to find himself described as a promising young novelist. I thought this a huge joke and possibly mentioned it too often. There was more money, and we acquired a car of our own, a 1934 Lanchester, with green silk roller blinds for the passenger windows, and door handles rather like pearl-handled butter knives, sunk vertically in the door panels. The car was always parked under a tree, and the running boards grew a cluster of laburnum seedlings. My father never bothered much about machines. He found them dull. He was also depressed in advance about them, because he was sure they wouldn't keep to their side of the bargain, the possession of compensatory qualities such as reliability and the exemplification of cause and effect. It didn't matter how new or expensive they were. Cars, boat engines, lawnmowers, cameras and chess machines – all acted towards him like naughty children with a weak teacher, as if they didn't have to behave. Alec, by contrast, had unshakeable faith in a determinist world. So any machine he had, whether or not he had built it, behaved perfectly.

Of course, boats were different. My father regarded boats as a mixture of his world and his father's – a focus, perhaps, of the opposition between them. That was part of their attraction. During our land-bound summer holidays we hired or borrowed sailing dinghies, and day sailing was a good compromise from my point of view. But my father's need for adventure, for voyages, was becoming ominously noticeable.

So, in the winter of 1955–6, we went to Rochester to look at another boat. *Wild Rose* was a converted Whitstable oyster smack, built in 1890, her delicate name touchingly at odds with her appearance, like a stevedore doing embroidery. She was massively built, about forty feet overall (that is, including the bowsprit), and broad in the beam.

She had a petrol engine that was inadequate. She had two masts, a ketch rig, and a bowsprit fastened through the deck to the keel with massive timber posts. There was a flush lavatory, always referred to as the heads in proper naval style. Life was intimate and we used to sing when anyone disappeared inside.

There was another, unexpected piece of equipment. Between the tiller and the main cabin's bulkhead (sea talk for wall), the deck contained a round recess, about six inches across. Sunk into it, flush with the deck, was a hinged handle folded above a steel cylinder. If you raised the handle up, put both hands on it and pulled like crazy, then the three-foot rod attached to it would come up a little. If you pulled long enough to overcome its reluctance, the whole rod would emerge, and bring level with the deck the stopper, surrounded with rubber, which made a near-seal with the cylinder. Above the stopper there would be a few inches of brown water, which would wash over the deck and out through the ports. This was the bilge-pump. My father was sorry that it was manual, and not linked to the engine. This turned out to be a huge stroke of luck.

My parents bought *Wild Rose* for three hundred pounds, and at once they had to spend great amounts on her. This was normal in our family with any large purchases – houses, cars or boats – since my parents found bargaining boring and embarrassing. In any case, my father was a sucker about boats, at least until 1967, and he lavished things on her, though fearfully. He bought her a red ensign, a proper one. He bought lots of wonderful new rope, and chunky if rather dim port-and-starboard lights made of copper.

Sailing was an experience of extremes. Some of it was terrifying, but there were nights when we sailed along the silvery path of the moon, or watched the sun go down in a stupendous array of colours. We were aware of the sea as something unique, a vast creature, indifferent but alive. Sometimes you saw a swirling curve of green light, awash with phosphorescence from micro-creatures. But these moments were not the point for my father. For him, it was the sense of voyage, the use of his skill and imagination. And his formidable strength.

It has struck me only recently that perhaps he was never scared, despite the many close shaves we had. I was scared a lot of the time, and I was not imaginative enough to realise that he was different. He was in charge at sea, and liked it that way. After all, it was barely eleven years since the end of the war. Given that no one was shooting at us, the situation for him was a marked improvement.

Wild Rose was the boat, of all our boats, for which we felt most affection. This was partly because of her idiosyncrasies, but also because her great strength saved our lives on several occasions. We felt that she was noble and strong. Somehow the way a boat goes through the water, holding you safe, has a human or perhaps better an animal quality. And a boat never looks like a machine. Nor is it like a house. It's quite common to love a house, but I don't think you ever feel that the house loves you back. With a boat, you feel a response.

So, in July 1956, we gathered up our sleeping bags and clothes, our provisions and a couple of books each, and drove down to Southampton, to Kemp's yard on the River Itchen, just below Northam Bridge. It was always a shock opening up the boat. It had a particular smell – a very specific mixture of oil, bilge water and decay. I was reminded of it recently when our washing machine flooded and the carpet dried slowly in the humid summer air. But the smell was too clean. It lacked, I'm glad to say, that faint, putrefying undertow. In *Wild Rose* there were always bits of paper soaked and then dried, stuck to the cabin floor. There was always some forgotten scrap of food, obliterated by a thick covering – fine, grey-green needles of mould.

The very next day we set off. We moored in Yarmouth, a nice little port on the western end of the Isle of Wight's landward coast, a few miles east of the Needles. There we waited for a fair wind and a good forecast, both of which we unfortunately got.

It was a fine afternoon, with a brisk north-westerly which was supposed to moderate after blowing us safely to Cherbourg. A few miles out from Yarmouth the engine began to cough. Then it stopped and would not start again. The wind became obtrusive, and the sea rose unpleasantly in great heaps. My father fastened safety ropes around the shrouds of both masts, and his cheerful, active demeanour became more abstracted. Then the dinghy, which we were towing astern, slowly filled with water. Once full, it began to drag *Wild Rose*'s stern down after it. Waves began breaking over our deck.

My father took his seaman's knife and cut the painter of the dinghy and it vanished astern with dreadful speed, soon lost in the distance among the acres of green waves. I began to wail. I was terrified by its loss, and the way it debunked our cockleshell seaworthiness. My father, under great strain and just possibly frightened himself, lost his temper.

'I can stand *either* the weather *or* you,' he shouted.

I looked at the swirls of white rushing past. I wondered what it would feel like to drop down into them. After all, there was no choice about the weather, so clearly I should jump. But I decided to wait. I remembered that my father was occasionally wrong, sometimes even foolish. I went below, crying messily. My mother, whose customary support for my father had puzzlingly morphed into steely silence, offered me a biscuit. I experienced something else novel – I decided I didn't want the biscuit. I was suddenly feeling dreadfully sick.

This was a blessing. Lying on one of the bunks in the main cabin, retching over a pudding basin provided by my superbly practical mother, I noticed the rising storm, but vaguely. She kept things going below, making hot drinks, pausing occasionally to throw up in her turn. My father was seasick too. He and my brother took turns to steer. David was not quite sixteen, and apparently free from sickness, but he later claimed – we would beg and implore him not to say this – that he had *swallowed it down*.

I was not allowed back on deck. Perversely, it was a sunny afternoon, and from the companionway I could see heaps of brilliant, jade-green sea, wind-flecked and piled far above the stern, as high as a house. Then the vast waves would sink under us, and I would see instead a wilderness vista of white and green stretching far away. We were utterly on our own. Even I could see that. I looked at David. He was sitting on an upturned bucket in the sunshine, steering with one arm wrapped tightly round the tiller, while the wind whistled nastily in the rigging, and the sails were drum-taut. I saw to my astonishment that he was utterly happy.

The extent of my courage – fully tested – lay in saying nothing. Neither my mother nor I was strong enough to hold the tiller, so my father and brother did it all. After a few hours on watch, one of them would spend a half-hour dragging the handle of the pump up, shooting the bilge-water over the deck and out through the ports. Oldmeadow's blisters in *Fire Down Below* are a personal memory. Even so, the floorboards in the cabin were awash. *Wild Rose* was taking in water. My father and David steered the boat and desperately pumped her bilges the whole of that desperate night. Mercifully, *Wild Rose* stayed in one piece.

At some point, my father and David had a conference – perhaps on deck, since my mother seems to have been excluded from it. They agreed that we could not make for Cherbourg, under sail, in the dark, beating against a foul wind – for by now it was south-westerly. To the east of Cherbourg is the port of Barfleur, small, hard to find and on an exceptionally rocky coast. To the west are the sinister waters round the Channel Islands. We needed to endure the storm longer. We must stand off, east, across the Baie de la Seine, well north of the eastern corner of the Cotentin – the Cherbourg peninsula – and then turn southeast for a safer patch of water close to the beaches of Normandy. And then we would wait.

So it was that, at some stage, during the day that followed that long, long night, *Wild Rose* began to make easier weather of it. The sound of the wind abated, as did the manner in which, every few waves, the bow of the ship seemed to strike something unyielding and bounce back again. I think I may even have slept. Vaguely I remember the sound of the anchor chain rattle-rattle-rattling for a very long time. My father was worried the anchor would drag, an anxiety that was part hallucination from exhaustion. He was probably not the only one. Finally, we were anchored. Peace and a strange sense of normality came over us and we slept for about ten hours.

When we woke, the sea was flat and oily-looking. There was fog, which lifted occasionally to show us we were within sight of land. My mother made us hot drinks and David and I polished off a whole packet of Marie biscuits. Then the fog cleared, and the wind rose, fastidiously it seemed by comparison with the roaring and whistling of that earlier night. The mainsail was hoisted. The bowsprit had been pushed back, past the timbers and right through its iron bolt, right up against the mainmast, by the force of the waves. The foresail was split. Since we couldn't use the foresail or the jib, we couldn't use the mizzen either. My mother took the tiller and my father and brother began to haul up the anchor.

They couldn't do it. They were worn out, even after a night's sleep. Instead, they lowered the mainsail, and we sat down to consider. A few hundred yards away there was a smallish trawler, and she began to approach. I realise now her crew wondered if we were sinking. Once within hailing distance, my father explained our difficulty in grammar-school French. Moments later there was an avalanche of boots on our deck, three enormous men in *bleu de travail* leapt at the chain and within a few minutes the anchor was swinging on *Wild Rose*'s bow. My father took out a sheaf of multicoloured French banknotes, *pour boire, pour les enfants, pour les dames*, all refused. It must have been farcical – our ludicrous boat, the bowsprit right across the foredeck, the split wood, torn sails, the much-used pump. Two children and a pretty but dishevelled wife. And my father, who always looked poor, even when he was well off. In the end they took a modest tip, and leapt off the boat again, wishing us well.

Reaching Le Havre, we half-sailed and half-drifted up to the outer mole, the huge man-made boundary of the outer harbour, and made fast to it. There were large notices saying not to do this. Passers-by and fishermen came to tell us we could not stay there. Then, they took one look at *Wild Rose* and implored us not to move. Ceremonially I was led to the edge of the boat to touch France, though really I was touching French engineering. Someone gave us a wine bottle full of hot coffee. The lighthouse-keeper gave me his lunch. It was a piece of cold, brown steak with a thick ruffle of yellow fat, sitting on a strange, round slice of yellowish bread with large holes in it. My mother looked at me firmly, told me to say thank you and *take it below*.

A launch sent by the harbour master towed us into the inner harbour. Later that evening my parents gave me some money, taught me the phrase *Du lait, s'il-vous-plaît* (which I thought meant 'a bottle of milk' so I added 'please' to it) and sent me off into the hinterland. A couple of hours later I was restored to my family by a posse of elderly Frenchwomen all in black. Heaven knows how they understood me, or how they found the boat.

The first few days I was so tired that everything seemed as if behind thick glass. Until I recovered, I thought France was always like that, as if it were another planet. Then my father's ineffably calm colleague John Milne arrived, and this coincided with the locals of Le Havre embracing us. I remember talking French, which cannot have been the case. We had dinner with the mayor of Le Havre (five courses, including one which was just *petits pois* and very small onions, all on their own). We lunched with a pair of mysterious elderly ladies, and for that event my mother triumphantly unpacked for me clean white socks and a seersucker frock, not much creased but slightly salty.

When we were not being wined and dined, my mother and John sat on a pontoon just astern of *Wild Rose*, chain smoking and stitching away at the torn foresail. My mother, very pretty, and tremendously chic in a striped sweater and hoop earrings, looked rather like Jeanne Moreau and people would stare. French engineers would come along, shrug about the engine and chat her up. My father astonished John (who had read French at Oxford as well as music) by asking if he should put the *bougies* (spark plugs) to *chauffer* or perhaps *sécher* on top of the Primus, the French for which I have alas forgotten. After a couple of weeks the engine sulkily began to obey instructions, the bowsprit with a new bolt and splinted timbers was back in its right place, and the foresail was patched but usable. With regret, my parents began to plan our return. We had become used to life in France. We have a photograph of the cabin interior. There are four empty wine bottles, one on its side. All are St Émilion.

My father and I went to look for a bank. My grandparents

had been terrified by the exaggerations of the local newspapers, which proclaimed we were adrift in the Channel for three days without food or water. We were never adrift, and had plenty of food and water. It was appetite we lacked. My mother was furious at the implications for her house- (or boat-) keeping, and telegrams had whizzed to and fro. Actually, mealtimes became rather exciting, because we kept the tins in the bilges, and in the storm all the labels had come off. Tinned pears with ham one day, potatoes and custard another. But Grandma and Alec generously telegraphed money to pay for repairs, and the two of us went in search of the authorising bank.

We walked for miles – my father got hopelessly lost, as he usually did on land. Our meanderings took us over vast flat stretches of grey rubble. This may in fact have been an early sign of the new prosperity, new building, the end of the grey old France. But to my father it was evidence of 'the war', aftermath of the D-Day invasion and the destruction he had helped to bring about. The locals gave no sign of resenting this – all the French people we met treated us like long-lost relations.

When eventually we found the bank my father pulled my pigtails affectionately and proprietorially while we queued, and I stretched out my hand to pull his beard. He laughed in a clubbable way with the other men, Frenchmen standing around, while he pushed my hand away. Later he explained that to pull a man's beard was a dreadful insult. I was mortified and near tears. I understood that my reaction had connected somehow with the few indecencies I knew of, and the greater number that I could imagine.

One evening, with a light southerly wind, we set sail for home. How flat the sea was, how calm the sky. The moon rose, John and my father stayed on deck, and I went to sleep in the fo'c's'le, with the sound of our progress a pleasant rippling whoosh, under the bow.

John had taken some pictures of us and sent them to the *Salisbury Journal*. The paper chose a jolly family picture, with my jovial bearded father, my lovely mother, David silent but heroic, and me eating. It was a long way from the buried fear and piled-up seas of that night. I see, half a century later, how truly heroic my brother was, and my mother too. And I understand my father. It was all too much, my thin wailing in the middle of those mountainous green waves. We never mentioned it again.

In the autumn of that year, 1956, my father's third novel *Pincher Martin* was published. Pincher fights against drowning, and the reader has a number of terrors laid out with great immediacy. Of course, our own storm was too late for that book, but I'm glad to say it wasn't wasted. It appears thirty years later in the Sea Trilogy, in the latter part of *Fire Down Below*.

That September, thin and brown from sailing, I moved up into the main school, with its two hundred and fifty girls, strange new rules, and many new people. There were boarders, who formed their own community, one made up of knowing, confident girls. They all went round in twos, and these pairings were usually kept faithfully, throughout the length of one's school career, like swans mating for life. Their language was different and remade itself spontaneously. It was crisp, and interlaced with strange terms, the brilliant, aristocratic jargon of their world. And they pronounced things differently. Lax, short for lacrosse, became lex. My pigtails, now almost to my waist, became plets. Nicknames emerged, for teachers and girls. It gave me my first sight of glamour. The senior girls were a race apart. They were the great figures – far older, far wiser than our teachers, who had bare, weathered hands, chalky and unenriched by a gold ring. Sometimes we were uneasily aware of pathos.

Aware in other ways, I began intermittently to pick up an unwilling acceptance that my father was unusual, not merely poor and eccentric, as he had been. But this was only among the pupils and lower ranks of staff. Our headmistress was the distant, regal Miss Jerred – an immobile, mandarin figure, even now more august to me than the Pope, the Queen, anyone else except perhaps John Gielgud. The mere name still produces a cooling effect between my shoulder blades. I never spoke to her, and if I had it would have been like touching the Ark of the Covenant. I doubt very much that she was aware of my father's bizarre habit of writing. To her, his main characteristic was his beard. There was only one other bearded parent, a gentleman farmer named Thatcher. Miss Jerred could not envisage a world where two of these beards existed, and she could not tell them apart anyway. So she addressed both of them, austerely and impartially, as Mr Thatcher. My father liked this. He thought he had merged. He was quite wrong. Mr Thatcher had acquired eccentricity.

One evening in March 1958, I came into the sitting room to find my father there alone, listening to the radio. It was producing strange, rather strangled dialogue, and a generous display of BBC sound effects.

'Oh good,' I said.

I sat down on the sofa with pleased anticipation.

'Is it the *Goon Show*?'

My father put his head in his hands, gasping with laughter. It was the radio adaptation of *Pincher Martin*.

7

Distant Rumbles of Fame

After 1956, life spread out. For one thing, it included London. We even went there for a weekend. My father became a member of the Book Society committee, and went up to London once a month for meetings to choose the 'book of the month'. He joined a London club, the Savile, and there were lunches and – I am sure – drink. He made friends – Peter Green, Michael Ayrton, Anthony Storr, Wayland Young. All this – or some of it – emerged in stories he told us. The traveller paid for his absence with tall tales, as is of course traditional. I suspect that the newness of it all dislodged and confused some of his beliefs, perhaps even assaulted the status quo. Also, he and my mother talked and, surprisingly, they don't seem to have concerned themselves with what I might overhear. Maybe they liked having an audience. In London, my father said, some people had mistresses, some people got drunk, some people in the Book Society favoured books written by their friends. I heard of hotel rooms being trashed – by writers, not pop singers. And there were other things. People, 'who ought to have known better', got girls 'into trouble'. Trouble to me meant trouble at school, and, puzzled, I visualised middle-aged men having to explain things to headmistresses. But I didn't ask about it.

Literary London changed him. I noticed he became less predictable, edgier. I became more careful. Also, instead of a schoolmaster struggling to be published, he became a writer who happened to teach some of the time. His headmaster, eager to keep him as a member of staff, gave him time off. I never heard the slightest grumble about this from his teaching colleagues. They must have been a generous bunch.

He had a curious set of clashing standards. He once described someone to me as 'a very wicked woman'. He explained that she had had 'lots of lovers'. He said this to me when I was about fourteen. Perhaps he was concerned – against all appearance of necessity – about my chastity, and was warning me off sex, about which my parents were ostensibly modern and broad-minded. It seems an extraordinary judgement to me, and I think it is possible that he really meant she had been destructive or hurtful as well as promiscuous. But I saw no sign of it. The allegedly wicked woman and her husband were most affectionate, although interestingly she sometimes seemed jealous if my mother happened to show me affection. I have wondered since if the real problem was that she was in love with my mother. A lot of people were, and some of them were women. But that was not a possibility I thought of then. After all, my mother was quite old, over forty, and what was the point of being in love with a married woman so clearly devoted to her husband?

We still lived in our nice, airy magnolia-painted flat next to St Mark's Church. We still had most of my parents' pre-war furniture; their yellow-varnished sideboard with its attendant biscuit barrel could now go straight into a Poirot adaptation – for Inspector Japp's semi in Tufnell Park, perhaps. But life became split between normal, daylight experiences and exotic, unpredictable evenings. There were many strange visitors. One, a thin, extremely attractive man, had a terrible stutter that he magnificently ignored. I thought he was thrilling, and assumed this was a unique discovery of my own. Actually, he was Kenneth Tynan.

Alastair Sim was going to star in my father's stage play *The Brass Butterfly*. He came to dinner, and when I was sent off to my early bed he got up from the table and bent gracefully from a vast height to kiss my hand. Everyone laughed delightedly, while I had an aggrieved sense of being a kind of stage prop. He and my father eventually fell out with each other, but there were signs of strain even in the fifties.

By about 1958, my parents were finding all these varied

projects hard to manage. My father went up to London to talk over lunch to a literary agent. I was always keen to make him laugh, and so – a cheap joke – I asked him if the agent had taken ten per cent of his steak. His face darkened.

'I wonder if you know quite how funny that is,' he said.

As usual, the question was rhetorical. I rather regret my silly crack now, since it's possible that it strengthened his prejudice against agents. He would have done much better, I think, with an agent, and certainly life for the rest of us after his death would have been far easier.

So the projects rained down on him from London – essays, reviews, radio plays, talks. Several BBC producers came down, all men, all charming and most with Scottish accents. They usually had a nice young woman with them – probably their visit entailed an overnight stay somewhere. Not with us – my parents would not have been ready for that. Their bohemian years were over, though they enjoyed as spectators the general blurriness it still gave to relationships around them. A friend of my mother's had bought a holiday home. According to my father, she started as she meant to go on by sleeping with its surveyor.

'But you don't know that,' said my mother loyally, despite deprecating her friend's actions, which she considered cliché-ridden, and unworthy of her genuine talent.

'Oh, *dar*ling . . .' replied my father.

But complexity was increasing for all of us. One BBC man brought along a young woman who had read Classics at Cambridge. She was extremely pretty, with boyish short dark hair in soft feather shapes round her neat little face. She wore a tight black sweater and a swirly full skirt.

My father corralled her into conversation with me. I had just started learning Latin, and the plan was that I should progress smoothly on to Greek. I was astounded that anyone so poised and glamorous could do anything as fusty and mannish as the Classics we were taught at school. So far, I suppose, that was what my father intended. She was puzzled by my father's attitude, but courteous, and gazed in a kindly manner towards me, as she assured me that, yes, Greek was indeed good stuff and she hoped I would enjoy it. My father hovered, apparently genial, but more or less pushing our conversation along. I felt we were both embarrassed.

For decades she remained my picture of intellectual success and confident female perfection, an example of what my father would have liked me to be. In 2003 my father's friend Peter Green told me she had killed herself in the 1960s. Over a man, he said gloomily. I could see he thought it an inadequate reason. I did not. By then, as we sat over lunch by the sea on the island of Lesvos, my one suicide attempt was more than thirty years in the past, made 'over a man' only a few years after her characteristically more efficient measure. I was glad I had survived, and I felt terribly sorry for her and her family. My own attempt had been made during my brother's first stay in mental hospital. What could I have been thinking of? I once put this to a wise friend, and she replied, kindly, that being suicidal was a delusional state.

So some of the colour and exoticism was dark as well, at least in retrospect. Given the subject matter of my father's novels, this was perhaps to be expected. He loved to laugh, and had a vigorous sense of humour, liking silly jokes, but preferably with a dark edge. One of his favourites, about someone in a road accident – 'So I put my head between my knees . . . and I didn't faint' – was so brutal that I did not understand it for nearly half a century.

Sometimes our London visitors would jovially ask me questions about him. They were actually making laborious conversation to their host's silent teenager, and I would have liked to be jovial back, but it was difficult. His writing was still something on which we must all be silent, or evasive at best. He had a special half-hearted and weary voice, used for unwilling discussions of his own work. The conversation would falter and turn elsewhere.

Inescapably, however, he was beginning to belong to a wider

set of people. Some felt that he was fair game whatever his attitude. But he never liked talking about his writing. Provided he had a book on the go he was cheerful, if ruthless. Annoying questions could be brushed aside, and I expect he was human enough to enjoy some of the results of fame, much as he distrusted them. It was quite understandable that he didn't like talking about work in progress – he feared it might vanish if he did, like Eurydice when Orpheus looks back at her. Work already done he considered irrelevant, as if it were dead or in another universe.

By now, the parents of my friends mentioned him often. Perhaps they had heard him on the radio. Soon, I became aware that people would listen to stories about him, keen to hear of his jokey normality – putting the dustbins out, doing the washing up. This was gratifying, but it felt dangerous to me, as if I were using up precious capital.

My mother began to take a more businesslike role. It was she who answered the phone, read his contracts as well as first drafts of his writing, and chose who would come to lunch. She protected him, but also she felt he should not get used to being above ordinary life – she was quick to debunk signs of veneration from journalists, students, even old friends. She was quite right that he needed this, and to begin with she did it with humour and a light touch. But as people became more comic in their deference, the humour dropped out of her wifely deflation. Some of the interchanges were uncomfortable for listeners, especially those who wished to see him as their own personal celebrity, and thought of his conversation as obviously more important than anyone else's.

One day in the late 1950s, we learnt that someone who worked for the local authority had observed, 'in a meeting', that flats such as ours, owned by the council, were not meant for successful novelists who had posh friends down from London. My parents were very offended by this, partly I think because it tore away the last shreds of their illusions of poverty. Aggrieved, they pointed out that they paid an economic rent. Nevertheless, it was clear that we had outstayed our welcome.

Our family had talked for years of living in the country, and now we had the need as well as the means. After all, we did own things. We had a boat, though not a sleek one like the Hilliard sloops or Atalantas we admired in Yarmouth or Beaulieu. We also had a car of sorts. The old Lanchester had died. A small leather washer (price twopence, I remember) had disintegrated in the heart of the engine. Repairing the car would have cost more than it was worth. Besides, you could hardly see out of the windscreen. We got rid of it, and for a few uncomfortable weeks it stayed, on the forecourt of the London Road garage, abandoned. We averted our eyes from JR 103, its shamefully familiar number plate – it felt like the cut direct.

We borrowed my grandparents' car, the 1934 Morris. But soon that gave out as well, a mere quarter-century after they bought it. And the successors were so unmemorable and prone to sudden death that I can hardly separate them. There were about six in three years.

Though we now had more money, my father's fear that it would all suddenly vanish had never gone away. He still had bad dreams in his sixties and seventies about his writing never being published. Early on, the anxiety was acute and open. This stopped him from buying new cars. We would carefully acquire yet another dismal wreck.

My father would set off, attended by both his children, with a folded chequebook in his trouser pocket. He always said that he had a large sign over his head saying 'sucker', and he was probably right. We usually went to buy cars in the rain, which was a good idea, or would have been if it had been intentional. In reality it reflected my father's refusal to waste good weather on something so depressing. I remember one car declined to start at all. The salesman was quite unembarrassed, and just loaded us all into another one.

Our new car often broke down on the journey home from the showroom. At that point my father would stick his head under the bonnet. This was a ritual. The sight told him nothing beyond the fact that the engine had not yet fallen out. He would stare balefully at the lumps of metal, sigh deeply and observe that he would have to crank the engine with the starting handle. This ghastly object was inserted through a hole in the front of the car which gave access to the crankshaft. The idea was that – by means of a gut-wrenching manoeuvre – someone with sufficient strength might actually force the engine to move. This was called 'turning the engine over', which always puzzled me since it seemed to stay in the same position. But, if it was done hard enough, long enough, the engine, caught unawares, might surprise itself into life. The handle then had to be withdrawn quickly, before it spun round, battering your shins. Then you had to leap athletically into the driving seat and press the accelerator, in order to catch the fragile combustion before it died of cold or wet. Once we were old enough, David or I would be given charge of the accelerator, a nerve-wracking task since failure would mean my father had to crank the engine again.

Many school mornings began in this way, sometimes with my father disappearing upstairs to warm the spark plugs on the gas stove in our flat. He had learnt this from life in the boat, not the other way about. Usually I walked or cycled to school, but it was always fun to drive with him on my own, and talk. The trouble was, if the car refused to start, I was stymied, sitting there biting my nails, since it would by then be too late to walk. I would pray earnestly if sceptically, and also tell the car how much I liked it.

By the evening, however, unless it had rained solidly, the car – by preference a late riser – was usually in working order. We would drive round the countryside near Salisbury, inspecting houses or even whole villages, deciding whether we liked the idea of living there. The long river valleys which run to meet each other in and around Salisbury, are dotted with places we nearly bought. Mills, manors, farmhouses, cottages – they all had charm and something wrong with them. Now, with hindsight, it feels as if my parents were waiting for something. Meanwhile, every Christmas and Easter we still went to stay at 29 The Green.

I had always talked to Alec a great deal, usually while he did something else at the same time. He was fascinating, and would explain without complaint everything I asked him, with demonstrations where necessary. He was practical and imaginative, a wonderful combination for a child. He also listened. When one day I said I felt sick, he explained this was probably because I was excited (my cousin Lizzie was coming to Marlborough later that day). He gave me some bicarbonate of soda, explaining that my stomach was producing too much acid, and the bicarbonate would help neutralise it. This was the first and last scientific experiment I conducted. It was completely successful.

I can see now that the look of surprised understanding on a child's face gave Alec pleasure, the sort that my father got from people laughing at his jokes, or listening to him playing the piano. And Alec was quite adventurous in his ideas. He showed me a map of the world and asked me what I thought about the shapes of South America and Africa. Sadly, I had no idea that science recognised such simple things and so I didn't say what was obvious – that the two continents fitted. I expect my response disappointed him, but he kept going, inured to such setbacks. His explanations were always clear and step by step. Soon I understood very well.

For years I thought I had somehow made this up, since I believed plate tectonics was modern, developed in the 1960s, and Alec died in 1958. But continental drift, as it was then called, had been suggested in the 1930s. Alec was fascinated by such a revolutionary view of the world, of the apparently immovable earth he stood on. He lived all his life in that brilliant world, full of possibilities and discovery and truth – a world where you could build yourself a radio, as he did, and then hear amazing things on it. This world, as colourful and dependent on imagination as my father's, did not really include my grandmother, though the two of them sat together, slept together, and shared every meal.

I realise now that Alec wished to give me particular memories, ideas that would lead me to good experiences, that might even protect me, and give me an intellectual heritage which would survive him. In countless ways he did. One day he showed me some drawings he had made as a boy. They were for an exam, pencil-shadowed pictures of cones, cylinders and spheres. He had copied a three-dimensional classical design made of flowers, swags and curls, with shading that made it look as if it was carved in stone. They were dull, he said, portraits of shapes, an exercise to show a technique. I thought they were beautiful. 'You can have them,' he said, and put them back in his desk. He meant I could have them after his death.

He got out his violin and bow, and showed it to me. He played it too, as well as explaining about the length and thickness of the strings. And he let me try to play it, which must have been a trial for a good musician. He played his flute, though he said he was out of practice. He would spread his hands over the piano keys, playing by ear. He told me that there was only one thing in his life he would change – he would learn the piano 'properly'.

When I was nine, I proudly announced to him and Grandma that I was learning the piano. Grandma asked me where I was learning.

'At school. In a room called Chopin.'

I pronounced it Chop In. My grandmother gave her short, barking laugh. I had no idea that the word was anything but a bizarre name for a very small room containing a piano and two chairs. Alec kept a perfectly straight face, and I told him about another room, called something long and difficult beginning with M. 'Mendelssohn', he said. I can still hear his voice saying it.

My mother told me, with her cupid's-bow smile of tight contempt, 'You used to follow him round like a little dog.'

Well, why not? Nevertheless, even I was growing older and more self-sufficient, growing away from my grandparents, whom I loved but took for granted, as children do. I hardly knew things were changing. Sometimes I would just leave the Marlborough house, close the green side-door behind me and be on my own, addressing the perennial problem. Who was right? Alec, whom I loved and trusted completely, with his brilliant but explicable world? Or my father? He was fascinating, unpredictable, some-times unfair or bad-tempered, and had at his elbow, at his beck and call, the world of mystery and stories, the world I most en-joyed. As I walked dreamily round the Common, or explored the edges of Savernake Forest, or even just looked in the White Horse Bookshop, I never consciously considered that the Marl-borough visits might one day end. But some suggestion of it was seeping in, like water under a door.

Once, I left my watch behind. It was an ordinary watch, but it had a lovely pink strap. I was already sitting on the bus, waiting for it to leave, when I realised. I ran back up the High Street, through the paved silence of Patten Lane, past the church. I pushed open the green door – it was locked only at night – then ran up to my room, grabbed it from my dressing table and tore off again. I hardly stopped to say a word to my startled grand-parents. I left them silent and bewildered. Despite my memory of not noticing them, I must have seen they were distressed – I collapsed into a seat on the bus and began to cry, as the enor-mous double-decker swayed off up the High Street and swerved to go past the Town Hall. We were leaving the bus stop where Alec had so often met me, where he and I in the old days had boarded the bus together, with him taking more care of me than my parents did. I felt brutal, as if I had broken something. The bemused passengers couldn't understand what was wrong. That was one of the last times, perhaps it was the very last time, I stayed in that house.

In 1957 my parents bought a three-piece suite. I came home from Marlborough and there it was, without warning, in stiff red plush. Our tatty, eccentric flat suddenly looked like everyone else's house. My brother, seated in one of the enormous red armchairs, added that my father was going to be on television, on the Brains Trust. Soon there was a proper, veneered hi-fi, which lasted us about fifteen years. And the new sofa and chairs outlasted my parents, staying at Tullimaar until we finally got rid of them in 2002.

During the late 1950s the actor Alan Badel used to come and visit us. My father liked him enormously and enjoyed hearing from him about the theatre, which always fascinated him. Badel was his idea of a real actor. He was charming and kind, breathtakingly handsome, and slightly but pleasantly stagey, almost ironically so. He had a voice like chocolate, liqueur chocolate.

Despite all these excellent qualities, the sight of him made me anxious. He had played Pincher in the radio adaptation, the focus of my most spectacular gaffe to date. I felt dreadful about it, and often berated myself for my stupidity, complacency, ignorance. At the same time I could appreciate its stunning perfection. It was frightful but splendid. So I was never sure my dad hadn't told Badel, who would in his turn have told the story brilliantly.

During one of these visits, my parents asked Badel to join us on an expedition. The cottage in Bowerchalke, their wartime home nine miles outside Salisbury, was up for sale.

I don't remember looking at the outside of the cottage or – what struck me later – the bareness of the garden, the lack of trees to climb. All I remember is Alan Badel sitting in a window alcove in the sitting room, his long legs crossed gracefully at the ankles. He looked around him. All the furniture had gone. The room was clean and spare, bigger than one expected. The floor was a good one, tiled with glazed terracotta. There was an inglenook fireplace, with an irregularly curved beam above it. My father said later, perhaps wishfully, that it had been shaped with an adze, like the timbers of a ship. There were three windows, set deep in the thickness of the old walls.

Badel said, 'This is a nice house. You should buy it.'

That was it. They did. In terror, my father got a mortgage.

The house was surveyed, the price reduced. Eventually, in the autumn of 1958, my parents paid just over four thousand pounds, a few hundred less than the asking price. That November we would leave our flat.

8

Alec

During the intervening summer of that year, 1958, we naturally went sailing in *Wild Rose*. I was pleased but surprised to learn that Alec was coming too. I knew he missed us all in the holidays when we were away. He had told me, though he later said he shouldn't have done. But it was still a huge step. Sometimes, friends of my father (and their wives, who hated it) had come sailing with us, but there was a dreadful lot of slumming and a huge amount of heaving on ropes and general mucking in. John Milne claimed his piano double thirds had never been the same again and he was probably right. Alec's presence at the age of eighty-one was revolutionary. However, another innovation was the presence of Jim Thorrowgood, a friend of David's. He would add strength and stamina.

But there is a hinterland to this story.

When my father was a young man at Oxford in the 1930s, he was absent for the whole of his second summer term, apparently directed by the dean of his college to stay away. My father's explanation was that he, a sprinter, had abruptly come to a halt in the middle of a relay race on the running track at Iffley – suddenly aware, he said, of the futility of running round and round. The race was an inter-collegiate one, which Brasenose, a very sporty college, naturally lost as a result. The dean, an affronted spectator, was vocal in his anger, declaring as well that my father had played the piano loudly every single night that year, directly above the dean's august head. I don't believe this was all, or even most of it, but the college records are silent on the subject, as are the university's.

My father didn't tell his parents. He went to Cornwall, his

place of childhood delight. He lived contentedly off his allowance, bought books second-hand in Penzance and read a great deal. He also had a love affair. It seems to have been a very good few months, possibly more valuable for him than the term at Oxford would have been. The love affair, seen by him as irresponsible, sounds benign, with no hurt on either side. I suspect he also acquired a belated sense of independence. The Goldings were a family who kept close together – my father was sixteen before he spent a night away from both parents. In another break from family habits, he hired a sailing dinghy and taught himself to sail. We still have an old, much-read copy of the E. F. Knight classic, *Small-Boat Sailing*. I expect it too was bought in Penzance.

But it couldn't last. Eventually my father was recalled from the magic of Cornwall to the dusty streets of Marlborough, probably because he ran out of cash. Once home, he found the courage not only to explain about the row at Oxford, but also to say he couldn't bear to go on studying science. Somehow I doubt that he told them about the love affair, but the books of poetry, not as illicit but quite as powerful, had had their effect. He told them he wanted to change to English.

Surely there must have been anger? But my aunt Eileen, my father's cousin and adopted sister, and at that time a child of only ten or eleven, heard the conversation. She was completely clear that the atmosphere was anxious, rather than bad-tempered, and she knew the participants very well. It may be that my father censored from his own account to me something powerful, something that would have affected his parents – his distress and desperation. Failure exasperated him. A competitive man, clever, decisive, energetic, he must have found the Oxford situation unendurable.

Alec, a scientist from passion and conviction, was understandably hurt. But he recognised that the fascination of science, the core of his own life, had failed to enthral his son. He had a good imagination, using it in teaching and, later, in his relationships with his grandchildren, possibly more than he had done with his own children. He could envisage difference. Above all, he didn't want my father to waste a third year at Oxford, doing nothing, perhaps failing his degree. He and Grandma agreed to fund my father for another two years while he pursued what was, for them, a subject for dilettantes. Generously, my grandfather wrote out the text of *Beowulf* for him, with translation and notes – we still have it. My father applied himself with astonishing concentration, as he always could if interested, and got through a year's work in a couple of months.

Then, as was customary, the family went on holiday. They went to Poole, and we have photographs of my father sailing there with his mother and Eileen, in a dinghy straight out of the Arthur Ransome books (not surprisingly, since *Swallows and Amazons* was published in 1930). The photos are on Alec's glass plates, and I imagine him watching curiously behind the wooden stand for the concertina camera, remembering the photos he had taken two decades earlier, pictures of his small sons and his nephew sailing their toy boats – made, of course, by him – in the rock pools of Newquay. It suggests a peaceful end to the summer's conflicts, and I hope very much it is accurate.

In 1958, the summer with Alec, we sailed west. We too were making for Poole Harbour, a place of memories for all the Goldings present.

More than a decade before, we had sailed to Poole in *Seahorse*, the time of our perilous entry to the harbour. And in 1944 my father had practised sailing manoeuvres here with the young men who were going to crew the 'little boats' in the Walcheren Operation of October–November 1944, the invasion of the German-occupied Dutch island at the mouth of the Scheldt. These boats were indeed very small craft, launches that were motorised but largely unarmed, designed to act as distractions to the terrible shore batteries, to draw their fire while the vital troop landings were achieved. Most of the men in the little boats were killed. 'These are memories to dim the sunlight,' my father wrote. David remembers how badly he felt about those young men. He had raced with them, back and forth across the harbour, everyone in high spirits.

We spent a few days in Poole Harbour, then we stood further west towards Weymouth, and the white cliffs of the Dorset coast. We had to sail round Old Harry, a headland battered by a notoriously rough sea, torn by opposing currents. We could see it ahead, tossing chaotically, the waves irregular and threateningly topped with white, like water breaking over rocks. Soon *Wild Rose* began to pitch and lumber in and out of the gulleys between the waves. Sometimes she swung so drastically that the boom would lurch across the deck and the sail would flap. My father regretted his course – characteristically, he had cut it too fine. But we couldn't change now – you couldn't turn in such a sea. The only way was onwards and through it.

He sent us all below, and we went – except for my grandfather. He sat on the round petrol tank behind the cabin bulkhead, holding on, I gather, tightly, but resolutely. My father, seated, in order to bring his centre of gravity lower so he was safer, was perched painfully on our helmsman's upturned bucket, with its raised metal rim. He held the tiller under one arm, while with his other hand he gripped the ropes running between the corner of the mainsail and the block or pulley that could slide from one end to the other of a bar bolted to the deck. This dangerous action was designed to keep the boom steady, but if it were too strong for my father, he could be swept overboard, or injured. The boat plunged on, twisting chaotically, swinging the sail in conflict with my father's grip.

Now, as my father struggled, most of his attention fastened to his task, he glanced occasionally at his father. Years afterwards he told me what he saw. Alec's face turned completely white, then grey, and then set in an expression my father had never seen before. He said later that Alec was having a heart attack.

Is this true? I don't know. But it had a special place for my father in the fraught mythology of Alec's death. It helped him. I felt something similar about a conversation I had with him the evening of 18 June 1993, the evening before his death.

We had come down to Tullimaar, their house in Cornwall, on that day, a Friday, for their party that evening. We met him on the front doorstep. I had not seen him since Easter, a longer gap than usual. Ironically, I thought it showed I was at last growing independent of my larger-than-life parents. He had just come down from the walled garden, where – in a gesture typical of his good manners – he had picked one of my mother's new roses for our deputy cleaner who was going to help at the party. Her name was Julia, and the rose, a curious browny-pink one, was called Julia's Rose.

I looked at him and saw he had changed. He had become threadbare. His beard was transparent. He had worn a beard since I was tiny. I could not remember him clean-shaven. Now, in profile, I could see the outline of his chin – with a quick jerk of pain I realised it was a weak one. Later, in the kitchen, I asked him how he was. He was fine, he said.

'You look pale to me,' I said.

He replied, with a bravura flourish, 'Then I shall wear *my rouge*!'

And he looked evasive.

In the bleak, unreal days that followed, that conversation provided me with some comfort. Why? Because it showed he knew? Because it made me – unlike my mother – privy to his condition? A secret between the two of us? Perhaps all of these. The heart attack story about Alec did the same for my father.

Why, one might ask, did Alec stay on deck? Did it not occur to him that he was a distraction, perhaps even a liability? I don't know. My father said about it, 'You can't tell your father what to do', a questionable statement, especially to me, who often told him what to do – phone the doctor, change the accountants, for God's sake *eat* something. Perhaps Alec wanted to be with his son in that struggle. Or he could have done it simply out of love and loyalty. He grasped what was going on – he was a scientist and a very intelligent man. We were in danger and my father was fighting to bring us out of it. I can imagine him remembering a phrase from very early days. 'Who will stand at my right hand, and keep the bridge with me?' The sea does make heroes, sometimes surprising ones. So he hid his fear as far as possible, and stayed, offering companionship to his son, and – maybe – silently enduring the pain of a heart attack. It may well have helped my father. People generally behave better with an audience.

Of course, we did escape. My father fought his way through the churning waters, as he did with so much in his life. That evening we docked at Weymouth, and from Weymouth we sailed to Cherbourg. My grandfather came ashore, remarked that France smelt just the way it did sixty years before, and refused to go again. When we all went off to eat, he stayed on board. I pressed him to come – it took away much of the pleasure for me if he wasn't there. But he refused – he had a mouth ulcer which made eating painful, because of his false teeth. In retrospect I see two things: he was touched; and the mouth ulcer was a minor problem, compared with what was really bothering him. He was starting to be ill.

France had changed a lot in two years. My parents had always spoken of it as a land of plenty – wine, butter, bread, tomatoes . . . I hadn't understood before. But the main thing for my father, I believe, was the sailing. Recently, Glenn Collett, another friend of David's and one of the two people who could make *Wild Rose*'s engine work (the other one was Viv, who was with us in *Tenace*), sent me a reminiscence of my father from Jim Thorrowgood:

> He was fascinated by seamanship. In Cherbourg (I think, though it might have been Le Havre), we were in some basin or other, and he wanted to move to the other side. We couldn't sail, and fuel was short (which is why David and I eventually ended up towing the boat up the Itchen using the dinghy), so he devised an elaborate skein of lines and springs, a cat's cradle, which at the critical moment he released so that all

twanged and we moved slowly, miraculously, across the basin. Worthy of Hornblower.

The cat's cradle was correctly termed a 'spring', I believe. It used a system of ropes under tension and then slackened. As in most seamanship, it used the laws of physics with maximum economy. Indeed, it may have been done partly to interest Alec. My father would have been gratified, particularly by Jim's reference to Hornblower, an unacknowledged source I am sure for his Sea Trilogy.

We had an idyllic night sail back from Cherbourg. I sat with Alec on the petrol tank, both of us wrapped in an old sleeping bag. The sun sank to port in a path of gold, and we looked at the fading coastline of France. Then Alec and I went below and slept, while the rest of the company sailed us home, across a benign English Channel. By the time I woke up we were skimming past Netley, and turning out of Southampton Water into the Itchen. Here the wind died. David and Jim must have worked quite hard, towing us up the two miles to Kemp's yard and Northam Bridge.

My father and I drove Alec back to Marlborough and delivered him safely to my grandmother. He had been away little more than a fortnight, and it had been a happy time for us. But now, restoring him to my grandmother, we stood guiltily in the hall of the old house and watched. Grandma, that small figure, was bent and weeping and came towards Alec with her arms outstretched. He embraced her and the embrace was almost as if she were a tearful child. I was shocked. I see now that I still believed it was her job to look after us. In truth, the roles were reversing with her. But not with Alec. With him, we never got to such a point.

In mid September the four of us drove over to Forest Row in Sussex, taking my brother, angry, silent and miserable, to Michael Hall, the Steiner school where my father had taught in the 1930s. They hoped that David would feel more relaxed there, away from the pressure of Bishop Wordsworth's School, out from under his father's shadow. I had no idea that David was enduring the first of many unwilling exits from home.

When we arrived at our new house that November, we found many of the electrical fixtures were broken. I was still afraid of the dark. Also, we were surrounded by the utter velvet silence of the night-time countryside, a silence punctuated by eerie owl-hoots and reverberant mooings from cattle. And it hadn't struck me until we actually moved that I could no longer walk out of the house, run a few hundred yards and see a friend.

However, these matters soon receded. News came from Marlborough that my grandfather was not well. He had seen the doctor, who declared that Alec should go into the little cottage hospital on the edge of Savernake Forest. Just for a few tests. My mother gave me a message. Alec felt *very honoured* to be staying in my birthplace. I laughed. It was going to be all right. Life would continue as usual. Christmas might be rather different but we would manage until Alec recovered. The cottage hospital was friendly and small and local. Grandma – helped by my kind aunt Theo, down from Grantham – could visit him daily.

But the picture darkened. Alec would have to go to Swindon, 'for an operation'. After the phone call, my father stood motionless beside the telephone in the sitting room.

'He won't die, will he?' I asked.

There was another pause.

'I don't know,' he said heavily.

My first feeling was outrage. Why didn't he reassure me? Alec mustn't die. But, even as I thought this, I had begun to recognise the truth. My father's reply, a brave one, was the best possible way I could be made to understand.

We visited him. He sat in his neat, clean pyjamas in an iron hospital bed, with the glazed brick wall behind him. My parents asked where he would like to come to recuperate. Would he like to go home to Marlborough? To the town? Or would he like to come and stay with them, in the countryside? We all knew my grandmother would prefer to have him back in Marlborough, in the old house on the Green. She liked to watch the town. It was what she did.

Alec thought for a few moments. Then he said slowly, 'I think I should like to go to Bowerchalke.'

I thought of looking after him. But even then I knew he would not come.

It was by now early December, and Alec had his operation. My father took me over to visit. We went into the ward. I don't know how I knew he was dying. Tears poured down my cheeks. I was embarrassed because I thought I was giving the game away. But I couldn't stop them. Down they poured, whatever I did, whether I blew my nose, looked at him, looked at the floor, tried desperately to think of something funny. He looked so diminished, in his pyjamas in the horrible narrow bed. The stony floor, the hard, resistant walls, all this gave me the clearest sense of death. I don't know why this should have been so. My father seems to have been surprised when Alec died. So how did I know then that I would never see him again?

Alec knew, too. He looked at me very directly, and told me that until he was engaged to Grandma he had never kissed a woman except his mother. This I can well believe. But then he added, 'And – I have been happy.'

I felt a sharp, painful compunction. He was lying, that truthful man, lying about his marriage at least if nothing else, lying in a good cause. It was the last time I kissed his cool cheek, with the sandpapery stubble. My tears must have wetted his face.

Now I am old enough to imagine myself in Alec's position, I suspect he was already sorry for my grief. Probably he had some idea of how heavy it would be. I don't know whether he understood the feelings of my father, that grey monolith, his sparring partner standing behind me in the hospital ward, observing and – maybe – weeping too. Here is a passage from my father's journal, written in February 1977, about six months after the birth of Nick, my first child and my parents' first grandchild:

I have done some letters and we have been in to the garden, then shifted Nicky's first Christmas Tree to the other end. (I have had a sudden kind of imagination of him driving over the bridge: Applespill Bridge – many years hence and saying to his companion about a huge evergreen 'that was my first Christmas Tree': and I felt a great wish to save him all the grief that would come with the thought. But he must undergo his journey like the rest of us.)

The last time my father saw him, on the evening of 12 December, Alec said to him, pointing to the cylinder at the end of the hospital bed, 'I've been teaching about oxygen all my life, and I've just discovered what marvellous stuff it is.'

Remembering this caused my father anguish.

The hospital phoned a couple of hours later. My father had just arrived home, after driving the forty miles or so from Swindon. He still had his coat on. He put the receiver down exhaustedly and said to us, 'I'm afraid poor old Alec's dead.' Then he stood up and walked out of the door, to drive to Marlborough and break the news to his mother.

Before I realised how forbidden the whole subject was, I used to ask him about Alec's death. He would tell me nothing, except that it was awful. He seemed unable to understand that once he had said that, I needed to know more. Many years later, when I was about thirty, he finally told me.

The day after Alec's death, he went back to the hospital to ask the doctor what had happened. The doctor didn't seem to understand my father's love for his father, or the grief he felt, or the sense of terrible waste at his death.

The doctor said that Alec had got out of bed for some reason (rather foolishly, he implied), and had then as a result collapsed on the floor. And my father said to me bitterly, and, as we all do, blaming himself, that he did not realise then that old people were regarded as of no account, just – he said angrily – thrown away. Alec, he was sure, had needed help, had realised he was having a heart attack, and – lacking help – had been desperately trying to reach the marvellous, life-giving oxygen. Instead, he fell dying on the cold hard hospital floor.

I don't know when Alec's funeral was. No one went to it except my father and his brother. When I asked my aunt Eileen – about thirty-five years later – why she hadn't gone, she said furiously, 'I wasn't *asked*.' His body was cremated at Swindon Crematorium, and as far as I know they left the ashes there. I heard nothing about it at all, until many years later my father complained to me that his brother had not said a word to him on that occasion – that day in North Wiltshire, wintry no doubt and devoid of music or ceremony, when the two brothers were there with their father's coffin. I did not dare ask him if he had said anything to Jose. I left it on his terms.

That was the first Christmas away from Marlborough. The idea of the house without Alec was outrageous. Besides, my grand-mother had vanished as well. In her place was a balding, fretful figure, a pitiable, unrecognisable, childlike person of indeter-minate gender and no speech. Her mind had frayed. Her usual connection to the outer world, tenuous at best, was gone. From now on she depended on her children, her sons and most of all her adopted daughter Eileen, for what little of that world she was willing to notice. The rest of us tried to get on with things. My brother came back from boarding school for the Christmas holidays to a new house, a world without Alec, and a family kept apart, not only by grief but also by the silence with which we met it.

After Alec's death, precious things got lost, his oil paintings, including a good self-portrait, his watercolours, books, papers, tape recordings. They melted away. It became increasingly dif-ficult to mention him. My father made it clear that the subject was unwelcome and after a while it felt indecent. I remember blushing heavily in an English lesson when we had to learn 'Full fathom five thy father lies'. The subject of a father's dead body, 'of his bones', was a terrible faux pas – a gross reference to the process of decay. I knew perfectly well that Alec's body had been cremated. It was still indecent, this sea change that had happened, if only in the mind.

Because Alec's things were disappearing, I realised I must myself claim the drawings he had told me I could have. No one would hand them to me. I reported the conversation to my father. He looked at me balefully. Nervously, fatally, I elaborated, saying that one of the drawings, the copy of a floral pattern, was taken from the covers in the drawing room. He said, with deadly but satisfied contempt, that what I had reported could not possibly be true. Jane Austen describes one of her characters as being 'full of angry pleasure'. That was exactly it. The drawings Alec had offered me, part of my inheritance of his knowledge and love, vanished for ever, gratifying my father in some way I still do not understand. I hope he regretted such cruelty, though I doubt, honestly, that he thought much about it. Once the immediate sensation had gone, I expect he forgot all about it.

But I was constantly aware of Alec's absence, and of my foolishness in taking his presence so much for granted. The house in Bowerchalke was coloured for me by what had happened and never lost its shadow. I thought it pinched and ugly. It had a few old rooms, but my bedroom was modern, with straight walls and metal-frame windows, lots of them. The roof was thatched and the house in general seemed to be populated with thumps and rustlings. Behind the walls and cupboards of the attic you could hear scrabblings. In the strange new room some shapes became threatening. I had a tall, narrow bookcase that now looked coffinshaped. Later I found that my father had a similar struggle as a child with the awful narrow height of a grandfather clock. But it was my mother who moved it.

I began to have ferocious nightmares. I awoke screaming one night. I had heard a voice whispering to me, just behind my ear. My ever-practical mother said I had probably heard myself snoring. In one dream my door opened slowly, and my father's head came round it, *three feet from the floor*. I screamed and screamed. My perplexed parents left their door open, told me about Freud, about parents being fallible – that is all it is, they said. You are growing up, they said. I doubted it.

After several weeks of fractured nights, my father tried a different tack. Confront death, he said. Imagine the Egyptian mummy unwrapped. Imagine your own body dead and decaying in the ground. Imagine it in detail.

That night, when I went to bed, I set about doing as he suggested. I saw my skin shrivel, my face sink, my lips stretch. I watched my flesh collapse on to its skeleton. Finally I let my long hair fall away from my head in great hanks, and lie around it in a sort of dark corona. I was unprepared for what happened next. I felt a rushing, like a storm. I dropped and dropped into a deep hole, where it was dark. But my thoughts were very clear. They were: first, this is really exciting; second, what on earth was my father doing, telling me to try this?; third, it has worked. Then I fell asleep.

9

The Cold Light of Day

I saw Alec's death, I hate to admit, as something that happened to me. I hardly took notice of it as a disaster for Alec himself, or for Grandma (far worse, in fact, for her), and I utterly failed to understand the scale of my father's sorrow. He wrote later that he had wept more tears over Alec than over anyone. I never saw those tears. Instead, I saw a dry-eyed – and dry – reserve, a retreat from many things and people, including me. Until that cataclysm (my father himself said it was 'like the side of a cliff falling away'), it seemed to me that he and I had talked unself-consciously, with reasonable openness and friendliness. I see this in retrospect, and I may exaggerate. But the effect at the time was almost as if I had lost two people rather than one.

Perhaps we resented each other, silently competing. Each of us felt like the chief mourner, both of us ignoring my poor grandmother's wretched claim to that role. But this was not the only thing dividing us – though it may have been the most severe and lasting. Family trivia also played its part, persistent irritations and unforgivable small misdemeanours. He had lost his loved and resented father, and in addition his little, malleable daughter was daring to grow up. Such a combination can hardly be unusual. But in my father's case, it coincided with him becoming slightly but perceptibly famous, a person to be reckoned with.

I was changing as well, physically and mentally. It may even be that, bereft of Alec, I was more needy than before, just at the point where my father was dealing, or trying to cope, with his own grief, and also becoming affected by his incipient fame. It must have been hard for him not to value his time quite highly.

Of course his response to me was not particularly rational, but all the more powerful therefore.

Most of the ground between us became dangerous or at least unpredictable. He used to find my robustness – even perhaps my demands – rather likeable, a sort of party trick. Similarly, he used to find me pretty, lively, human and animal. However, as I reached puberty things became more fraught. There was the kind conversation when I started periods. There were many polite, distant acknowledgements that I was a woman. He would open car doors for me, take his hat off when he met me. But when I was a teenager he found the reality of my femaleness difficult and – it seemed to me – unpleasant. For years I thought this was because of my extreme, unique ugliness, something that I can see from photographs existed principally, though tenaciously, in my mind.

Now, I think it was a combination of two factors. First, it would be inconvenient to find me attractive. He found incest both natural and absorbing – in theory. He often portrayed it comically, but then he did so with other subjects of great seriousness – love and death, for instance. Pretty Flower in *The Scorpion God* fails in her dutiful attempt to seduce her father, the pharaoh who will be ritually poisoned later that night. He does not respond to her dance of enticement. 'Very good, my dear. Most exciting,' he says, with deadly dismissal. I remember laughing at that passage, reading a pre-publication copy at my parents' home. He wanted to know – all authors would, I am sure – what I had found funny. When I read it out, his face fell. Poor Pretty Flower. 'Oh the shame,' she cries, 'The burning shame of it!' Sophie in *Darkness Visible* also fails in her approach to her father – in her case partly an attempt just to make contact. Perhaps I am imagining things. But the possibility of incestuous approaches from a daughter to a father evidently existed in my father's imagination, that realm where he spent most of his time. The father declines the approach, a position of great power.

Also, he knew, as I did, that my mother was capable of jealousy towards her daughter. It had often appeared. Once, he said to me what a nice mouth I had. My mother shot him a look of such startling venom that I initially thought she was joking. His expression closed instantly. No one spoke.

I had always taken for granted the idea that he and my mother were equals, neither afraid of the other. But in this I was wrong. A thoroughly married man, he was willing to pay a high price for peace at home. And he depended greatly on my mother. She was a crucial support in his writing. He says himself that without her he would not have written the books. I believe him. Also, like many wives she provided a link for him with the outside world, and this saved him a lot of time and effort. His need of her was very great, and his understanding of her was, to say the least, incomplete. Some of it was pure guesswork, endearingly naive and frequently wrong. I think it is true, and perhaps rather comic, that he found women hard to fathom. Many outwitted him, some affectionately – I have done it myself many times – some with less friendly aims. He learnt to play pretty safe. Besides, tranquillity around him was crucial if he was to stay creative, the state in which he was happiest and most fulfilled. It often set him free to be anything but tranquil himself.

So, if his teenage daughter seemed to be making difficulties, too sure of herself, too feminine, he would withdraw coldly. I would know I had to be careful. I was not to be sexual, and I was not to disagree, which put me as a teenager in rather a quandary.

In a flight towards warmth, I concentrated on the things we shared. Shakespeare. Greek. A slightly contemptuous appreciation of Latin – nice poetry but not as good as Greek. I developed an instinct for what he would like – the spare intensity of Donne, the simple-seeming beauty of Edward Thomas – he loved the 'first white violet' poem. But there were awful moments. I quoted the Tennyson lyric 'Now fades the crimson petal, now the white' – which I loved. Naively, I connected it with my mother's scent-filled garden and the cool dusk by the river.

'Nonsense', he said crisply. 'Don't you see? It can be paraphrased in three words. *Sleep with me!'*

Everyone laughed, and of course he's quite right. I just hadn't
noticed, and went as crimson as the petal, both at the appalling-
ness of having failed to read the poem with enough sensitivity,
and, even worse, having precipitated a reference to sex.

Such contempt burnt, and began to be expressed more often.
With more money and more fame, and famous friends, he began
to drink more. If he had a lot, it made him unlike himself – harsh,
baffled, humourless, and desperate in a way I didn't understand.

And of course I did offend him. I caught some of David's left-
wing beliefs. Despite or maybe because of my father's flirtation
with the fringes of 1930s communism, he came to loathe my
opinions, or at least the fact that I expressed them.

Politics in the 1930s, that time of fierce commitment, had
brought my parents together. But their beliefs soon diverged.
After 1945, my father grew distrustful of politics and in a curious
way resentful of socialist ideas. They were, he said, incredibly
boring. I think he felt that he had been bamboozled into a position of simplicity, something he always distrusted. He treated
socialism like a discarded infatuation, with all the consequent
embarrassment and scorn. He raged, quite nastily, against my
wishy-washy socialist ideas, and laughed at David's more deeply
felt communism. Later he argued fiercely with me and with my
husband over Mrs Thatcher, the miners, the *General Belgrano*,
the CIA. Terrell, a political theorist, used to having arguments
on a reasonably level playing field, eventually grew irritated, and
asked him why in that case he had ever done things like belonging to the Left Book Club.

My father smiled unusually, with lots of teeth. Then he said,
'Because I wanted to sleep with the Pasionaria of the South-
East.'

My mother made no acknowledgement of this tribute, and
continued getting the Sunday lunch.

Meanwhile, I was progressing steadily towards the point when

studying Greek would be inevitable. Inexorably, these two subjects, Greek and politics, became linked, if only by the idea of
rebellion.

My father had many volumes in Greek, and one of these was
a copy of the New Testament. Keenly, pressingly, he lent it to
me, and I rather enjoyed deciphering the familiar in a foreign
language. For a while Greek seemed something that could, like
other languages, become translucent.

But this book had particular relevance for him. It brought back
what he described as a crucial part of his political education.

By the time I was fourteen or so, he was firmly prejudiced
against anything left-wing. He referred to Harold Wilson as 'my
hero' precisely because he thought Wilson wasn't a real socialist,
and he had a lot of fun with this. He used to tell us a story from
the 1930s, when he was canvassing with a candidate who was actually Communist, a man of pugnacious party conviction. They
visited a clergyman, full – both of them – with youthful confidence that they could explain to him just where he was mistaken.
The clergyman mildly asked the candidate if he had actually read
the gospels, and the man replied, 'Yes, in the original Hebrew.'

This was a flat lie and a fabulous bloomer. Our earliest version of them is written down in Greek. Even if the gospels had
survived in the actual language spoken by Jesus, they would be in
Aramaic, not Hebrew.

My father and the clergyman gazed at each other in shared,
horrified hilarity. It put them squarely on the same side. 'In the
original Hebrew' became shorthand for self-importance, deceit,
for presumptuous ignorance. Even for conviction itself.

His hatred of my harmless left-wingery was extreme, and
harshly expressed. Sometimes it seemed to me as if he had invited
me home, or out to dinner in London, with the conscious intention of having a go at me. He would lay a temptingly reactionary
statement there, before me, like a lonely pawn. If I took up the
challenge I would be crushed. If I didn't, I would be despised.
Some of these encounters reduced me to self-hating tears, or

made me flee my parents' home in the middle of a visit. I felt cornered and harried. Eventually I just gave up and kept quiet. Even now I avoid admitting to any belief – I am frightened.

The worst thing he could say about any of us was that we were boring. The word came with its own heat-seeking deadliness, striking one's weakest points. The fear of being in the way, disliked, disapproved of, made me incapable of rational thought. To be constantly entertaining from the age of thirteen to thirty is an impossible challenge. I took cover.

Of course, he reserved the right to be inconsistent. One day in 1985 (I was nearly forty) he rang me up. Clive Ponting had just been acquitted. He was a civil servant who was charged under the Official Secrets Act with revealing classified material about the Westland defence-contract negotiations in 1984. Ponting claimed to have acted in the public interest. But the prosecution had tried to dismiss the public interest defence, and the judge's directive in his summing up had supported this, declaring that the public interest is what the government of the day says it is. The jury dug their heels in.

My father said to me, 'Isn't it amazing how, every so often, a jury gets things dead right? You wouldn't expect it, but they do. Dead right.'

He also told me that he had once been on an American tour in the early sixties where he had given a talk at a place that was also hosting a conference of physicians. By this time he was a reasonable draw as the author of *Lord of the Flies*, and many of the doctors came along to hear him. During the questions, he was asked by a member of the audience to provide an example of a contemporary Christian act.

He took a deep breath and replied, 'The establishment of the British National Health Service.'

He told me proudly that the hostility was palpable.

After his death, I read in his journal that he had always voted Labour.

My reaction, I am afraid, was one of rage. If all this was so, why had I been so attacked? As for being boring, did he really imagine he was fascinating all the time? But this was much later, when I was fifty. As a teenager, I picked my way past the contradictory signals. In my turn I adopted preoccupation. Soon everyone in the house was abstracted. We avoided each other – we provided cover for each other. Conversation in the home was silently acknowledged to be a danger and became rare. Television was a refuge. So was playing the piano. My mother gardened.

When we moved to Bowerchalke he acquired a study, something new to him. He was finishing *Free Fall* (published in October 1959), and he mentions in a letter to the producer of the BBC Brains Trust that he is finding it hard to finish. He had written his first three novels at snatched times, in staffrooms, on buses, at the kitchen table. In solitude and silence, the task seemed harder. And the study was probably cold – certainly a lot of the other rooms in the house were. But the real thing, the real poison, was Alec's death.

Free Fall contains a portrait of Alec. He becomes Nick Shales, the science teacher of the anti-hero Sammy. He exemplifies one of Sammy's two irreconcilable worlds. Nick's world is matter-of-fact, humane and humanist, the world of cause and effect, optimistic and limited, as my father apparently believed Alec's was. Sammy goes to tell Nick that he, Sammy, has worked things out, that Nick is wrong. So there is a description of Alec on his deathbed, utterly recognisable to me. It was written less than six months, probably less than four, after Alec's death, and it contains a faint suggestion that Alec's world at last revealed itself to my father to be both richer and more complex, as he watched him facing death.

But Nick was in hospital dying of a tired heart. Even then it seemed to me he had less than his share, a bed in a ward in a town he always wanted to avoid. I saw him that evening from far off down the ward. He was propped up on pillows and leaned his immense head on his hand. The light from a bulb behind him lay smoothly over his curved cranium, snowed on him like the years, hung whitely in the eaves over his eyes. Beneath their pent his face was worn away. He seemed to me then to have become the image of labouring mind: and I was awed. Whatever was happening to him in death was on a scale and level before which I felt my own nothingness. I came away, my single verse unspoken.

In 1958 the Society of Authors unexpectedly awarded my father a science fiction prize for his short story 'Envoy Extraordinary'. He always said he had been given 'The Infinity Award Second Class', a misquotation that he relished. He could be heard muttering it as he banged his head or dropped his wallet. Actually it was the Infinity Award, Special Merit, and the brass plaque, set slightly crooked on its wooden background, has stayed in our various downstairs lavatories since he got it. It came with a two-hundred-pound travel scholarship, which would help fund our next family holiday. This would be his most extravagant escape from Marlborough yet. Alec was dead, and he, my father, would go to Italy.

But some of the money went elsewhere. Soon after we moved to Bowerchalke he bought a 1912 Bechstein, a grand, something Alec would have guiltily enjoyed too but agonised over. Not so my father. He would have rummaged in his store of Shakespeare. Oh reason not the need. In 1971 he forced himself to write by giving up the piano and he found it horrible. It was somewhere to *go*, not just something to do, and I think pianists, bad or good, will understand this. On holiday, I would sometimes see him get up and walk purposefully off. Then he would recognise the piano-shaped hole in the house and return sombrely. At our house in Bowerchalke the music room was just long enough for the Bechstein and a chair. It was a great distraction but also nourishment. Our old piano, with its bruised varnish and worn keys, disappeared.

In the spring of 1959 I had been given permission to be absent from school for the end of term, so that we could have more time in Italy. My teachers were clearly conscience-stricken about this, and gave me many warnings disguised as encouragement about how educational it would be. But as the end of term approached I began to feel terribly ill. I crawled through each day, slept like a log and then dragged myself up in the morning for another dreadful struggle. Finally, one evening, I decided to give up. I let my head sink on to my history homework. It was painful but restful. My father found me, soothed me with a kindness I perhaps unfairly think of as unusual, and told me to go to bed. I burst into messy tears and said that the school would not let me go away to Italy with the family if I had already been absent. This was vividly clear to me in what I now realise was a delirious light. My father said, patiently again, that it would be all right and I would not be left behind. I was terribly shocked by his understanding, and – oddly – it made me feel more vulnerable, not less. I took his advice, partly as a way of avoiding further conversation. Steadily, in turn, we all three sank into terrible bouts of flu.

Barely recovered, a couple of weeks later we packed and got into the car. It was a heroic effort, accomplished with terrifying patience from all of us. My brother had come home from boarding school and luckily he was spared the infection. His map-reading, always good, was a life-saver for my father, who later found difficulty getting from Cornwall to Devon. We crossed the channel overnight by ferry boat. Next morning, at about six, the day with several skins too few, we fragilely began the long trek through Europe.

All the way south we drove through an accelerating spring. My father described it as being like a miracle – we watched the mist of green grow deeper over the branches, as the aftermath of flu lifted from us and the sun came out and melted away our winter.

At Pisa I decided I was absolutely obliged to go to the top of the Leaning Tower and walk down it thoroughly – I had a bet with my cowardice. It never occurred to me to consider anyone else. So I carefully – and visibly – circumnavigated each rung, on the outside, no cheating. When I got down, my father – terrified of heights even by proxy – said reproachfully that he had spent the time lying on the ground, chewing the grass like Nebuchadnezzar.

But some subjects could not be joked away. We went into the Pantheon in Rome, stepped round the puddles on the floor and came across a long stone box with the single word Raphael on it. 'Look,' I said. This was unquestionably one of the educational reasons for our trip and I was proud of finding it. My father turned his back on the hated shape.

We stayed in a *pensione* in Florence, and visited three pupils of Annigoni, the artist who had famously painted the Queen's portrait three years earlier. I don't recall how this came about – an introduction, I suppose, though I wonder now who it was from. Two of them at least were amazingly lovely young men. They referred to Annigoni as 'the maestro', and their unselfconsciousness seemed to me a bit put on. Now I realise from this how young they were. Did we actually meet the maestro himself? Possibly. But I definitely remember the three long, dark, talkative young men in suits, and my father gravely explaining to me later that he thought it had been a pretty – by which he meant considerably, not decoratively – homosexual set-up. I gazed at him in astonishment, not at the idea but at the implication that this was news.

Of course, he assumed from my expression that I didn't understand, and the rest of the Italian trip is filled in my mind with his explanations of this – to him very puzzling – idea that men sometimes loved each other. It wasn't puzzling to me – I was desperately and silently in love with a girl in my class at school. She epitomised all nobility, wit and grandeur, even though she had a rather bumpy nose and straight brown hair. She made a magnificent Tybalt in the school drama competition, swirling her cloak with her square shoulders. Since then I have always grieved more over Tybalt's death than Mercutio's. But it led my father to harp, rather, filling Italy for me with men in desperate love with each

other – Shakespeare, Michelangelo, other great names. His con-
cern – a generous one – was lest this should reduce their stature
in my eyes. He had forgotten how puzzling adults always are to
children – puzzling but to be accepted.

I was much more puzzled by my parents' fecklessness. In
Rome my mother had a sudden bilious attack, throwing up in
the washbasin, poor woman. This unsurprisingly blocked it, a
circumstance I had never come across before. She then began
a desperate, painful and absolutely flooding period. Later she
told me it was 'almost like a miscarriage'. Later still, she told me
she was sure it had been one. I did my best, rather pompously,
to ensure we stayed put. After all, I now knew about periods.
But my observations were ignored. My father was nearly always
restless, and in any case the Infinity Award hadn't lasted nearly
as long as one might have hoped. My mother – a brave woman
– dragged herself up out of bed and into the car, away from the
blocked washbasin. Off we went north to Milan. I have often
wondered about that life – a third child, born in September or
October 1959, conceived I suppose around the time Alec died.
The child would have been fourteen years younger than me, another daughter perhaps, a rival. I never asked my mother if she
wondered, but of course she must have.

We drove around Milan many, many times. I feel despairing
hatred for it even now. Eventually we fetched up in a small, grim
hotel, a tall unending staircase with rooms more or less hanging
off it. Here a change was made in room allocation. I slept with
my mother and David with my father, which must have been
shy-making for them both.

Next day, as we ate our boiled eggs for lunch – it had been a
very disjointed night, with much banging of doors – my father
explained in liberal and soft tones, looking me in the eye to show
he wasn't embarrassed – oh, no – that he thought the hotel, the
only one we had been able to find with vacancies, had been, as he
said, 'a bordello'. I took in this word, and decided that it was such
a pretty one that my initial and unvoiced belief must be wrong.

I wished, as all children do, to protect my parents from the dangerous subject of sex, so I had kept quiet about my impression that the hotel was full of prostitutes. A brothel could not possibly be called something as jaunty and foreign as that.

We paid a formal call on my father's Italian publishers, to see if they could give us some money, over the counter as it were. With great charm, they announced happily that they had not sold any of his books. They invited us to participate in their amusement at this fact, which was generous, really, since it meant that my father's small advance was still unearned. We left, washed out of the building on a wave of absent-minded delightfulness.

There was nothing for it. How many times, I wonder, did my father realise with heavy heart that Alec was no longer there to send us five pounds? Luckily, it was compulsory – for mysterious currency reasons – to buy coupons for petrol before you left England. Otherwise we would have been completely stranded. So we drove on through northern Italy, Switzerland, France, desperately short of money, and living off more boiled eggs cooked for us by the cheap hotels we stayed in.

As we drove across the enormous plains of France, my father decided it was time to bring out our own vast subject. But he had overestimated his ability.

'It's going to be a real loss,' he announced firmly. Then there was an audible falter.

He cleared his throat, pushing through our family reserve.

'A real loss. Not being able to talk to Alec about all this.'

None of us replied, not even my mother. We recognised the effort those words had cost him. We sat in respectful silence. I thought of Alec and his painting. He had never been to Italy, never sat six feet away from the *Primavera*, never seen Botticelli's little angels. I had looked in astonishment at their full, blue smocks, rather like our school pinnies, but covered somehow in a subtle veil of gold. The blue and gold flared out behind each small figure, as they skated across the glassy sea towards the crowning of the Virgin.

But I couldn't feel anything. I tried more purposefully. He would have known how you could paint that veil. He would have known what the curious black thing is across the lips of Flora. But he was gone, and I had been to Italy at an age when he had probably gone no further than the centre of Bristol.

I tried to tell myself that he would be glad – glad for me, that is. Yet he was the most curious of men, the most capable of enjoying the sight of things, things to learn from. Being sorry for the dead was extremely difficult. I was sorry for the living, myself in particular. In a dim, vague way I was even sorry for my father.

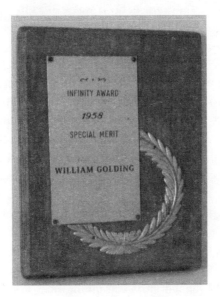

10

Goodbye to the Old House

One Saturday in November 1959, soon after the publication of *Free Fall*, and almost a year after Alec's death, my parents and I drove over to Marlborough and went for the last time to my grandparents' house. They had rented it for nearly fifty years, since my father's birth in 1911. It was soaked in memories.

Some more tangible things had vanished already. Before we arrived, my uncle Jose had a two-day bonfire on the lawn. According to Theo, he burnt a lifetime's accumulation of receipts, bills, letters, exam certificates. There were all the papers a family might have, letters from the war years, letters from before my grandparents' marriage in 1906. He did keep a few things – my grandfather's diary, the cards David and I had sent our grandparents for their golden wedding. Also the last note which my grandmother wrote to Alec. 'The usual scrawl but just a line to send you my love.'

Now, the larger contents, furniture, books, crockery, linen, curtains, were to be shared among the three families: Jose's, Eileen's and ours. The discussion took place, it seemed, above my head, on some inaccessible adult frequency.

Puzzlingly, my parents seemed to be taking nothing. My grandmother was very ill by this time, too ill to say who should have what. Earlier in the year, while she was with us at Bowerchalke, there had been a flurry of phone calls, visits from the doctor and the district nurse. Then, late at night, Eileen and her husband Bill arrived with my cousin Lizzie. The grown-ups thought Grandma was going to die. Lizzie and I slept that night head to toe in my single bed, talking and laughing, while the grown-ups watched over Grandma.

But she didn't die then, poor woman. She recovered enough to be taken to Southampton, where Eileen nursed her for the next eighteen months or so, a process so exhausting that it ruined Eileen's own health, which Grandma herself had so anxiously protected, mindful of the premature death of her younger sister – Eileen's mother Estie.

Grandma finally died in August 1960, in her sleep, when we were away in *Wild Rose*. I was told of her death almost casually, almost as an afterthought, as if she had been gone some time. Her retreat from the world had always lent her near-invisibility, and she had managed at last really to fade to nothing, at least for those of us who had not been looking after her.

So that November day in Marlborough was bleak, even by Wiltshire standards. We knew it was the absolute end of the previous life – ours, as well as Alec and Grandma's. The house, our house, would be lived in by strangers.

When we arrived, the electricity had been turned off, and we had to work in daylight – in that house which always had dark corners. The short day wore on, and the visibility became a real problem. Still our car was empty. I couldn't understand it.

Later my father told me, angry and perhaps defensive as well, 'Jose wanted me to buy that house. I told him I hated it . . . wouldn't touch it.'

Perhaps the bonfire is not surprising.

I took matters into my own hands. Without asking anyone, I carried Grandma's chair out of 29 The Green and round to our estate car. I loaded it into the back. I went back indoors, and somehow got my arms round Alec's davenport, the little desk that stood in the drawing room. When you opened the lid, there was a smell of mapping ink and violin rosin, a way back to Alec. I don't quite understand how I carried it. But I managed, and soon it lay on its back beside the chair in our car. I should have told someone but I didn't. I had some vague idea that, since they meant more to me than anyone else, I should have them. But I kept quiet, gathering up Alec's four-volume edition of Scott's novels, and some crochet work that Theo had given me. I waited, sitting on the bottom stairs in the hall, as the old house grew completely dark. The feeling of an ending was so strong that it wasn't even creepy any more.

Soon, my parents had finished. My father announced cheerily that he would come over the next day to finalise things.

We drove back to Bowerchalke. No one said anything about the chair and the desk. Decades later I realised that my parents assumed Jose and Theo had put them in the car. And Jose and Theo must have assumed that my parents had simply taken them – without saying anything. It would not have occurred to anyone that I had done it. It was entirely uncharacteristic of me to do anything so bold. I can still hardly believe it myself.

Years later, I confessed to my mother. I was probably about forty. She listened, folded her lips for a moment, and then told me magisterially that I certainly did not need to worry. But she claimed to be surprised, nevertheless, that *nothing had ever been said*. Of course no one ever said anything. We were not the sort of family in which things were said.

Pleased, she put the chair and desk in our sitting room, where they looked quite at home on the nice tiled floor Alan Badel had so admired. Next day, my father went over again. Afterwards, I heard him and my mother talking. There had been a bit of a to-do about a nice pair of red velvet curtains from the drawing room. Lizzie and I had used them as a sort of theatre curtain, bursting out from behind them to recite poems to our admiring families. Happily, it turned out that Theo and my father each just wanted one. So the argument, probably conducted in the most civil, you-have-them-no-you sort of way, was painlessly resolved. No one seems to have said a word about the things we already had. My father hung his half of the curtains over the garden door in his study. It kept the draughts out till 1970, when they knocked down the study and music room and built a new, bigger room instead.

He also brought something else – Alec's long woollen dressing gown, a traditional one, plaid wool, corded round the edges, and with a cord belt. I remember Alec sitting up in it, when he was recovering from flu. It was far too small for my father, but then its usefulness was not the point. It was the first, tentative sign of his feelings. It hung on the back of my parents' bedroom door from 1959 until the late 1970s – until, as my father said, Alec had died out of it.

So, in November 1959, my father and his brother Jose became the older generation. I believe they never talked unreservedly again. There are some letters – jocular, ostensibly open, frank in a brotherly way. One should never judge a relationship by its letters alone. About two years after we gave up 29 The Green, Jose and his family came to visit us at Bowerchalke. Jose's children chased Lizzie up one staircase and down another, while Jose sat silent in his mother's chair, the one I had taken. We still have it at Tullimaar, the Cornish house where my parents moved in 1985. The varnish of the right armrest is worn away, down to the wood. Recently I found one of Alec's glass plates, a photograph of his mother-in-law, my great-grandmother. She is seated in it, her hand on the armrest as I remember Grandma's. And I don't remember Jose saying a word. Theo talked, my mother and father and Eileen talked, but Jose sat silent in the chair, just as his mother had.

It was not a good family moment. And it cannot have helped at all that our lives were triumphantly different. It was obvious that we were well off. We were well settled in our charming thatched cottage in the picturesque, much sought-after village of Bowerchalke. We had an Aga and *two* bathrooms. The three-piece suite had new covers.

To my parents it was a homecoming after exile. They remembered being happy there. In April 1940, a year after their first meeting, and seven months after their marriage, my father left Maidstone, where they had met, to take up a job at Bishop Wordsworth's School in Salisbury. He had done his teaching practice at the school a couple of years earlier.

I was always puzzled by this move. In Maidstone, my mother, pregnant with her first child, could have called on her family for help. She and my father surely knew by 1940 that he would have to go and fight. Why move to Wiltshire, where their only relations were hostile and had refused to meet their son's wife?

When my parents married in September 1939, it was only a couple of months since my father had jilted his fiancée, Mollie Evans. He and Mollie had been engaged several years, and they had been to school together. Alec had taught her, Grandma and Jose knew her well. The marriage had been long expected in Marlborough, and indeed by Mollie's parents, who kept the village shop in the nearby village of Great Bedwyn. It was a small-town scandal, and made my grandparents furious and ashamed. Mollie herself suffered acutely, and never married, though I am glad to have learnt recently that she bravely rebuilt her life. Jose himself was coldly disapproving, not only of his erring and ruthless younger brother but also of that brother's new bride, clever, glamorous, and assumed to be complicit in the break.

Relatively recently, and a decade after my father's death, I found the reason for the move to Wiltshire. He records it himself, with a characteristic mixture of honesty and self-dislike. The school had sacked him, the grounds a mixture of women, alcohol and politics. His account of the whole business was written after my brother David's first admission into mental hospital early in 1969. It is a confession, a hard one to read. It gives a picture of how he saw himself, ruthlessly selfish and – in spite of his guilty awareness – happy in the fruits of that selfishness, his marriage to my mother.

It would have seemed to Jose, on that visit to our new home, that my father had chosen the house in Bowerchalke over 29 The Green. More than twenty years before, he had chosen life with my mother over life with Mollie. Our move to Bowerchalke was another break away, and together with Alec's death and the loss of the old house it became radical.

Next to Bowerchalke church and its peaceful graveyard, with

drooping yews and lichen-dappled gravestones, is a handsome house, the former vicarage, built, like Salisbury Cathedral, of Chilmark stone. In the 1940s my father's friend John Milne and his wife Daviona lived there with their two small sons. The Milnes' presence made the village more attractive, but it was a lovely place anyway. In May 1940, a few weeks after my parents moved into their cottage, the hedges would have been white with hawthorn. For my mother, used to the orchards and hop fields of Kent, it was new and strange. But she soon grew to love it.

At the bottom of their garden ran the Ebble, which rose clear and very cold nearby, through the chalky soil. There were elm trees in the next field, hawthorns across the river. Higher up the village were tall clumps of beech, with their echoing rookeries. The silvery, quiet road ran down towards Salisbury past my parents' cottage, beside the stream and its cress-beds. A mile further down was the bigger village of Broad Chalke.

In 1940, the cottage was called Little Thatch. It was a two-up, two-down. But by 1958, when we moved there, it had five bedrooms, two bathrooms, a study and a music room, as well as a small dining room and the beamy sitting room where Alan Badel had delivered his verdict. The previous owners had added another wing, and with the old bit of the cottage it formed an enclosed space about ten feet by ten. Grandly, we called it the courtyard, and my mother decorated it with tubs and pots, and a tangled honeysuckle that held birds' nests and soaked the place in perfume.

Perhaps Alec's bitter judgement about his two sons – how Jose worked but my father achieved success – had truth in it. Both sons worked hard; it was in their family nature to do so. Jose was a well-loved, effective teacher, someone – like his father – who improved hundreds, perhaps thousands, of lives. But my father was the one who took risks and they paid off. Just as Maidstone gave him the push in 1940, Bishop Wordsworth's offered him a job. This enormous piece of good fortune placed him in and around Salisbury and its cathedral for the next forty-five years.

It also gave him two of his closest friends, the musicians John Milne and Tony Brown.

John Milne, who often came sailing with us in the 1950s, had been at Oxford the same time as my father. In 1940 he was conductor of the Salisbury Orchestral Society, the group with which my father had played *Eine kleine Nachtmusik* so memorably. He was also on the staff of Bishop Wordsworth's.

He and my father were very different. Once, when John was sailing with us, I did exactly what you are not meant to do with a pair of signal halyards, thin cord rather than rope – I let one end go, and it instantly flew away in the wind. John, very tall and mostly silent, stepped dangerously on to the slanting cabin-top just behind the bellying sail, recaptured the flying piece of cord and handed it to me without a word. I don't think anyone else even knew. If he hadn't done that, the cord would have worked its way back up the mast, and unrieved itself through at the top. Then someone would have had to go up the mast. As his godchild, I could not have asked for a better model of decency and kindness.

Their friendship was a constant for nearly forty years. Late in life, long after John's death, my father had a nightmare about being on his own in prison. He says himself that it reflects the fear he felt at the possibility of going into the navy without John. In fact, his luck held and they went in together, and no doubt some of the strength was on my father's side. But you could not miss John's goodness. John was a far better pianist, a better musician, but for my father his great talent was dealing with people's fears, a quality he shared with Alec.

In December 1940, my father and John Milne were called up. They left Bishop Wordsworth's to join the navy. My mother, with my brother, who was four months old, moved up to the Vicarage, to live with John's wife Daviona and their two boys. The school bade my father and John an official goodbye in an impressive send-off. Another member of staff, by then departed in a very different manner, had been a conscientious objector, and I suspect, perhaps unfairly, that Freddie Happold, the school's ambitious headmaster, was using the occasion to make it quite clear that the rest of his staff were full of the right stuff. My mother – a truthful person – told me that, at the end of the head's exalted valediction, my father said, firmly and very audibly, 'The bravest man has already left.'

Of course, he liked to go against the grain, and prided himself on being subversive. He may also have been challenging himself to be awkward. But I believe his admiration for his former colleague was genuine. So was his acknowledgement of complexity.

Tony Brown was another member of staff at Bishop Wordsworth's. He too became a close, loyal friend until his death in 1977. He was married to Fiona, a fellow-musician. They had four children, all musicians too.

At the end of 1940 she and Tony were expecting their first child. The baby, named Iona after the island where her parents had honeymooned, was born in Salisbury. Soon after, Fiona had a visit in hospital from my mother and Daviona. Fiona often told her younger daughter Sally and me how gorgeous her two friends looked, how they both had pageboy hairstyles, Daviona blonde, my mother dark. They were smartly dressed, each wearing a stylish beret set at a fashionable angle. The story concluded with Fiona saying that they were off to meet their husbands, home on leave from the navy.

I knew that my father had enlisted in December 1940. But we have an enigmatic photograph. In it, my father, dressed as a naval rating, stands with his own father outside a window at the old Vicarage in Bowerchalke. My mother and grandmother sit together on a bench between them. On my mother's knee is a very small baby – my brother David.

It has always puzzled me. Clearly this was the great event – the eventual rapprochement between my mother and the Goldings, of which she told me. But my father was in uniform. Surely the navy hadn't granted him leave so soon after joining the service? David, born in September 1940, was still tiny, only a few months old. But Fiona's story makes it clear. Iona was born on 7 January 1941, and my father's arrival on leave must have been soon after that.

I cannot imagine what our lives, David's and mine, would have been like if this rapprochement had not happened. Most of my early years, and my brother's too, were rooted in our life at Marlborough. The steadiness and love of our grandfather, and of our retreating and silent grandmother too, gave both of us a better start than we could possibly have had otherwise. I doubt that my parents would have denied this. About a year after Alec's death, my father, speaking formally to us because of the effort it cost him, made a pronouncement.

'Alec,' he said, 'thought his greatest quality was his brain. Actually it was his goodness, his soul.'

In January 1941 it was sixteen months since the start of the war and my parents' marriage. My father had jilted Mollie in the summer of 1939. Alec and Grandma had firmly declined to meet my mother ever since. But things changed, even for them, the most conservative of socialists.

My father told me that soon after the outbreak of war, he and his brother went for a walk together. They agreed that it was unlikely they would both survive. And they promised each other that the survivor would look after their parents.

In 1957, when I was twelve, my father took me to buy a school raincoat. We went to the Salisbury tailors, just by the Market Square, where they did a good trade in used school uniforms. My mother had given us instructions, particularly about room for growth. The navy mackintosh we chose was almost down to my ankles. It was faded to a bluey-grey, but I remember it had a soft, pleasant texture that draped nicely and always lengthened my small frame. I thought it elegant. My father, often touchingly paternal but naive in matters of clothing, was no doubt unobtrusively steered towards it.

The shop was run by Mr Whaley, a tall man with a large head. After my father paid for the mackintosh, custom dictated that there should be a short burst of conversation, one of those so-cial positioning interchanges that the British navigate with such exactitude and pleasure. But the conversation veered off course. 'How am I?' repeated Mr Whaley, in reply to my father's anodyne question. He paused for a moment. Well, since both his boys had been killed in the war, life didn't seem to have much point some-how. He didn't sound angry, just honest, with the dreariness of a daily grief. There was then a moment of quivering danger when I think he could have wept.

My father turned away from the counter.

'I'm sorry', he said.

He didn't sound sorry, he sounded annoyed. Mr Whaley gath-ered himself together. In effect he had been told not to bother my father with his grief. 'No, no,' he said. 'It's all right.' He re-treated and became the shopkeeper again.

It was dreadful. I'm sure my father knew just how dreadful. But I think he had glimpsed, in those few seconds, my grandparents bereft and mourning their sons, my widowed mother struggling with her two children. He and Jose had got away with it, and of course he could not be sorry. Poor Mr Whaley, uncomforted, *and* with the feeling that he should not have spoken. We left, shamed, father and daughter.

For my grandparents in 1940, my brother's birth changed every-thing. Whatever they thought about my mother, or about the marriage and the jilting, they knew she would need help. There was a future, even if their son was killed. They felt, I suspect with relief, that their distance should no longer be maintained. An expedition was planned.

In general, they would not drive the car in wartime. My father said they felt it was 'using the sailors' blood'. So the car had been mothballed, as the navy would say, in the garage. But the com-plexities of getting from Marlborough to Bowerchalke by bus, two buses each way – and also I think some sense of the impor-tance of the occasion – overcame their scruples.

They navigated to Salisbury in safety, and out through the country lanes to Bowerchalke, with my grandmother at her most august, a vigilant passenger. She wore a hat, of course, a mannish-looking trilby, and her scraggy fur coat (later a burglar in my London flat pointedly ignored it). I can picture the car driving noisily up the hill in Bowerchalke, with my grandparents looking at the surroundings of their son's new life, the countryside, the neat cottages, the grey old church with its square tower and the downland behind it. I can imagine the arrivals, the introductions, the unspoken thoughts.

It was a sunny day. The shadows fall sharply in the photograph. The family group is gathered outside the east-facing window of the old Vicarage. Nowadays you can peer from there over the hedge into the churchyard, and catch sight of my parents' grave.

I am not at all surprised that a good six inches of open window is letting in the January air. But the day seems calm, and might even have had a tinge of spring among the bare branches. There is a bench under the window, and my mother and grandmother sit side by side at their first meeting. It cannot have been easy, despite my mother's charm, my grandparents' kindness. Mollie's name must have hung in the air. My father in his ordinary seaman's uniform is at ease, but my grandfather looks austere – he at any rate has not forgotten Mollie. My mother does not seem herself at all. She has a tamed, almost daunted air, quite unlike the cheerful confidence I remember. She is holding my brother on her knee. He is well wrapped up, though you can just see his silky blond hair and his little warm head and face. There is something squarish – a splint, perhaps – on one foot, underneath the baby blanket. My grandmother gazes down at him, absorbed in the sight of her first grandchild. Alec and my parents look at the camera.

In the summer of 1991, my father stopped me on the landing at Tullimaar. It's a large space, almost like an upstairs hall. He and I usually talked when other things were going on, in a car, or with the burr of family conversation around us. The silence was unnerving.

'I need to tell you something.'

I turned to face him. He was looking straight at me.

'You see, you do – *eventually* you do get over the death of your parents.'

This was awful. I was so embarrassed that the blood drummed in my ears. And – what was that?

'You do, but it takes a long time.'

There it was. Without my leave, or my intention, the flesh on the back of my neck was stiffening, the hairs were rising, lifting against each other almost audibly, rising in rows, as if marked out by a hairdresser with a tail-comb.

Then he said casually, turning to go downstairs, 'It has taken me thirty years.'

11

Greek to Me

When I was fourteen, my cousin Lizzie and I put on one of our plays at Bowerchalke. As usual we made everyone in the family come and watch. Its best bit of dialogue was the following:

LIZZIE: Who's Calliope?
ME: The Muse of epic poetry, of course.
LIZZIE: Oh.

This got great laughs, though we never understood why.

Our scenery consisted of two cardboard pillars. The linoleum for the music room had luckily come in a large cardboard tube, which I opened myself. I could see its potential. It tailored our material to classical themes, and our scenes mostly to temples, but that was all right. Sometimes the pillars fell down, with improvisation from us – 'An earthquake! The Gods are angry!' – and stifled laughter from our audience.

We used the attic. It had cupboards and a window with a fire escape, useful for exits and entrances. We charged sixpence, and the not very sizeable proceeds went to Oxfam. It was a rowdy affair, with terrible singing, and thunderous applause at the end, increased no doubt by the audience's relief. When we came downstairs afterwards, the Coombses, who lived over the road and kept a jaundiced eye on strangers, told us that Freddie Happold, my father's bête noire, had called on us. He was retired now from Bishop Wordsworth's, *désoeuvré* and, I expect, lonely. He had *gone away again*, unable to make anyone hear. My father, with the air of someone missed by a falling rock, gave Lizzie and me a ten-shilling note.

But it wasn't just the cardboard pillars. The classical theme and the learned reference to the Muses were a way of pleasing my father. And it worked, however much he laughed.

Latin was easy. I enjoyed the simplicity of it, the paucity of synonyms, the thuggish bareness of it. I liked the way it was all bolted together. No wonder the Romans built roads and bridges. When, later, my children started playing with Lego, I was strongly reminded of it. Everything fitted, and the components came in regular sizes.

But Greek was different. It seemed to me to fall apart in my hands, like wet newspaper. Bits of it morphed extravagantly – verbs, particles, accents. Greek grammar has one more of almost everything than Latin: passive, active and middle voice; single, plural and dual number; indicative, imperative, subjunctive and optative mood. Admittedly, it doesn't have the ablative case. Perversely, I quite liked the ablative.

Moreover, unlike Latin, in Greek we studied dialects, which meant the language we knew was often cunningly, almost maliciously, disguised. If you didn't understand, you couldn't read the literature, which was allegedly the point. Homer, Sappho, Thucydides, Xenophon – each one was different. Reading them required the sort of elasticity that comes only with technique. The process, difficult but possible at first, soon became something I refused to acknowledge to my parents and teachers – an impossibility. I got through O-level mainly because my set book, Homer's *Iliad*, Book vi, included the farewell of Hector and Andromache. I still look at it now. Sappho too. Her poems were blessedly short, intense, and apparently simple. They were about things I recognised – unrequited love, the shocking beauty of young girls, the ordinary day and its happenings:

> You, evening star, bringing all that shining dawn has scattered, you bring the sheep, you bring the goat, you bring the child to its mother.

I tried extremely hard to like Thucydides. My father often told me how good he was – how important, how admirable. He charted, said my father, the descent of a civilised nation from decency to cruelty. He told me how, at the beginning of the Peloponnesian War, the Athenians condemned the rebellious people of Mytilene to a ferocious punishment – the men would be killed, the women and children enslaved. A ship was sent across the Aegean, to impose this terrible judgement. But then the people of Athens repented of their fury, and sent their fastest ship, with the best rowers, to overtake the earlier vessel and countermand the order. By the end of the war, said my father, Thucydides shows us that such a punishment had become commonplace. Of course, the subject lay close to his heart. Not, I'm afraid, to mine. I didn't want to read about conflict and what it did to people. I spent my life avoiding conflict at home. Why should I want to read about it in Greek? Penelope avoids conflict in the *Odyssey* by weaving her tapestry – now, that I could understand. Awful as it sounds, war bored me.

So did the grinding persistence needed to learn the wretched language. My father told me that 'one day' it would all become translucent. There would be no foreign language – I would look straight through it. No longer would I need to think *about* it, I would think *in* it. Did he have a sense, I wonder, of how far away that was?

'Samuel Johnson said Greek is like lace,' he announced. 'A man gets as much of it as he can.'

I had never seen my father trying to acquire lace. The sententious quote annoyed me, because he was, after all, talking about a choice in my life. I knew he really wanted me to do Greek, to acquire it, to be at ease within it. But it was still not important enough to him to warrant real scrutiny, so he just threw literary quotations at the whole business, as if that would fix it.

And of course it didn't. In my struggles with this lacy, intractable word-fabric, important things stayed out of reach, notably – shockingly – the great tragedies. Those, I was told, were the pinnacle of literary, and even spiritual, achievement – apart, of course, from Shakespeare, said my father, his loyalties briefly and comically torn. But I could not make them come alive. They bore no relation to the gripping stories I had known since childhood. I knew they should seem magnificent – the tragic progressions of noble characters towards their inescapable fate – but they shrank grubbily to the status of a puzzle, sometimes a ludicrous one. They brought into my mouth the unmistakable taste of boredom mixed with despair. And I couldn't say so. I yearned for my father's approval. I knew that I used to have it, that affectionate admiration. I used to surprise him by how clever I was; I had always been so absolutely right on the money. Now I had lost the easy knack of being the daughter he wanted. All I could do was try again and again.

He compared learning Greek to playing the piano – something he had struggled with since the age of six.

'You have to break your hands on the instrument.'

I hated this phrase, at least as interpreted by him. He thought it meant 'break' as in fracture – presumably so that they could be re-formed in a shape that suited the activity. Surely this was rubbish? I believed the expression, incautiously adopted by him and repeated often, terribly often, like the idiotic lace business, was actually a metaphor from the breaking of horses. I said this to him once, daringly, and his face assumed a completely blank expression. He went on as if I had said nothing. The entrenched phrase gave him something, I have no idea what. He had applied it vigorously to himself, it appeared, and now he would apply it to me. Even at the time I felt horror at his reiterated acceptance of the need to break my hands. My father was actually very squeamish, and so loath to see me physically hurt that when I was eighteen, and had finally left Godolphin, he tried for several hours to dissuade me from getting my ears pierced. But he couldn't acknowledge my horror at the idea of broken hands.

He would frequently remind me that Classics gave you 'mental discipline'. He told me that most of the high-ranking civil servants had done Classics degrees. I really didn't want to be a high-ranking civil servant. I suspect he would have been greatly depressed if I'd become one. But such a response would merely lead to his killer shot.

'Do you want to end up working in Woolworth's?'

I thought I might prefer it to learning Greek. But I never said so. I just kept chipping away at the coal face. I was, in fact, mildly talented at some subjects, but with Greek I was hopeless, humiliatingly so for someone whose other inadequacies were usually explained away by 'being clever'. Any small progress I made was down among the foothills, whereas I was meant to scale mountains.

And there was certainly no help from the school – not then, at least. The poor deluded management was absolutely thrilled to have a Greek class for the school's Classics department, whose teachers had taught the same bits of the *Aeneid* repeatedly for the last twenty years, and generally endured the plugging of gaps in their timetables with divinity, history for scientists, and Scottish dancing when it rained.

Why could my father not bring himself to notice my struggles? After all, he had changed from science to English. He even told me that doing English was 'like getting into a warm bath'. Why didn't he want me to do the same? I assumed it was because he didn't care that much.

Long after the whole dreadful business, I came to understand that his strange obsession with the magic of Classics came, in part at least, from something in him that he could not afford to recognise. If his daughter had read Classics at Oxford, he might have seen the fading of that vengeful ghost, Oxford in the 1930s, the place where he was not quite a gent. But he could no more put this together than I could. His daughter had been to the proper school. Now she would do the proper degree.

So I battled on, astonished at my own stupidity. I had always found school work ridiculously easy, requiring nothing more taxing than stratagems to fill up the acres of spare time created by finishing early. But I was not surprised by my inability to say I wanted to change. I would have felt like Oliver Twist holding out an empty bowl.

However, it turned out that my inventive father did have something up his sleeve, something better than lace, better for both of us. In the spring of 1961, he and my mother took David and me with them to Greece for a holiday. My father was writing articles for an American travel magazine called *Holiday*, so there was extra money. We would go through France, Switzerland, Austria and then Yugoslavia, the first time any of us had been to a communist country. David was twenty and I was fifteen. It never occurred to us that we were rather old to be going off on holiday with our parents. We were still the family. Neither of us had broken away or showed any sign of wanting to. And, oddly, our parents also seemed to want us with them.

The voyage had its perils, different from sailing ones. We drove down the Adriatic coast, on roads that were sometimes surfaced for a few miles and then dissolved into dirt tracks. Every so often there were police barricades, and at one of those – we thought we had been waved on – a policeman suddenly pulled out a pistol and aimed it straight at my father. He braked extremely sharply, and stuck his hand out of the window in an imploring gesture of utter surrender, which I thought cowardly and humiliating. I still thought of guns as make-believe, things in films, and I suppose I thought he should have responded heroically. But my father had had a gun in his cabin as commanding officer during the war. He knew they were real, and he knew what they could do. I was also unaware how often guns are fired by mistake. My dad knew all about the cock-up theory of history. He could have given lessons.

The policeman looked at our passports and then, ignoring my father's cringing protest, *took them away*. We waited in miserable tension for about twenty minutes before they brought them back. I expect it was just a piece of bureaucratic bullying, the sort of thing I've encountered at airports, where the people at the desk occasionally pretend to lose your documents if you complain about anything.

Further south we saw women dressed in baggy trousers and

long, Eastern coats. We drove past churches with onion domes, through ravines and wild mountains. Sometimes the road would fray into the countryside, after part of the hill had slid down below us. We tasted real wildness, expected wolves, bears, eagles. We were in darkest Europe, Carpathia, Freedonia, Ruritania . . . Then, rather like a train bursting from a tunnel, we came to northern Greece. We drove through tame villages to Thessaloni-ka, a matter-of-fact town, and then down the eastern coastline of Greece. Here we saw for the first time what is really the most extraordinary thing about Greece. We were quite unprepared. I'm glad to say it still shocks me, even now, fifty years later. It wasn't the ruins that lay around, sometimes ignored, sometimes banal, often far too familiar. On the contrary, it was the defiant beauty of the landscape, dry, characteristic, often empty, and resonant.

One hot afternoon we visited Thermopylae, a lonely, washed-up site. It has a level, windy plain to the east, which lies where the sea was in the time of the great battle. My father wrote a fine essay about this, and called it 'The Hot Gates', his translation of the name Thermopylae, though now I wonder (what cheek – thinking my Greek is better than his) whether it should actually be The Pass of the Hot Springs. There is a smallish burial mound. It has a contemporary look, as if the battle were only fifty years ago.

Thermopylae is where the heroic Spartans – a mere three hundred – held out against the vast army of the Persian king Xerxes, buying time for the remaining cities of Greece to unite in a common defence. More, says my father, was won than that.

Neither you nor Leonidas nor anyone else could foresee that here thirty years' time was won for shining Athens and all Greece and all humanity.

The Spartans are not generally the good guys. That role is reserved – as he implies – for shining Athens. But my father had fought, had done at least one thing in the war which he thought would quite likely kill him. He knew what he was talking about

– he knew that such sacrifice should not be taken for granted, whoever made it.

In that essay he is alone, the solitary, meditative passer-by. But I often saw him carefully pocket another's experience, tuck it into his writer's stash. On the sun-hardened path across another battlefield, at Marathon, my brother saw a long brownish thing like a stick. As he bent down to pick it up, my father cried out.

'Leave it!'

David turned round angrily, thinking he was being reproved. But the brown stick moved, and slithered away into the grass. The snake – 'a sound as of a rope being pulled through the little jungle under the flowers' – went straight into the essay on Thermopylae. And from it I can see how my father did feel alone there, in a way – how the place reverberated for him. He was often quite shocked after such visits, to find that we had been there too.

Simonides of Ceos wrote a famous epitaph for the fallen, the three hundred Spartans and their leader Leonidas. His words are usually translated something like this:

> Go tell the Spartans, thou that passest by,
> That here, obedient to their laws, we lie.

But my father's version is different. The Spartans were not enamoured of words, and the poem is written as if they are speaking. And, adds my father, who himself, as he aged, moved increasingly towards a kind of passionate, distilled understatement, it has been translated a hundred times 'but can only be paraphrased'.

> Stranger, tell the Spartans that we behaved as they would wish us to, and are buried here.

Rather British Spartans, perhaps – but more moving, to me anyway, than the nineteenth-century version.

The Greek landscape and the stories that hung in the air above it affected all of us. Many times we were confronted by a name bursting with legend, to be succeeded by a scene of the everyday.

Driving past an oil refinery labelled Eleusis, or a tourist trap called Corinth, sweeping through the Vale of Tempe past the grey heap of Mount Olympus, deciphering in Greek the sign for Arcadia – it was funny, but somehow it was also something else, something a bit like vertigo. We looked over the sheer drop of those thousands of years, and felt – at least I did – an acute sense of belonging.

Nowadays an understandable knowingness has developed about all this, rather as Lyme Regis in the sixties had a greasy spoon called Jane's Café. Far from Austen country, in the baking summer of 2003 I stopped for a café latte in Mycenae. It was a dazzling, fiercely cloudless day, and the dark assortment of legends – the sacrifice of Iphigenia by her father King Agamemnon in exchange for a fair wind to Troy, his subsequent murder by his wife Clytemnestra and her lover, a horrible deed done as he soaks in a nice warm tub after his return from war – they seemed far distant from the smart little line of cafés. Nearby was a sign for the Hotel Clytemnestra. With bath. And I thought, with an abrupt jab I hadn't felt for quite a while, how my father would have enjoyed that. 'With bath,' he would have murmured, on his way upstairs to have one.

So Greece in 1961 obstinately refused to disappoint, both for us and him. The resonance was there in the background like a steady hum from electricity pylons. And I began to realise with astonishment that it was I who shared this experience with him, that he and I in the family had the deepest store, not only of knowledge but also emotion, about Greece. I began to wonder – might I make a go of it, of Greek, after all?

We went to the supposed centre of it all, Athens itself, prepared for disillusionment. It was still very small, as capitals go, almost homely. You glimpsed the white ruins of the Acropolis by accident. The Agora was dishevelled and grassy. Often you could not tell if a piece of stonework was two thousand years old or fifty.

One morning I was wandering with my father round the hot streets of the city. As usual we were lost, as usual in search of a bank. We happened on a rather dull-looking church, with a smaller, much more ancient one next to it, so old that its walls sprang from two foot below ground. It had the old Byzantine cruciform shape. It was dark and cool, and there were serene oval faces, almond-eyed, on the walls and ceilings. It was full of incense and lamps and shadows. There were photographers, and lots of rich-looking people standing around, clearly waiting for something. But no one told us to leave, so we stood bashfully near the door and waited too. Then a shiny black limousine drew up. A very modern bride – suntanned, thin and swathed in blazing white organza – stepped in her high heels down from the harsh sunshine into the dark interior. And suddenly, without warning, a huge bass choir boomed out from behind the gilded screen. Outside in the sun, my father dried tears off his face.

All of Greece astonished, even the dirty bits, even Piraeus, the port of Athens. There the water was clear like glass, and you could see ten feet down where the heads and guts of cleaned fish lay, watched mordantly by the skinny cats on the old stone walls. Small boats with huge eyes painted on their bows moved gently at their moorings; old fishermen sat and smoked, with their catch still twitching in baskets beside them. The city of Pericles and Socrates, Plato and Aeschylus, lay just up the road.

We drove along the southern shore of the Gulf of Corinth, turning south into the woods and hills of Arcadia, noisy with birdsong. We saw Olympia, with its fallen columns, their drums still in a line where the earthquake had toppled them. We saw its racetrack that looked so recently abandoned. There wasn't a museum, or even a proper road, and you could wander freely among the ruins, disturbing the odd sheep or rabbit. People camped there. Visitors were few and dedicated, wandering round like us in a state of awe and, it must be admitted, frustration. Nobody had a map and there was no guidebook. We had done well to find it at all. My brother was responsible for that. There was one café, where the locals sat, drinking water with a spoonful of sugary stuff in it. The establishment did not have much else, and in its perfect innocence had not yet learnt how much the foreigners like to drink.

We drove past the River Ladon, and my father, who preferred poetry to guidebooks any day, quoted Milton's 'sandy Ladon's lilied banks'. Usually quotations for him provided a latent context that he felt should be exposed. Astonishingly, in Greece you didn't need the poetry. It was there already.

Back on the mainland, we drove to the little village of Delphi, then just one narrow road hanging over a precipice, with the ruins at one end. Above us soared the rocky sides of Mount Parnassus, the Phaedriades, the Shining Rocks my father mentions so often in *The Double Tongue*, the novel he was writing at his death. Even then, in 1961, a couple of shabby hotels clung beside the road, and there were houses with doors hung round with postcards, woven bags and black and red pots. There were some concrete posts waiting to become part of a building. But that was all. There were no serious artefacts. As with Olympia, all that could be moved had been carted off to Athens.

Around the village the herds of goats still surged as they had done for centuries. Traffic gave way to them, though occasionally a lorry would honk and they would swing off, all of them together, leaping into the scrub on the hillside. The cafés had earth floors and awnings of grapevines, and were still for locals. They kept a special, respectful bemusement for our requests, bringing cups of black tea and separate cups of warm milk for the bizarre foreigners. The houses were largely untouched by the nineteenth century, never mind the twentieth. I suspect there were no drains whatsoever.

We had lunch in a hotel, built straight out over the edge. These villages are likened to swallows' nests, and the birds swoop all round you. The hotel dining room was empty except for one other man, a Greek. He seemed to want to talk to us, but my father was discouraging. He didn't like talking to strangers – often, he didn't want to talk to anyone. He feared it might bring complications, a fear I think he learnt early from his parents, with whom I saw it in action – no playing with the children next door, for instance. Also, he had been depressed to find that his knowledge of ancient Greek gave him hardly any help with the modern language. It felt like an eroded landscape, and he resented it – it had managed to spot a deficiency in him. So there had not been many conversations with the people of the country unless they spoke English. But the stranger had no English. Instead, he spoke German, not a passport either to my father's good humour. We could tell, however, that something important had happened.

That was how, in a near-empty hotel in Delphi, we heard, in German, that the Russians had put the first man – Yuri Gagarin – in space. Old loyalties abruptly came back, and politics became a jolly jape. We drove straight back to Athens, chortling at the Russian success. Once in Athens, we went straight to the American Bar and ordered Russian tea.

Then, the last thing, there was Marathon. More poetry, of course. The mountains, we are informed, look on Marathon, and Marathon looks on the sea. Right, as far as it goes. But of course Byron was making a political point about Greek independence from Turkish rule, the equivalent for him of going into a café in Istanbul and ordering Greek coffee. Our experience was more personal.

If you are not running there, but going by car, the distance seems quite short. We went one cloudy afternoon, threatening thunder. We looked at the mound which – like the one at Thermopylae – seemed pathetically recent.

My father, standing with us, began to tell us the story of the battle, the way Pheidippides did *not* run a marathon, he ran all the way to Sparta, a hundred miles, to beg them to put aside their traditional rivalry with Athens, and join with them against the Persians, the common enemy. He told us how the Spartans agreed they would come, but only after they had completed a few essential religious observances. Slowly, reluctantly, they put their well-drilled war machine into action and marched towards Attica, the countryside around Athens. But before they arrived, the Athenians, fighting stubbornly under their general Miltiades, and with only a few Plataeans as allies, had defeated the whole

Persian army, helped it was said at various places on the battlefield by a huge figure who bore archaic armour and dissolved
into a golden haze at the point of victory. Among Athenians, the
term 'veteran of Marathon' became the most honoured title.

When my father had finished, there were twenty or so people gathered around us and, as he was fond of saying, not a dry
eye. At last I saw the point. I had seen the real Greece. This
was the reason for those irregular verbs, those impossible, loose
constructions. I would do it, I would bury myself in it – and my
father would see.

But I had miscalculated. My father, swift in action especially
when full of feeling, leapt in the car with my mother and brother,
and sped off back towards Athens. I am told – and this is rather
touching – that the subsequent, one-sided conversation consisted entirely of his asking whether the visit had inspired me with
my Greek studies. O levels were little more than a month away.
When I did not reply, he apparently thought I was sulking, and
grew quite tetchy. My mother and brother, hysterical with silent
laughter, waited for the penny to drop. Finally, my father looked
round to the back seat, and nearly drove off the road with shock
when he realised only one of his children was there.

By the time they came back, I was surrounded by a posse of
black-clad women just like the ones in Le Havre five years earlier. The car screeched to a halt. Then, in all the chattering (we
did, of course, know the Greek for thank you), my parents and
brother somehow got in the car and drove off without me again.
But this time they came back quickly, and the journey back to
Athens was a quiet, thoughtful affair.

We were all great devotees of Technicolor epics, especially
my father, who sat entranced through many of them and often
quoted, with embellishments, their worst lines. A former Mister Universe named Steve Reeves was a stalwart of such films,
and we had admired him in many guises. We were personally
gratified to see a billboard in Athens advertising Ο Γιγας των
Μαραθοντων – The Giant of Marathon, or, strictly, The Giant

of the Marathonians – of which he was the star. Alas, it did not open till the following week, by which time we would be driving back to England. We would simply have to imagine him, his chin, his chest, his golden armour, his wonderfully wooden speech. And the story would stay imagined, as my father told it.

We had been lucky – we had seen many of the glories of Greece, and had seen them at a time when we did not have to airbrush tourist kiosks or new motels to get a good view. But that was not the main thing. All such journeys – our gimcrack sailing, the voyage to Italy, to Greece, even perhaps the journeys to Marlborough, the walks up to the forest – I believe they were undertaken even then, before the years of real difficulties with his writing, as voyages – escapes – which fed my father's imagination. He didn't know where the books came from, so he lived in fear that they would just stop. Perhaps it was not a matter of feeding. Perhaps the voyages, the wanderings, gave his imagination permission to wonder – the activity he once said he wanted on his tombstone. He had a feeling this was the state he needed, the receptive state, a fallow state. It was, interestingly, a habit of mind he shared with his father. The fallow state needed to be filled with things that engaged him and moved him – sailing, or visiting places that resonated for him. That way he didn't fret. He was pleasantly distracted, he had his family with him for company, and he didn't search anxiously for the next book.

12

Far, Far Away

It was a longer voyage that produced the next book. During that trip of ten months, my father, thousands of miles away from loved and resented Wiltshire, and from his children – about whom I think he felt much the same – set to work on the novel most rooted in his own neighbourhood, the novel about the building of Salisbury Cathedral spire. Distance lent him freedom, rather than enchantment, a freedom to build the cathedral as he wished.

In the autumn of 1961 he was going to be writer in residence at Hollins College, near Roanoke in Virginia. A girls' college, it was small and rather posh. I suggested I might go as well. Patronisingly, we all assumed that an English A-level student was capable of pursuing a first-year college course in America. I have no idea if this is true, or was in 1961. In any case, my parents didn't agree. Hollins wouldn't do Greek. From my point of view it would have been perfect.

But the true reason was they wanted to go away on their own. They had been married more than twenty years, most of it in what felt to both of them like poverty, either separated by the war, or occupied in looking after their two children. So far, the only member of staff from Hollins whom they had met was Louis Rubin, an English lecturer and novelist. He had appeared the previous year in our village, rather like a visitor from outer space. He told them Hollins was a nice, friendly place. This turned out to be an understatement.

My brother was at Oxford, in his second year. I was sixteen. The American salary would allow my father to pay my boarding fees, a large expense that suddenly neither parent seemed to begrudge.

My parents were looking forward to the trip very much,

though they tried to hide this from us. They were, as almost always, enough for each other. And it was easy for them to believe I would be fine. I should have been. It was much more common at that time for parents to leave their children at school and vanish to the other side of the world. One friend of mine went to boarding school when she was four, while her parents disappeared to sort out Africa.

In my case, I was going to a school I'd attended since 1953 – eight years. I would be in a boarding house where I had one close friend already. Besides, it had always been my brother who had difficulties. I was the one who was all right. My mother in particular was loath to hear of problems in my life. She would listen politely but sceptically while making no comment. Then, a few days later, she would invite me to agree that I had exaggerated.

David and I quarrelled more fiercely than usual that summer. His unhappiness was more complex than mine, but quite as intense. He disliked Oxford thoroughly, as my father had, and maybe for similar reasons. He always hated going back to it, and as ever hated leaving home.

Boarding school, even though I had dreaded it, was a shock. The abrupt amputation of many freedoms I had taken for granted made me furious and – something new – disobedient. It was years since my parents had limited my reading in bed. When I was about ten I read all night, to see if I could. Nothing happened except a rather surreal memory of the Enid Blyton I'd been reading. At boarding school I was not even allowed to read a book in bed in the mornings, even though it was light enough, even though I was in the sixth form. And this was a *school*. The silliness of it, the twice-daily prayers, the dust storm of rules – walk on one side of the stairs, not the other, don't put your hands on the banisters (what were they *for*, then?), prefects must go first through a door, then sixth-formers then fifth-formers – the bruising boredom of it all still frustrates me. It was enraging to be so hedged about, and by such stupid people. It was a place to be endured, and I did so with a very bad grace, skimping on work, making it trivial. I had wanted to please my dad, but now he was thousands of miles away, teaching American girls.

Godolphin seemed to me then an intrusive place, at once prying and unhelpful. We had to tick a column in an exercise book – a red one, actually – when we started a period. In early December my housemistress called me into her sitting room. Why had I not done so? I replied with carefully calibrated insolence that it was because I had not had a period. She sent me away, and then she appeared round the door again and called me back. Did anything, she asked, *happen* in the holidays? I looked back over the weeks of packing, the farewells as my invisible parents left aboard the *Queen Elizabeth*.

No, I said, nothing happened. We were planning to go away to North Wales, but there wasn't time.

My housemistress smiled, I thought as a dismissive gesture, but now I see with amused relief. No one, certainly not me, saw the abrupt ceasing of something so banal as an indication of unhappiness. Subsequently, in the disasters of the following year, my mother complained that the school should have let her know. She also pointed out that my letters were very cheerful. I don't doubt it. I thought I should protect them from my feelings.

Strangely, in view of our quarrels, I wrote to David, admitting to him how miserable I was. He wrote back almost immediately, kindly including a packet of crisps with his letter, in a large manila envelope, which he decorated with communist slogans to cheer me up.

This caused a furore. I had to open the crackling envelope in my housemistress's presence, and to my horror she immediately took his letter and read it. He wrote sympathetically and at length about my misery, the boredom, the ugliness of my surroundings, the ludicrous pettiness of the rules that engulfed us, the stupidity and narrow-mindedness of the boarding-house staff. She gave me the letter without comment, and as far as I could judge did not penalise me for its contents, which was good of her. She confiscated the crisps.

At Christmas David and I fled gratefully to my aunt Eileen's house, where she cared for both of us, put up with the over-full household, cooked, washed and listened to our stumbling attempts to explain how we felt. She tolerated my bad behaviour. She knew we were both unhappy. She had had far worse to contend with – by the time she was sixteen her parents and brother were dead and she was wholly dependent on her aunts and uncles, adopted by two of them, my grandparents. Heroically, she did not remind us.

The distance between us and our parents seemed colossal, as if they were on the moon. I had spent my whole life with them, apart from Marlborough. It was a shock to be with people who weren't much interested in Greek poetry or Keats or Schubert. And I missed them.

One of my strongest school memories is of waiting after breakfast for the housemistress to give out the post – how every morning I was worn out with hope, how, when I got a letter, the others would congratulate me, relieved that at last one had arrived. Most girls got one every week, regularly, Monday or Tuesday. My mother, inexperienced in this particular field, simply had no idea that was how she should behave. She wrote as she habitually did to people, when it occurred to her, perhaps every three weeks or so. My father wrote none at all, and I found out later that this year was a time of turmoil for him. Drink was plentiful and they had money. He was surrounded by people who admired him, many of them young women. This was the moment when an evocative phrase entered our family's language – someone else's description. A flappy-eyed girl student. As in, 'The bastard's gone off with . . .'

At Hollins, and then on American campuses generally, he became a bit of a star, something he enjoyed but nervously. Puritan Marlborough was there, at his shoulder, ready to show him that pride cometh before a fall, a favourite saying of my grandmother's. Designed to breed anxiety, and perhaps even to take revenge, it did a good job on him.

He and my mother – snobbish Europeans, at least in that context – actually expected to find most Americans a bit dim. What was worse, if possible, was my father's unselfconscious belief that a pretty and pleasant woman could not be intelligent. This was in spite of my mother's striking combination of good looks and cleverness. It's a good example of his unwillingness to change his ideas merely to encompass facts. But it worked both ways. Saying a girl was not bright often meant she was attractive. Sometimes he would say to me affectionately, almost admiringly, 'Darling, you *are* a nit.' It felt warm, and to my shame I never challenged it.

But Hollins was going to overturn many assumptions. The following September my mother would be fifty. My father was *at least* normally susceptible – unconsciously so, which is far more galling for a wife than the response of a practised old flirt. The more famous he got (which of course coincided with her getting older) the more he attracted women. This wasn't coincidence. To him, the resultant flirtings were detached, single events. He never saw them coming. Because he didn't recognise such behaviour as a come-on, he was puzzled by my mother's snappish reaction, a measure, I think, of how little he understood her. Curious, I think, since he had noticed that she was jealous of me.

It's a delicate job, describing a marriage. I'm relying on what I heard and what I can guess by inference from later and less light-hearted times. I might be very wrong. But I don't think so. He was never agile in social situations, and I suspect my mother did not have the confidence to stand in his way at Hollins, to become a tough and efficient gatekeeper, especially when confronted with a tall, glamorous twenty-year-old with nice clothes, lovely hair, beautiful manners and *intelligence*. There were fireworks, I think.

Many social situations panicked him, and the threat of her absence, or distance, was powerful. But he was naturally unwilling to rebuff the many pleasant young women, his pupils. Also, I think for the first time in his life he found teaching easy and enjoyable. So the answer was for *him* to change, rather than his ideas. He began to build himself a kind of elaborate hide. He started turning into a guarded and mysterious figure, a tormented and sensitive artist, and that gradually became the person who had written the novels.

One of my father's colleagues at Hollins, a slow-speaking artist from the Deep South called Lewis Thompson, painted a portrait of him, a half-length in oils. In many ways it is still the best portrait of him as novelist. It makes him look older than he was at the time, thoughtful, preoccupied, forbidding. It foretells the future.

But, of course, this is only part of the story. When occupied, he was an upbeat person, tormented, yes, but quite jolly with it; anxious, even obsessive, but surprisingly cheerful. He had speedy access to despair, and could plummet with alarming speed. Or the reverse. Once in his seventies, and by then distinguished, he became very depressed. It turned out that a youngish doctor had agreed with his suggestion (warding off the worst, he hoped) that he probably had emphysema. I told him that the doctor would probably have agreed if he'd suggested he was pregnant. He laughed, said he'd rather have emphysema, and bounced right up again.

If he happened to be amused – thinking about the Infinity Award Second Class, or the advert he had seen as a child, 'They Laughed When I Sat Down to the Piano', and many other repeated and not very good jokes – his mood would shoot upwards in no time, way past mere equanimity, sometimes as far as outright joy. This, I am sure, came straight from his childhood, from that socialist, teetotal sternness and austerity, which was combined, slashed across – like an Elizabethan doublet – with streaks of warmth and colour. At Marlborough those streaks were tantalisingly rare.

On their arrival at Hollins, they were welcomed enthusiastically, as is traditional. But soon they were appreciated for themselves. The president of the college was Jay Logan, a pleasant

historian, and he and his wife Ann, a New England heiress, became lifelong friends. There were many other friendships, some
rich, some fraught.

As ever, their stories were colourful, but they were guarded,
as they had not been earlier – we had been allowed to overhear
extraordinary things. Now, there was hesitation. He would be
conscious of my mother's reaction. You could sometimes hear in
his voice that he was wary, like someone inching along a dodgy
plank. Life at Hollins was fraught as well as fun, and so were
their travellers' tales.

We heard there were households in Virginia where you could
not mention Franklin D. Roosevelt's name at dinner parties.
There were parties they could go to because they were foreign,
while most of their Virginian friends were insufficiently blue-
blooded. There were horrible stories of lynchings, bullying, vic-
timisation. My father, a lifelong hater, and connoisseur, of the
British malady of class, began to see that other places had related
diseases. My mother told me that on a visit to New England she
could not work out what was wrong. Then she realised. There
was a white man sweeping the street.

Some experiences were absorbed ruthlessly into his novel. My
father repeated to me a conversation he had with the wife of
one of his Hollins colleagues. It went straight into *The Spire*,
apparently without scruple, as Rachel's speech to the outraged
Jocelin:

> Rachel, face shaken like a windowpane in a gale, was explain-
> ing to him why she had no child though she had prayed for
> one. When she and Roger went together, at the most inap-
> propriate moment she began to laugh – *had* to laugh – it wasn't
> that she was barren as some people might think . . .

What would she have felt, reading it?

Other moments were lighter. My father, slightly drunk at a
party, and wearing sandals because of the heat, was surprised to
find one of the faculty wives carefully varnishing his toenails. She

was attracted, she explained – probably rather flappy-eyed – by their gorgeous size and flatness.

At Christmas, they took a train up to Connecticut to stay with the Logans, who had inherited Ann's father's house near New Haven. On the train, I was told, they drank Ohio State champagne, and it or something gave my father his worst hangover to date. Suffering dreadfully, having sinned both against God and good taste, they found themselves listening to an English radio voice, reading the football results from a genuine English Saturday. The familiarity – Arbroath, Sunderland, Crystal Palace, Plymouth Argyle – made them weep for home, they said, even by implication the boring bits. I can't help wondering if that category included us, and over the holiday we talked on the telephone, the first time since September we had heard each other's voices.

Things improved after Christmas, for me at any rate. I crawled out of the dark as the year did. I cautiously enjoyed myself. People told me extraordinary things – what it was like to be kissed by a boy, whether the girls at school were virgins, who on the staff knew about sex.

Also, people seemed to like and trust me. I learnt to tell stories that made them laugh. I accepted that I was bizarre but not hopelessly so. For the first time in my life I was in a choir. I saw a professional ballet company.

But I still couldn't bear to stay as a boarder. My parents were coming back during May, before half-term. I started negotiations. I wanted to be allowed to stay after the Easter holidays in the house of a friend of mine who was a day girl. Untruthfully, I said it would help my work. I went along to see the headmistress, a kindly, modest but astute mathematician called Gladys Engledow. 'I hope,' she said, 'that you are not unhappy as a boarder?' This was, of course, a joke, and a question with only one answer. 'Oh no,' I said, lying again.

Then suddenly there was a flurry of letters. It appeared that my brother and I would go to the States for the Easter holidays. We were, after all, to be part of the voyage. Eileen announced she would fleece David for his Party card. During the spring half-term she bought me new clothes. My English mistress said she would expect an account of the trip for the *Godolphin Gazette*.

We changed planes twice; the third one was tiny, landing us bumpily at the grass-bordered runway just outside Roanoke. There were my parents, jolly and somehow glossed by it all. We and they were shy. Also they were uncharacteristically happy about money, even my father. They were affected by the optimism around them, the presence of possibilities. During their stay they bought hundreds of paperbacks, literally hundreds – shipping them home cost a vast amount. Many of these I subsequently knew well in those editions – Henry James's short stories, Darwin's *Origin of Species*, Trollope. They had an un-English digestible quality in Signet Classics, as if all this literature was easier than you thought. Some of the Marlborough belief, that you could not have it all or even most of it, had taken a knock. In America, you clearly could, at least for a while. But buying the books was a little like their freedom from their children. It had seemed easy and cheap – but the eventual cost was unexpected.

At the airport, my mother appeared in a snappy brown suit with a fur collar. Her hair was different; her nails perfect, almond-shaped and the colour of strawberry ice cream. She had new high heels. Her darkened eyebrows had an air of delighted surprise, which made her eyes bigger. Her eyelashes had grown and were darker too. She looked both younger and older.

I had been invited to a big dance later that spring, and my mother decreed that I should have a new dress, to be bought under guidance from Eileen. This was so important that she telephoned Eileen about it, an unheard-of extravagance. When Eileen and I bought the dress, it had all the characteristics of my mother's taste, being dramatic, simple and expensive. It was a knockout.

My parents had bought a Chevrolet, dark green and comfortable, several years old. It was like something in an Edward Hopper painting, not that I knew so at the time. An automatic, it started every time without fail and had a forgiving shabbiness. My father learnt actually to love a car. We liked it too. Others thought us eccentric, which was probably intended.

Early the next morning we left Hollins. My father enjoyed lecturing. He had always loved making people laugh, and at that time looked forward to doing so without any nerves whatever. I don't believe he thought of it as teaching. It was performing – a throwback to his love of theatre. So we were going to drive round the States, together, to California, Seattle, Chicago . . . a Great American Road Trip, reminiscent of our sailing voyages, though without the squalor and, mostly, the danger. When I met Terrell, my future husband, an American student at Oxford, we discovered I had seen far more of the States than he had.

We went through Tennessee, stopping at a place called Athens – as my mother said, 'the Athens of Tennessee'. Here we stayed in the first of many cheap motels. I noticed then – I still find it true – how one becomes nostalgic for last night's ephemerally rented home, for the cosy familiarity of something which had been just as unfamiliar at six o'clock the previous evening. I shared a room with my mother, and David with my father. My parents did ask me once if I would mind sharing a room with David. I said I would rather not, which impresses me now, both with my strength of mind and the fact that my parents asked me in such a way that I could refuse.

Day after day we drove hundreds of miles. Day after day we passed the same telegraph pole, the same stretch of stony wasteland to right and left. Occasionally, tumbleweed really would bowl across the road.

Serious tourists, we naturally went to the Grand Canyon, but we could hardly look at it – my father hissed with terror if one of us went within ten yards of the edge. There was a Navaho jewellery store, where my mother bought a beautiful silver-and-turquoise bracelet and matching earrings. Then we drove south for a while, still past our very own telegraph pole, and eventually, late in the evening, we came to a deserted hut with a sign. Meteor Crater This Way.

The place was eerie but inviting. It made the landscape seem ours in some way, though I think we all understood the feeling was temporary. Do I exaggerate? It's hard to be sure. It was such a smooth, huge shape, saucer-like, with the rock sides puckered like scarred skin. There was a stiff breeze, and the delicate light was going. The evening birds wheeled overhead. My father, intrepid when curious, started off down the wooden steps into the depths, his fear of heights temporarily placed on one side, as the builder, Roger Mason, does in *The Spire*. We followed.

Then, a clear, disembodied voice broke into our silent twilight. It was so close it might have been inside our heads. We were startled, all of us, and the steps shook dangerously beneath us. We were informed that we were small in the face of the cosmos – a reasonable idea but greatly diluted by the voice's ineffable complacency. You often hear that measured, secure authority now in voice-overs, but nothing for me since has matched its stupefying incongruity. We never worked out where the loudspeaker was. My father looked very carefully. I think to him it sounded like the everyday, homely – and American – voice of God.

It was on a timed loop and, alas, there were diminishing returns. By the time we got to the bottom of the crater the light, together with the mystery, was sinking fast like water in a sieve. I now feel the best bit was the fright – the utter wilderness quiet and the sense of millions of years. And the voice. It comes back, I believe, in my father's novels – in *The Paper Men*, added to his own dream of the Spanish Steps, even in *The Double Tongue*.

Did we drive through Las Vegas? Hard to know. It could just as easily have been a theme park of itself. I know we drove through Death Valley, because my mother told us stories of explorers dying of thirst, horridly misled by the sight of rock formations that looked like cornstooks in the white and shimmering heat. Police cars appeared at intervals, checking. They searched as if for pioneers.

At last, we arrived in San Francisco. We gazed at the Pacific, where an enormous bank of fog on the horizon looked solid, a ghostly continent reflecting the one we had crossed. We wandered through Chinatown, where my mother bought a dress-length of raw silk. It was turquoise which matched her new Navaho jewellery which matched her eyes. The shop made it up for her in half a day and she looked stunning. But more and more she found herself in an unfamiliar position. Young men may be hoodwinked or flattered, but young women know the score. They certainly did at Hollins. They know it is their turn now. Or most of them do. I had no idea it was mine.

13

Breaking Down

In San Francisco we conducted some business. My father's accountant at that time was a Plymouth Brother of great if obtrusive rectitude. After an avowedly religious critic had said that *Lord of the Flies* might have an undesirable influence on its readers' morals, our accountant debated within himself as to whether he could continue in conscience to advise its author. Eventually, he concluded that he could, but the tempest of his moral struggle unnerved my father greatly, and reinforced in his mind the association of money and retribution placed there long ago by my grandparents. This was at the same time as he laughed at the chap's fees, probably the only time in his life that a bill cheered him up.

With some spiritual agility, the accountant had suggested that my father form a limited company to avoid paying tax. So we held the first ever meeting of the board of directors of William Golding Limited in a restaurant in Chinatown, San Francisco, in April 1962. My brother and I celebrated by blocking the election of the chairman, until my father remembered, or invented, that the company secretary presiding pro tem (my mother) had a casting vote. Later, my tax-avoiding correspondence would arrive at school, addressed to Mr J. D. Golding, Godolphin School, Salisbury, given by my father as my place of work. My teachers, whose sense of humour I had never previously suspected, mischievously placed the small brown envelope all alone on the shiny table outside Miss Engledow's office, and I would collect it furtively when I hoped no one was looking.

After San Francisco we turned north, driving past the silver Pacific, past redwoods and mountains. We arrived in Seattle, where my father was booked to give a lecture. Seattle had the World's Fair on its doorstep, and the enormous site was being finished off. We went up the Space Needle (you can see it in the Warren Beatty film *The Parallax View*). This was in spite of my father's fear, and the fact that it wasn't really open yet. The stomach-melting view from the top, the terrible suspicion of slight but perceptible movement, went straight into *The Spire*.

We were guided round by a nice man from the university, and he brought his daughter along. She was poised and sophisticated and wore red lipstick. I was mortified to discover she was only thirteen, three years younger than me. Looking at her nice short curls, I took a huge step. I said I wanted my hair cut.

About ten years earlier, six years old and demanding a fringe, and having my request refused, I had taken a pair of scissors and cut the front of my long hair into a wobbly line across my forehead. My parents were furious, and told me reproachfully that I would have to go to the hairdresser's, a punishment that I of course enjoyed. But it was the last such visit for ten years. My fringe was carefully grown out, and the lengthening bits pinned back with tortoiseshell hairslides until they could be incorporated in the rest, slicked straight back from my forehead, which gave me an unpleasant, quasi-spiritual look, rather like a boiled egg with eyes.

My parents liked my long, thick plait. My mother remarked complacently that it was reminiscent of a Renaissance portrait. It also made me look about twelve. Both she and my father tried to persuade me that it was much more *interesting* to look as I did, much more distinguished. Nonsense, I thought, and we went to the hairdresser, who cut most of it into a nice bob. Suddenly, a normal face, even a mildly attractive one, looked back at me from the mirror. I returned triumphant to the hotel, where my chagrined and outmanoeuvred father said, well, he supposed it was all right – if, he added, and not at all as an afterthought, *if* you want her to look as if she hasn't any *brain*. Yes, I thought. That's exactly what I want. It was completely clear, after all, that my innocent father tended to equate absence of brain with sex appeal. And, if he did, presumably the rest of the world would too. A couple of nights later there was an extraordinary event, which I can still hardly believe. At supper in somebody's house I sat next to a nice, good-mannered American boy of about nineteen. I found myself talking happily, amused and apparently amusing. Possibly we were leaving my mother out of the conversation. She was on his other side, and certainly I've always found it difficult to switch from one side to another at a formal dinner. She probably felt neglected. She heard me say something to this boy about boarding school, about my dislike of it and how much I'd missed my parents. She broke in, with an embarrassing roguishness veiling a huge rage we could all see. Oh, she exclaimed, turning her shoulder, couldn't he see the *daggers* in her back, where I had stabbed her?

I was aghast, full of apologies and protestations that I hadn't meant anything bad by what I had said. I might have added that it had just been *my* feelings, nothing to do with her whatsoever. But that would have been disingenuous. Once I thought about it, I realised that my remark implied that my parents didn't care about my feelings. Of course, what I'd said was treason. But that treason was compounded by my revolutionary appearance.

After my apologies had begun to embarrass her, my mother told me across him that it didn't matter. Then, more repressively, that I should *stop talking about it*. We never did talk about it. It would not have occurred in the first place, if we had been people who could talk about such a thing.

The next day we went on a boat trip and my mother said she would stay in the hotel. I was aware of the weight of this decision. She conveyed unambiguously that something had brutally removed from her the capacity to go out and enjoy herself. Luckily, I was not very good (I'm still not) at joining things up, and didn't realise that she meant me. She said goodbye to us, and walked slowly and wistfully back into the hotel. Suddenly my father ran back after her, and a few minutes later they both returned, my mother smiling, especially, embarrassingly, at me. Over the next few minutes I realised to my indignation that I was being forgiven.

But gradually we became a family again. Even in those days, when foreigners visited American universities, the practised machinery made sure you arrived with a bundle of information attached to you. Part of our bundle was the sea. Hence the boat trip, a thoughtful attempt to put us at our ease. But people never understood how ramshackle our sea was. They apologised for the small size of the motor launch that took us round Seattle's harbour, unaware that we were impressed simply that its thudding diesel didn't break down. They asked if we raced at Cowes. Did we have a skipper? Crew? Did we sail in the Med? My parents answered as neutrally as they could, and David and I tried to keep a straight face. It pointed up the difference, the way we expected to rough it, the way our life in Europe was still makeshift. It made my father homesick.

I know now that he was also thinking about *The Spire*. He may have feared – he often did – that a book would get away from him if he didn't write it soon. There may also have been people he wanted to see again at Hollins, people who would disappear at the end of the semester. My mother was very calm.

We drove past thousands more telegraph poles on the road to Chicago. My mother decided I should have my hair permed. Afterwards, it shot into nasty little corkscrews, tight as nuts, and I'm happy to report that I threw the most incredible tantrum, my very first, and about four years overdue. I stayed in the bathroom for hours, sniffling, with a book and a huge sense of grievance. The evil perm, I learnt, would take six weeks to grow out. I had had a week of looking tolerable, only to be cruelly returned to my previous ugly state by my mother's insistence on the stupid perm. My shaken parents decided we must go to the cinema.

They bought the paper. There was a double bill, *Breakfast at Tiffany's* and *The Guns of Navarone*. My brother had seen *Breakfast at Tiffany's* at Oxford. It had made him cry, he said. This was recommendation indeed. We ordered a taxi and gave the driver the address. He looked at us. Were we sure we wanted to go there? It made no difference, not even his suggestion we'd find it hard to get a cab back. Off we went.

It was an unforgettable drive. At first, the roads were unremarkable, the streets full of moving cars and figures. Then things changed. We drove through empty streets of tall grey houses with steps up to the front door. The steps had motionless figures on them and every figure was black. Their stillness was intimidating and reproachful. The taxi stopped outside a picture house and we went in, got our tickets and sat down. Everyone but us was black.

We all cried, not just my brother. In the interval, my mother and I went to the ladies' loo. Everyone was charming to us, asked us politely where we came from, and told us we must be extremely careful going home. The management, we were told, would call for a cab. We *absolutely must not* walk anywhere, even to the train. We did as they said. When we described our adventure at the hotel, the receptionist turned pale and clutched the desk. We were told we were lucky. I have no idea if that was true or not. Actually, our travellers' tale is a variation of a certain genre. The usual location for it is Harlem, and the Brits, innocents abroad, come out of the subway at the wrong station, at which point they are escorted to safety by the scandalised locals. Our interval visit to the ladies was one of the hundreds of occasions in America when perfect strangers turned hospitably to my mother, smiled and said, 'I jus love the way you all talk.'

David and I flew home to Blighty, our memories stuffed with gorgeous pictures, of unequalled landscape that stretched from sea to shining sea. I forgot my ghastly perm in the excitement of my new dance dress, and felt ashamed of my tears in the Chicago bathroom. I had no idea how normal they were.

In England, without the fear of boarding school, I found the mundanities of life delightful. I enjoyed staying with my friend – it was like having a twin sister. I bluffed my way through the term's responsibilities, my school pinny decorated for the first and last time with a prefect's badge. For the first time in my life I did my homework on the sofa, watching the television, and simultaneously watching my work get worse and worse.

At last, I admitted to myself that Greek was impossible. I mugged things up, minutes before my lessons. I cheated, misleading my teachers, lying about the time I spent struggling with Thucydides, Euripides, the arcane elaborations of the optative mood, the principal parts of the opaque, impossible verb 'to stand', and its sister irregular verbs. I believed at the time that vindictive fate gave these contorted forms to the most useful verbs (those for 'to go' and 'to be' are similarly gnarled and worn down, as of course they are in most languages). Now I see it as part of the miraculous geology of a language, something to spend your life excavating, like music, perhaps, or astronomy. But then I just thought it meant I would never, ever, achieve what I must achieve. 'It is too much for a woman's brain,' says Mr Prettiman, the dangerous radical and proto-feminist passenger in my father's Sea Trilogy. Mr Prettiman believes that his affianced wife, Miss Granham, must meet every sort of challenge for her future life as his assistant. But he accepts that she cannot learn Greek.

When my parents came back, the holes in my expensive education were visible. Odd things happened. My Greek teachers began to show open anxiety. One of them went so far as to say that there was 'still time'. My history mistress read out one of my essays to the A-level class in the year above. Surprisingly, no one seemed to hate me for this. She then wrote to my parents, suggesting I might get a scholarship to Oxford if I applied to do history. My English mistress, though annoyed at my refusal to produce the expected American travelogue, took an essay I wrote on Keats and read it to my year's English A-level class, which I wasn't even in. I told my father this as we drove home that day, and he was so thrilled he went straight through a red light. Now I see that these were messages from my teachers. Change, they were saying, before it's too late. But I didn't have the words. My school report triumphantly said how much being a boarder had improved me. I had been a capable and efficient form prefect. I was not so shy. But about some things I was tongue-tied.

That summer we did go away to North Wales, as we had planned the year before – ages before, it seemed. It was a holiday with great constraint. Alone with my parents, in the wet, green landscape, I felt we were all bored. When we returned, the new term came closer and closer like the brink of an enormous waterfall. I began to have attacks of claustrophobia in lessons. My guts ambushed me, protesting on their own with long, embarrassing growls. When I couldn't stand it any more I would put my hand up. *Please may I be excused?* This was rather a poor show for a sixth-former, but mostly my teachers agreed absently, and continued talking while I shot out of the door, bitter with failure but helpless. I would waste as long as I dared in our old cloakrooms, wandering round the pegs and shoe boxes, or locking myself in one of the ancient brass-trimmed lavatories.

Then one day I asked to go out during divinity, a 'continuation' subject (the others were English and French – no maths or science, unnecessary for young gentlewomen). For some reason a number of our maths teachers also taught divinity, and Miss Engledow herself was teaching us, since we were now in the upper sixth. Miss Engledow, a good if unexciting head teacher, had her finger on the pulse. She had heard about my frequent exits. No, she said. The normal hum lurched to a complete hush.

'Read this passage aloud to us instead,' she said.

I was furious, and read as if I was declaiming from the rooftops. Afterwards, you could have heard the dust fall.

In break, she sent for me. She was a nice woman. 'I didn't want you to have a failure,' she explained. If I had been brave enough I would have replied, 'Sometimes there just *is* a failure.' But I couldn't. I bided my time, touched by the sympathy of friends who were outraged at her treatment of me. But I knew she was right.

Once home that evening, I considered things. It was clearly impossible to go back. Something must be done, something violently necessary. I drank half a bottle of Milk of Magnesia, which gave me diarrhoea. Later I put a finger down my throat and threw up. I announced I was ill. Over the next two weeks I skilfully contrived a succession of illnesses. At the end of the fortnight there was a polite showdown with my parents. I produced an idea which was fresh to all of us. I don't want to go to school any more, so I shan't. There was a thoughtful pause.

They sent me to the doctor. I cycled down to his surgery in Broad Chalke. I explained I felt trapped in the classroom. 'But you're not really the outdoor type, are you?' he said mildly, perceptively. 'Why do you find it so difficult?' I couldn't answer, couldn't mention the vocal stomach, the desperate fear. After due thought, medical science concluded I was having a nervous breakdown. I took small green pills which, oddly, made me cry. The label said Valium. I became an ordinary teenager, monosyllabic, truculent, staying in my room.

Soon I was seeing a psychiatrist and my parents bowed their heads in shame. I was enrolled in correspondence courses for Latin, Greek, and history, and I diligently failed at all of them, even history and Latin, which were easy. My parents assured me that it was all temporary, and I would go back after Christmas, when I was better. I would progress smoothly towards the summer exams. Sometime in the autumn my father and I had the terrible conversation about my wanting to die, with his level, bitter reproach – 'I know you're *sick* . . .' There was the hate and contempt.

My maternal grandmother made little forays at her beleaguered daughter.

'What use,' she asked, 'will Greek be to Judy when she gets married?'

That settled it. Greek became a feminist goal and my mother lined up with my father.

But I didn't go back to school. I just blandly stayed put. I wasn't good at conflict but then neither were my parents, so for once we were well matched. I read *Little Women*, Arthur Ransome, and other books that made me feel safe. I felt horribly guilty, but I preferred the guilt to going back to school.

In January 1963 my father went away to the US for six weeks, on his own because my mother stayed with me. I missed him terribly, crying hysterically when he left. I still thought of him as that large, comfortable shape from my childhood. In reality it had not just gone to America – it had vanished altogether. Of course, none of this was said, even to the psychiatrist, a kind, puzzled man who did his best. Sometimes he implied to my parents that they had not been perfect. Who is? Nevertheless, my mother afterwards referred to him as 'that stupid man'.

Meanwhile, Britain disappeared under the harshest winter since 1947. The ground stayed cold and hard. Even the edges of the flowing Ebble froze, and the sparkling cress-beds towards Marleycombe iced over completely. Starved birds fell dead out of the air. Roads shrank to a single lane, their sides creeping inwards under banks of dirty snow.

My father came back, hoping for a change in me. The only change was that I had given up working. We cancelled the correspondence courses and I sent back the books. By now I was taking fourteen pills a day, six blue tranquillisers, six red antidepressants, and two white tranquillisers as well, in case the antidepressants made me too lively.

Then, another change. There was neutral but recurrent mention of my becoming an in-patient, since I was 'not making progress'. I was not going to school, not doing Greek, not even working in Woolworth's. I suspect what would have followed my going into hospital – as it did for my brother – would have been ECT. Electro-convulsive therapy. But I escaped it, quite unaware of this grim possibility. Thank God, with wonderful irony, for boarding school – I had had enough of institutions, where people had real power over you. Never again. I began to realise I must . . . what?

My mother had my room redecorated. My father tried to discuss the future – I could see him carefully censoring his habitual gloom while he did it. Not surprisingly, the conversation lacked vigour. But there must have been signs of recovery. Then my brother decided he had had a nervous breakdown too, and consulted the doctor, who was most unsympathetic. Actually, I think the doctor was mistaken. But he took his cue from my father, who was angry with both of us, and wanted the whole matter resolved as quickly as possible. He was desperate to be preoccupied with his new novel, knowing his imagination needed to be sunk in it. He didn't wish to come out of it but we were forcing him to.

Then there emerged the prospect of another, very short voyage. A voyage for two. The film rights for *Lord of the Flies* had been sold fairly early on, outright, for a thousand pounds. My father regretted this, as well he might, though my mother pointed out that he was glad enough of their share of the money at the time. But, for some years, the project had languished. The censors would give the film an X certificate, and in the late 1950s that meant the whole project was hopeless, since no one under eighteen could be admitted.

However, films were changing with the decade. Horror films became more profitable. *Film noir* now attracted American money, and subsequently American films tackled situations that would earlier have been considered taboo. There was, for example, an American film about a love affair between two young patients in a mental hospital – *David and Lisa*, starring an unknown young actor called Keir Dullea.

Eventually the project went ahead and, by a huge piece of luck, came to involve Peter Brook, whose version of *Lord of the Flies* astonished and gratified my father. Its fidelity to the novel was awe-inspiring. The young actors were convincing, the music sharply moving, the photography startling, with the black and white brilliantly showing the heat and blood. We saw the finished film in a dusty little auditorium in Wardour Street during

March 1963. And then came the news that it would be entered for the Cannes Film Festival.

My father was invited to go, and decided he would. This was uncharacteristic. He didn't usually do publicity. But he was still full of amazement at how good the film was. Naturally, it was expected that my mother would accompany him.

Generously, perhaps desperately, she decided I should go instead. She put aside our rivalry and made a leap of imagination about what might help me. And it did help a great deal, though in a way no one could have predicted.

We had just sent back the correspondence courses. I was still heavily drugged, calm almost to immobility. My mother bought me some lovely new clothes, I bought a mud-coloured lipstick, and off we flew to Nice. My father hired a very small Fiat, and he crashed the gears all the way into Cannes. I noticed him drinking with abrupt determination. I saw him change. He became angry. He missed my mother, and resented my presence in her place.

We had a nice couple of rooms, a suite, in a posh lemon-coloured hotel on the sea front. Sometimes I went across the road to the sullen gravelly beach in my dull black swimsuit. There were lots and lots of people. I could hardly believe how many it took to make a film. Even two of the boy actors, Ralph and Piggy, were there. They seemed sober and confident, matter-of-fact about this extraordinary world.

But my father and I were much less capable. We didn't have a minder. In the absence of my mother we were helpless. Strangers, who all wanted something from him, were always approaching him. It produced a perpetual smoulder. Almost anything set him off. One evening there was a party on board a yacht that belonged to Sam Spiegel. Spiegel himself was absent, a sort of Gatsby figure, and the deck was crowded with fabulous-looking girls. One had mud-coloured lipstick like mine, but she had gone further. Her whole face was made up in the same colour. She looked as if she was moulded out of some ultra-modern pale pink metal. My dad said that *she* had the courage of her convictions.

The nicest person around was Lewis Allen, one of the film's producers. He had a thin, lively face, and masses of kind-hearted charm, which showed in his capacity to seem charmed by me. Despite liking him, I found talking to him difficult. Replies to his kind questions and observations stayed in my head. It was like having to leap off a high-diving board. Over and over again my courage failed me right at the very edge. After my silence at dinners, parties, receptions, my father and I would return to the hotel, his despair rising like a fog, his thinning patience timed to give way completely when we were alone. One night I could see at the dinner table that he was drinking ridiculous amounts. Eventually he began to do it in a manner I saw later. He drank as if he hated the stuff. By the end of the meal he was – as he would often put it himself – beastly drunk.

I remember someone, perhaps Lewis Allen, asking me if I could manage. Naturally I said I could. Any Godolphin girl would have done the same. There my father was, flat on his back in his bedroom, holding up wodges of brightly coloured French banknotes. At first I could not see what he meant to do with them. Then I had a sudden intuition. But I lacked strategy.

'Oh, Daddy, don't tear it up, *please!*'

So of course he did, masses of it. I got some away from him, took off his jacket, braces and trousers, and pulled the quilt over him. I went into my own room and listened. I even wondered if I should get a doctor. Might he die? I left the doors open and soon I could hear him snoring. Eventually I slept too. Next morning he kept his sunglasses on the whole time, and drank coffee with desperation.

We flew home that day. I don't know how much he told my mother or how much she guessed. But her plan, formulated or not, had worked – finally, the huge figure from my childhood had begun to shrink. We were sent some photos from the yacht party. I look quite normal, and so does my father, except for his wasp-eyed sunglasses.

The Palme d'Or was won by *Il gattopardo* (The Leopard) – an adaptation of Giuseppe di Lampedusa's novel. The win was well deserved, I gather, though the only film I remember seeing at Cannes was *David and Lisa*, which of course had great resonance for me and for my father as well. I have often wondered since whether he had a sense of foreboding about it – a sense that our family wasn't finished yet with mental hospitals. In any event, *Lord of the Flies* was on the move.

14

Breaking Away

My parents had looked forward to their years without children – freedom to travel, no school fees, a quiet and empty house, and lots of peaceful conversations, one to one, over cups of instant coffee. The years after 1963 must have proved something of a disappointment.

David and I did go away to university – in my case for more than seven years. I was away much of the time, but until I married in 1971 I had a tendency to come winging swiftly back for the occasional weekend and most of the holidays, immersing myself once more in TV, playing my father's piano, and reading the family collection of Georgette Heyers. Despite our much-insisted-on poverty, I already had many expensive tastes. So I drank up their good white Burgundy and enjoyed my mother's cooking. Polite and hostly, they made me very welcome. They were also generous with money and presents. Home was hard to leave. For David the break was even more difficult.

So, in the 1960s, we both knew we should leave, knew we needed to – and couldn't. I had understood the need very well, from my eighteenth year onwards, from the months after that trip to Cannes, when I crept nervously towards recovery, watched anxiously and without comment by my hapless parents, who longed for the good old days when they merely had to worry about school fees.

In 1963 David graduated from Oxford with a very respectable history degree. He hated the place but had made friends. Most of them were communists, and his activities at home in Wiltshire were also heavily involved with the local Party branch: folk-singing, selling newspapers and organising protests. He had a world to settle in.

I found some of the language of that world engaging – 'Are you going to Tolpuddle this year?' – but my father did not. David borrowed my parents' car when he deemed it necessary, and his friends also had cars or motorbikes, or access to them from their mostly middle-class parents. They often drove out to Bower-chalke, to our house, which they found comfortable. My mother, hospitable as well as charming, was still very left-wing. Often the sitting room was full of young men keen to smash the system, and it feels rather cheap to cavil at them now. I suppose I am joining in my father's scorn.

He certainly fizzed intermittently about it. He resented being roped in to the cause, much as he resented my leaning out of my attic bedroom to address the Wilton Hunt, as its hounds and horses walked decorously down the river at the bottom of our garden.

'Ban blood sports,' I yelled. One of the riders put his hand to his hat in a courtly salute.

'Ban blood sports in your own bloody garden,' said my furious father.

Later he apologised for swearing at me, and I said not at all, it made a really good phrase. So the two of us laughed and made up. But things were not so easy for David. Unlike me, he was serious about wanting action, though it must be admitted that all our family tended to regard changes in language as tantamount to actual change, and this included him. From the sixties on, he called our parents Mum and Dad. He said Mummy and Daddy sounded middle-class, and I suppose he was right. But it grat-ed, with my father particularly. He thought of himself as Bill or Daddy – those were his two personal labels. 'Dad' was what he had called Alec. Steadily, he and David accumulated more and more things to disagree about, trivial things that mapped on to matters of harsher conflict.

Since the return from America in the summer of 1962, my father had worked and worked on his new novel. When later I tried to write, he gave me several pieces of excellent advice. Apart from the caustic remark that novelists were people who finished novels, rather than those who started them, his most helpful comment was his admission that some days he wrote easily; some days it was a struggle. So, he said, he often felt he should reject the easy, thinking it facile; or the writing that came with a struggle, thinking it grubby, halting and forced. But, he said, when he looked back he found the quality of the two roughly equal.

I would love to know what passages of *The Spire* came easily. I suspect not many. There was a great deal of rewriting. He started with a group of three stories, one of which was set in modern times. But gradually he narrowed the book down. He wrote and wrote, polished and cut, made many changes. I was rather scandalised to find that Jocelin's deathbed inspiration, '*It's like the apple tree!*' had originally been '*It's like the cherry tree!*'

Finally, he was modestly confident about its quality. Some decades later, he told me he thought it one of his three best. Before publication, while he was correcting the proofs, he suddenly said to me, 'You've had a hard time lately. And I've had a hard time writing this book. So I'm going to dedicate it to you.'

I was taken aback. Most things went by seniority in our family. My grandparents were the dedicatees of *Lord of the Flies*, and my mother of *The Inheritors*. The two subsequent novels had no dedication. One would have expected David to be the next recipient, and indeed my father dedicated *The Pyramid*, the novel he wrote after *The Spire*, to 'My son David'. But I had jumped the queue. I doubted somehow that this was a good thing.

It was published in April 1964. At the time I was studying English and history A-level, at a technical college in Southampton, staying with Eileen during the week just as my brother had done a few years earlier. But I was home for the weekend after publication. In those days there was a Sunday morning radio programme called *The Critics*, in which pundits discussed a book, a play, a film, a concert. That week *The Spire* was the book, and one of the critics described it as 'wuthering depths'. My father barked out a kind of gasping laugh, and turned greyish white.

The radio words hung in the air, indelibly. For a moment he covered his face with his enormous, blunt-fingered hands. Then he walked quickly out of the room, but carefully, as if he was carrying something. My mother let loose a stuttering, rage-filled volley of the most extraordinary swear-words.

I heard the other critics admonish their colleague. He mumbled an apology. But the damage was done. We were suddenly in a different world, a pale, awful one, like the atmosphere when someone is gravely ill. I believe my father's confidence never completely recovered. That remark, made by a man whose name I forget, and of course attracting to itself all the other bad notices he had ever got, gave him a sort of intermittent stage fright. Crucially, I believe he became most strongly frightened about his imagination, about allowing himself that freedom in thinking which had produced the remarkable early novels. He no longer roamed among his own ideas in an unselfconscious way. He had to work much harder and for a result which he himself found less convincing.

Most writers find aspects of struggle, I imagine, in what they do – however good they are. For my father, his increasing dread of being, as he would say, 'without a book', meant that he was assailed by a monstrous conviction of his own appalling turpitude, temerity, and squalid pretentiousness, both when he wrote and when he couldn't. Either way, he felt terrible. The self-contempt burnt him, and he had learnt to fear that fire long before. While one might see the radio critic as a kind of wicked fairy, this was not a story with a magic wand.

Actually, I think *The Spire* is as near perfect as any novel can be if it is not by Jane Austen. However, a few weeks after publication, my mother privately informed me that she believed it would have been a better book if I hadn't been *ill*. I remember thinking how neat it was – I couldn't go and complain to my father about her saying this, because then I would have to explain to him that she thought the book was flawed.

'Ill' was their word for my breakdown. About ten years later

I told them I was ill, and they went into complete panic. They only recovered when I told them I was being tested for sickle-cell anaemia. Sickle-cell anaemia is incurable and not a good thing to have, but my parents thought I meant tranquillisers and psychiatrists, and that to them threatened a far worse disaster. (The test was negative – not surprisingly, since it usually affects only people of African-Caribbean descent. The doctor in Oxford was intrigued by the possibility, and ultimately slightly wistful at the result.)

In the summer of 1964, when I had finished A-levels and more or less recovered my equilibrium, we went off to Greece again. To all outward appearances, my parents had with them a pair of completely normal children. My father's friend Peter Green had taken his family to live in Greece, where he supported them by writing reviews and novels, and translating authors such as Sartre and de Beauvoir into English. He had the old-fashioned idea that if you knew Greek and Latin you could just reach out and grasp modern languages as they whizzed by, and in his case, with his extraordinary gifts, that might have been true.

The Greens had settled in a remote and unspoilt village (I suppose we were the ones to start spoiling it) on the north-west coast of the island of Lesvos, until 1912 ruled by the Turks. At the top of the village, just below a ruined castle confusingly ascribed to the Genoese, stood two large fortified houses. They had been built, we were told, for the Turkish rulers, and had enormous wooden doors bound with iron, presumably to keep out the angry natives. The Greens lived in one of these, and we would rent the other.

A few weeks before the holiday, David told us he would like to bring a friend, a girl. Strangely, my father reacted to this with anger. He was generally very keen on either of us making connections with the opposite sex. David's friend was sixteen, not very articulate, and in terrified awe of my father and perhaps my mother as well. It was hard for her, and her parents, to reject the idea of what looked like a marvellous holiday. We should all have known better. However, my father, possibly a little off-balance because of the reception of *The Spire*, spoilt his arguments by speaking contemptuously of David's feelings. My mother and I came to David's defence, and my father's doubts were brushed away.

By 1963 or so, my father finally had to acknowledge the fact that he was not poor. Sales of *Lord of the Flies* had taken off. Of course, he didn't feel at all secure about money – he never did. But he paid off the mortgage on their cottage. He bought my mother some serious jewellery. And also, with fear, guilt and glee, those family friends, he bought his first ever brand-new car – a white three-litre Rover, which Peter Green christened the White Wonder. We would drive it down to Brindisi in Italy, get the ferry across to Patras in Greece, drive up to Athens and then take a ferry to Lesvos.

We had four days to get from Calais to Brindisi, which should have been ample. However, a few miles in from Calais, the Golding luck with machines reasserted itself and the timing chain – an apparently important component – fell off the engine. The White Wonder lay immobile for two whole days, a white disappointment, in the local garage. My father phoned someone at Rover in a theatrical rage – he told me he thought of Donald Wolfit – and a new part was flown out.

When we started again, we needed to make up lost time and my father drove at speed. This was partly fuelled by his anger, since David and he had quarrelled about the best route, and then about the driving. On one occasion, he fell asleep at the wheel, and swerved off a tree-lined avenue in rural France. Luckily, we went into a ditch rather than a tree.

But we made up the time and caught the boat to Patras. In Athens we met up with Peter, whose practised eye soon spotted the aftershocks of a terrible family row. It gave him an obstinate and bouncy, almost rubbery, cheerfulness, which made David angry.

Our ferry was small-scale. Once across the Aegean, and at the port of Mytilini on Lesvos, the Rover was hoisted in a rope hammock out of the hold and on to the quayside. My father would earlier have scorned feeling affection for any car, but the sight of this expensive object swinging precariously over the green water of the harbour drove him – literally – to drink. He had a few ouzos, a substance which I have noticed often brings out a nasty side in people. By the time he had driven us across the island, on dirt tracks with ruts, donkeys and occasional large groups of islanders sitting in the middle of the road so as not to miss the bus, he was in a chaotic and destructive mood. My mother got him off to bed and for a day or two life proceeded without him.

The next five or six weeks were a mixture of fearful rows, idyllic settings, wonderful outings to deserted beaches and long, enthralling evenings in Eleftheria's, the local taverna. There was a swirling crowd of bronzed ex-pats, confident, bohemian and articulate. They were unsettlingly sure of the correctness of their views, informing me, for example, that I should make more of myself, put on eye make-up, wear uncomfortable shoes, go to bed with someone, learn how to have a good time. It was all a bit unsubtle. Such ideas came, directly or indirectly, from my father, who longed hungrily for his children to be normal. I have no idea if any of them talked in similar style to David. I hope not.

Actually, I *was* having a good time. It was a long way from drab old Wiltshire. I loved the arguments in the taverna, and got on brilliantly with Peter, his wife Lal, and the other visitors to the stony, picturesque little village. 'Darling,' said my father, pleased in spite of himself, 'You're a pseud too.'

I even picked up shreds and snippets of modern Greek. Classical Greek at last became something interesting, because Peter would recite it in a sort of machine-gun delivery, talking about it for hours, making it like a film, giving it drama and glamour, a *Shakespeare in Love* version of the language.

However, once I had got used to feeling happy, it struck me that my father was still curiously morose about me. It was as if he expected me to plunge back into inconvenient depression at any moment. It even seemed as though he *wanted* me to. I began to feel indignant. Finally, we had a row, during which I told him defiantly, and probably rather rudely, that I was quite all right, and would be out of his hair by that September, and off to the University of Sussex. He said little, adopting a misleading expression of fair-minded scepticism, a brilliant way of avoiding conversation.

For my mother, life was harder. Under the wonderful island sun, she went browner and browner. Inwardly, she seethed more and more about the deteriorating relationship between her husband and son, and also between David and his friend. She was angry – this was clear. But we all had to get along, at least in public, till the end of the holidays. Conversation within the family, never an easy business, became impossible. We all talked to others. It was like an international summit conference, with mediators.

The Greeks in our village, perhaps recognising a tragedy, or alternatively a soap opera, took our family in its fissile state to their hearts. It was obvious they yearned to help us, their expressions showing completely how they identified with my parents, how they sympathised. I don't think much could have been hidden in that village. Their sympathy lifted the whole interaction above the level of gossip. They tried to take care of us.

When my mother developed a terrible stomach bug, and she needed to see the doctor, the consultation took place with him in public, in the shade of a huge plane tree near our house. Peter (our usual source of Greek) was away in Athens. My mother knew no Greek, the doctor no English. My father's Greek was inadequate, nor could his expertise in any language cope with the pitiless physical detail. So the whole interchange was interpreted for us by a pleasant Greek American, on holiday from Chicago. Soon, his Greek responses to the doctor were echoed by a small group of middle-aged Greek women, some but not all of whom we knew. Dressed in black, they all repeated how many times my mother had been to the lavatory, whether she was passing blood, whether she was vomiting.

The doctor gave her some pinkish powders wrapped up in folded waxed paper (she said they tasted just like strawberry jelly), and instructed her to restrict her diet to rice and tea. For the remaining weeks of our stay, every adult Greek in the village would admonish her, and sometimes us, with 'only rice and tea' in a special sing-song voice, whether we were in a bar, in a restaurant, on the beach. This was quite unselfconscious – they were not becoming a chorus for the tourists. It was the way they behaved.

The Greek American, who clearly fancied my mother despite all the details of her ailments, which I think was a comfort to her, would repeat the injunction in the most unlikely places, in English, charmingly, winningly, with a raised finger. And the first time she was well enough to have a glass of beer, the Greeks around the place burst into spontaneous applause. She bowed graciously, a perfect curtain call, and I knew she was touched.

I made friends with the daughter of another ex-pat. She and her father took me off to Hydra, with its sugar-white houses and scarlet bougainvillea. This was a kind deed, and an immense relief. We danced in the garden of a bar, and walked home in the near-dawn to their friends' house high on the hill. Slowly, away from my parents, I began to see the point and the possibility of a good time. Back on Lesvos a week later, I threw my remaining pills into the sea. I had recovered. But, precisely as I did so, my brother did the opposite. We were like the inhabitants of those little houses that predict the weather. When one of us was out in the sun, the other retreated indoors, miserably.

I spent the next three years at Sussex University. I learnt a great deal and not just academically. I made some good friends. And I did my best to be out of my father's hair, as I had promised. My parents needed me to be all right, and I worked hard, window-dressing my life for their benefit, making much of boy-friends and a farcical job in a coffee shop (I broke two coffee pots my first week, and emerged with pay of one pound seven and sixpence, which for some reason delighted my father). I tried to amuse them with my stories, and to some extent succeeded. I went to dances, I told them of the excitement of being at a new university. I did not admit how insecure I felt, how inadequate. I acquired friends who would, in effect, look after me, clear away some of my chronic confusion, and introduce me to the kind of relationships I had no chance of having at home. They did an excellent job and I owe them much.

They encouraged me to break the tacit rules that our family lived by. Sometimes they did this through simple astonishment. They wanted me to be vocal, noticeable, attractive. They helped me see that I was clever. In many ways they helped me *be* clever. So, my life cautiously became richer, unpredictable and yet all right. My Irish friend Anne took me hitching round Ireland, where we visited her scattered, astonishing relations, and went to Yeats's summer home, Thoor Ballylee, not a ruin exactly, but open and deserted, beside the willows of a stream, with a door banging in the breeze.

Besides, my parents liked them too, and welcomed many of them to our Wiltshire cottage, where they were received jocularly by my dad in informal mode, and fed extremely well by my mother. Everyone adopted the unspoken rule – no questions about the novels. I don't remember anyone crossing this line until my English tutor Stephen Medcalf came to stay in 1967 after the wreck of *Tenace*. He later claimed to have been extremely nervous, but he was bold enough to crash straight through the barrier in grand style. They became friends.

Without their children at last, my parents' lives broadened as well. They went to Russia with a writers' group which included many European writers. One evening, discussing the new drama in a hectic mixture of French and English, my parents taught Sartre and de Beauvoir the British convention of 'rhubarb, rhubarb' for crowd scenes in a play, something which the two French literary stars benignly intoned. My father said de Beauvoir reminded him of a gym mistress, unfair I should imagine to both sides of the comparison. But the Russian visit had a darker side. There was something about a hotel room being trashed. It was hushed up by the authorities, to my father's relief. My mother was prone to remind him of this, if he became heated about free speech in Russia.

He began lecturing on British Council tours. This would provide huge interest, travel, and a number of good friends over the next three decades. And he continued to write essays and reviews. But around the writing of novels there gathered an enduring cloud of gloom.

The first three novels seem to have leapt on to paper once his imagination conceived them. Almost, he said, as if someone or something else had written them. By contrast, *Free Fall* and *The Spire* both took much work, and both incurred harsh criticism. He had learnt to be frightened. Even my mother found it hard to help him.

In the past, he had been criticised for failing to create convincing female characters. Sometime after *The Spire* was published, he decided to experiment with this idea. He wrote an autobiographical piece called 'Men Women & Now'. In it he examines his relations with the women and girls who meant much to him. He starts with his mother, and his portrayal of her is sympathetic. He is able to acknowledge the fact that they share something – a life inside the head. He seems to understand some of the restrictions of her life, some of the sadness he hints at, a realisation that his parents retreated into 'their poor fortress'. He doesn't explain that phrase, but I think his understanding took him nearer to them, and a step away from the passionate young novelist of the fifties – a step that had disadvantages.

Much to my father's relief, the composition of 'Men Women & Now' led to his writing *The Pyramid*, his sixth novel, published in 1967. And during the late 1960s, as if he had prepared for it, his relationships with women were particularly fraught.

At about this time, my brother became preoccupied with fore-telling the future. I thought the whole business idiotic. Now I see it as part of his heroic attempt to control his life. Already, things were odd. There were unexpected connections in his thoughts and beliefs. We were all uneasy, including him.

He became enthusiastic about *I Ching*, a set of ancient Chinese texts that the reader consults by throwing three sticks or coins on the ground and then finding a passage in the book which has a sign corresponding most nearly to the pattern produced by the sticks or coins. The texts themselves are poetic, mystical and of-ten uplifting, though frustratingly obscure. For a while he gov-erned his life by the commands he saw in them, a practice we tried to comply with, though it was often very inconvenient and, worse, sometimes comic. Then, in 1966, he became interested in the Tarot, which I had read about at university because of T. S. Eliot's references to tarot cards in *The Waste Land*. I found them sinister.

My mother, the only person he could rely on to encourage him, allowed him to tell her fortune with them. He shuffled the pack, and put several cards face down according to a specified formula. Then he turned a card face up. It was a picture of a beautiful woman with long dark hair. My mother told me she was deluged with an unreasonable foreboding.

In the mid 1960s, a PhD student had written to my father. She was studying his work in America, but intended to visit England, and wished to discuss some of her conclusions with him. At first, he refused, as he usually did such overtures, but she was very determined and he did eventually agree to meet her for lunch in Salisbury. His reaction, guilelessly reported to all of us when he got home, was quite favourable. He said she was intelligent, quieter than he expected, dark-haired and rather boyish – per-haps a little like a Red Indian, he added, still unselfconscious. A few days later, she wrote to him angrily. She had felt fobbed off, patronised. My father was greatly upset. I knew then that he felt for her, that he would find her impossible to ignore. My mother went about her usual activities but watchfully, warily. Our family spoke to each other even less than usual.

The student and her husband came to lunch. Subsequently, she said she had found my mother unwelcoming. My mother, she felt, was being possessive, not so much about him as a man. Rather, she was behaving, apparently, like someone who claimed the right to control access to my father as a writer. Over the years my mother had acted as gatekeeper. Usually he was content that she should. Now, all of a sudden, it seemed this was not required. And, though my mother seemed confident, especially to a young and challenging visitor, this was misleading. Women, in particular, could frighten her. I don't know if he realised this.

During the next few years there was a tremendous struggle. My mother was miserable, especially since the struggle coincided with her growing older and my brother becoming increasingly withdrawn. She felt that she was a failure both as a mother and a wife. The great pillars of her existence, her sense of her attractiveness and her belief that my father loved her, began to show signs of fracture.

My father could not empathise with her, although – or perhaps because – he too was losing faith in himself. He did not see why his affection for this personable, intelligent young woman should be thought to diminish his much-declared love for my mother. There was great plausibility in what he said – and I heard it said openly, in the kitchen, not just the bedroom. Whether I would or no, I was witness to their discussions. 'Why not help her?' he would say. 'That's all I'm doing,' he would add – with all the reasonableness of the thoroughly infatuated. He could not listen to my mother's version of the story. And she too was reluctant to say it, to make it real.

I wonder if he remembered enough of those conversations to see later the extent of his self-delusion. He was a famous older man, approached by a younger woman because of his writing. I do not doubt she liked him – he was very likeable – but I believe that the foundation of their relationship, however affectionate, was his literary pre-eminence. After all those years as a novelist, exploring and portraying the human heart, he fell hook, line and sinker for what I perhaps unfairly assume was the first sizeable temptation.

> Old, inflammable men,
> Who should be at their prayers,
> Must make love by the pen
> And climb forbidden stairs,
> To fumble at the flower of things
> That never can be theirs.

He recited that poem to me, treating me as a sort of proxy for my mother, always his first reader. Even he understood that he could hardly recite it to her. Actually, I think it's quite good. I remember it, which is a tribute of sorts.

In June 1967, during my finals, I went home for a break. My father took me out for a drink, and I assumed we would talk of Shelley or Tennyson, Dickens or Shakespeare. He would often generously try to do me a bit of good, pass on something for me to use in my exams, not realising that I had for years been wary of his judgements. It sounds carping to say this, but frequently his ideas were not very fresh, however generous, and besides I often didn't agree with them. However, my assumption was quite wrong. He spent the whole time talking about this young woman – how she needed him, he could help her, he *wanted* to help her and surely that was reasonable? Over and over again, he assured me that he was not going to roll in the hay with her – it was a phrase he seemed to like. Was he reassuring me? Or was I to be the messenger? I was out of my depth.

I knew my mother was deeply unhappy, and I knew my father was taking advantage of the inequality of their life together. Actually, she was still very beautiful, with charm, wit and intelligence. But my father was fond of saying that a woman is as beautiful as she feels. He trotted this out to me so often that I eventually retorted that it was a pity the same could not be said of men. I was unsympathetic about the young woman too, which surprised him. He should have realised. My mother and I were often wary of each other, cool and unintimate. But, when the chips were down, I as a female lined up squarely with the wronged wife.

I don't know whether they rolled in the hay or not. No further bulletins were issued. My mother, aware as my father was not that I had anxieties of my own, reassured me that nothing could ever break the two of them up. But she said this with forced calm, her face showing signs of weeping.

This was only one of their sorrows. Soon there were many. My father's partly autobiographical novel, *The Pyramid*, dedicated to my brother, did not do as well as earlier ones. Humiliatingly for my father, especially in the midst of his troubles with my mother, critics made fun of his attempts at sex scenes. Did she, his usual source of comfort, discuss them with him? Or did she leave him to it, as I think she did in America if he had friendships with young students? His later attempts in this field are either comic (Talbot and Zenobia in *Rites of Passage*) or used to show a warped taste in the participants (Sophie in *Darkness Visible*). The subject became painful. His reaction was to ally himself with a punishing memory in the way he treated it.

But readers and critics actually seemed offended by the novel's modern setting, and its single-level narration. I suspect he too believed it was not as good as his earlier work.

In 1966, the year before *The Pyramid*, my parents bought their last boat, the beautiful *Tenace*. Perhaps sailing would bring back the old feelings, the old days. It was ten years since the first summer in *Wild Rose*. My parents knew that by now they had made good. Their days of ramshackle boats were over, so why not have a proper one, as they now had a proper car, a proper house? They bought her from a boatyard in Reedham in Norfolk, and the first job was to sail her back to Southampton.

I had gone to Italy that summer and found it heavy going. English girls had such a reputation that a refusal to have sex with someone was seen as a gratuitous personal insult. It was the only time in my life someone propositioned me at breakfast. I left, and managed to catch my parents at Reedham before they began their voyage. I felt, correctly I think, that they were not particularly pleased to see me. I shared a cabin with my mother, which was hardly ideal for a couple trying to revisit the best aspects of their marriage.

We set off downriver to the sea, together with my parents' old friend Viv Lewis from *Wild Rose* days, now a widower. John Milne joined us too, and as ever in his genial company my father started to settle down to the task in hand, laughing at his own foibles. But there were unpleasant things. At Harwich, somebody set us loose from our moorings in the middle of a moonless night. My father woke up, alerted even in his sleep by the boat moving. When he went on deck, he saw we were drifting, without lights, into the main shipping channel, with the ferries passing to and fro. We thought of that later.

Tenace had a berth on the Hamble, the posh river. Before, we had slummed round in the River Itchen. My father ordered repairs. As usual, he had bought something too trustingly, and there was more wrong with *Tenace* than he suspected.

He and my mother had an extraordinary plan, which they called by a secret name. We would enter the French canal system at Le Havre, de-mast *Tenace*, cautiously join the Rhône and ultimately the Med. As a bonus it would allow us to continue the family passion for life in France. They would moor *Tenace* at some idyllic small port (unspecified), and alternate living on board with occasional visits to Wiltshire. It was a plan that suited everyone, and maybe once more gave Marlborough a rebellious two fingers. My father loved the sunshine and could take any amount of it, at least at European levels. This way, my mother would share his sailing life as much as his writing. Crucially, there would be few visitors. Things would be as they had been decades ago. Of course, none of this was actually *said*.

Intermittent flashes of discord appeared during the spring and summer of 1967. My mother could not stop herself being suspicious, checking the post, asking why he had been out so long. I had enough experience of jealousy to see why she was so miserable, and why my father refused her nothing except the one thing she wanted. He could not give it – nothing could reassure her except, perhaps, time. In July, I graduated from Sussex and set my sights on the following year. Oxford.

So it was that we set off from Shoreham early that July morning in 1967, without David but with two men, Viv as engineer and another of my parents' friends, James Anderson, as crew. My friend Paulette Sainsbury, a fellow graduate from Sussex, came too. In my mind, that one day lasts for weeks. *Tenace*'s gradual sinking stretches out like a prairie of experience, with the final closing of the dimpled, swirling green water over her bow as a resigned, gentle moment. Hard to believe, but we were at home later that night. My parents took to their beds. My mother developed bronchitis.

The doctor called every day. Before, he had urged my parents to give up smoking, and they had tried to do so. He himself had given it up, after a heroic struggle, since he didn't think he could ask his patients to do what he had not done. But faced with my parents' misery, my father's retrospective terror at the lives that might have been lost, his grief over his beautiful boat, his shame at belonging – as he said – to that most exclusive club, of captains who had survived the loss of their ship, the doctor told them not even to try.

Soon, Paulette went back to her life in London, and Viv to Southampton, though before this he and I had an embarrassing conversation in which he tried to discuss with me the constraints my father felt in his marriage. Conscious of my mother coughing away upstairs, I froze the conversation to a rigid standstill, with an irritated realisation that Viv was enjoying himself. I thought I had seen cautious overtures towards me, and I suspected these came with my father's world-weary approval. Although I'd had several boyfriends at Sussex, I hadn't been to bed with any of them, which, in an annoying backwards flip from their previous attitude, had rather scandalised my parents. My father had even offered to buy me a book, never an idle threat in our family.

As soon as they were well enough, I flew off to Athens with another friend from Sussex, a very bright girl called Diana, whom my father always called Di the Finger because of the way she pointed haltingly at the dartboard before flinging a dart. We spent a week or so travelling round the Greek islands, arriving on one in the middle of a pilgrimage, where elderly ladies were climbing up a hill on their cardboard-covered knees. Diana stared at them with undisguised rage, and I was very glad she knew no Greek. We eventually went back to Athens and met Paulette. Then the three of us went to Crete, where we hitched round the island, sleeping on beaches and avoiding the local men. One evening we had a really bad lift and ended up jumping out of the car and running away. It was dark and we hid up in the trees while the car lights went back and forth, looking for us – at least, so we assumed. Then we walked to the nearest village, got a room above a café and saw the men we'd run away from sitting downstairs drinking coffee. Next day we took the bus.

The following evening, running out of daylight once more, we got a lift in a lorry. Paulette sat in the cab, more comfortably, but she had to deal with the men. Diana and I were in the back, open not only to the sky but also the road, which you could see disappearing with terrible speed below us. We held on for absolute dear life, and it was astonishingly difficult. It was hard even to breathe. But when I did at last look up I saw that the entire sky was fuzzy with stars – there was no sky, really, it was a mass of gold pinpricks. I remember thinking, 'I must tell Daddy about this.' Then I thought, 'Of course I can't. He'd be terrified.' The idea of living my life for myself – instead of looking for things to tell him about, to show him how sensitive, literary, or intense I was – this was new.

But I began to understand. Before Paulette's arrival, Diana and I had gone to Mykonos by ferry. A few miles out of Piraeus, black smoke began to emerge from the wheelhouse. The Greek crew had been reading a newspaper, which they spread on top of the engine. This had led to a political argument (it was, after all, the summer of the Colonels), which meant they ignored the smell of burning. Finally, the paper burst into flames. In the end the cook, a Turk, threw water over the fire and smothered it with a fire blanket from the kitchen. Diana went to have a look, but I sat down on the deck under a lifeboat, arms round my knees, thinking of *Tenace*. Later that year I told my father about this. He listened politely and walked out of the room. On my way to the loo I passed him in the passage. Immobile, face to the wall, he had his hands either side of his head.

Mykonos was exquisite, all blue and white, breezy and fresh, still a recognisable Greek island rather than the holiday village it would become. In a matter of seconds we were picked up by a nice Englishman and a youngish Greek man who was quite extraordinarily good-looking. He reminded me – but at least I had the wit not to tell him – of the famous bust of Pericles. The evening became confused, and that was the first time I really had too much to drink. The handsome Greek asked me to marry him and wanted to write to my father, a fantasy which I enjoyed tremendously until he tearfully confessed that it was his fortieth birthday. He got rather drunk too, and did a stumbling Zorba-type dance. Then the Englishman turned out to have been tried for murder and acquitted, at which point he had married his defence lawyer. This was terrific and we stored it up for home. I have a feeling the Greek proposed to Diana as well.

They were very good company, and kept buying us drinks, though after a while the Greek took to grabbing my arm and pulling me towards him in a way that was surprisingly painful. I found it difficult to make him understand that I didn't like what he was doing. When I finally did, there was an odd, rather childish and very disagreeable flash of anger from him and Diana laughed, which he liked even less. Subsequently, we seemed to have parted from them, I can't quite remember how, but I

guess through Diana's decisiveness. She was far more sophisticated than I, not a difficult achievement. We then found we were
lost. We walked round and round the small town, peering at the
whitewashed walls and the dazzling, clean little streets until we
found the open window of the room where we were staying. We
climbed in, finding such a procedure quite natural.

As soon as I lay down, I felt most tremendously ill, with my
head feeling as if it was a bucket being whirled round and round.
If I shut my eyes it was worse. Luckily, Mykonos was well lit,
because of the tourists, and our house was next to a street light. I
got up to use the outside loo, stumbled out of its wooden gloom
and found myself in a small square garden with white-painted
walls. There were flowers everywhere, oleanders, creepers, sun-
flowers, perhaps bougainvillea. There was a huge shadowy fig
with vast leaves. Next to it was a walnut tree. From one of its
branches there hung a swing. I sat on it for hours, gently moving
to and fro while the branch creaked overhead and the big leaves
rustled around me. Eventually my poor body managed to deal
with what I'd thrown at it, and I found I'd been asleep, curled
round one of the ropes.

I thought of our swing in the garden at Bourne Avenue, of my
father pushing me to and fro, of a time the swing broke and I
saw compunction on his face, compunction and guilty awareness
because he'd have to explain to my mother. I understood then
that I had finally reached the point when I would no longer tell
him everything.

The next day I felt absolutely fine, fit as a fiddle and really well
rested. Youth isn't always wasted on the young. That autumn I
went off to Oxford, where I acquired a husband, a job, a house,
some friends and eventually even a BLitt.

But David was still at home, and the situation did not improve.
In the autumn of 1968, after years of struggle and unhappiness,
he finally descended into a psychotic breakdown. In early 1969
he was admitted to a mental hospital. A few weeks later my father
wrote his account of their relationship, certainly the bleakest and

most self-condemnatory piece of his writing I have ever read. However complex and unfathomable the causes of David's illness were, my father saw himself and his behaviour unsparingly, as a contributory factor. I wouldn't wish such a belief on my worst enemy. I am very sorry for him, all the more so because I think he was at least partly right.

In his journal for 1976, he wrote a description of Alastair Sim. It was many years after the production of his play *The Brass Butterfly*, in which Sim had played the Roman Emperor, an urbane and charming Caesar. For one reason and another they had lost touch and Sim was now dead. Defying traditional piety, my father's comments are critical. He describes Sim's tendency to trivialise – 'oh, so winsomely' – any modern plays that he did not like, even those by Beckett and Pinter.

And then my father writes, '*De mortuis nil nisi veritas.*'

Nothing but truth about the dead.

'So may it be with Caesar,' he continues.

This is Mark Antony, busily winding up the crowd to vengeance after Caesar's murder. Of course, Mark Antony does not mean what he says, but my father evidently does, because he adds, 'And me, too, if anyone bothers.'

15

Grown Up

In the summer of 1970, Terrell and I were on holiday in Paris, staying in a sleazy hotel in the rue du Maréchal Ney. I had an appalling stomach bug. One day we went for a walk in the Jardin du Luxembourg. Fragile but determined, I announced that I must organise my life. I needed somewhere to live, somewhere settled. I was fed up with bedsits, tents, cheap hotels – especially cheap hotels. Also, I had an uneasy awareness that I could not prolong my time at Oxford indefinitely. I might even have to get a job. Terrell correctly interpreted this as the equivalent of a Victorian father asking him about his intentions. We returned home engaged.

My mother asked me privately how I would like to get married. Did I, for instance, wish to be married in Salisbury Cathedral? I said I thought Oxford registry office would be fine. But I was curious. Did she, my modern mother, married in Maidstone registry office wearing a nice tweed suit, actually want me to be married in the cathedral? Well, she confessed, she did have – as she put it – 'an atavistic desire' to see me walk up the aisle of our very own cathedral, on my father's arm. I was surprised. Any ambitions she had harboured for me had been kept very quiet, though it's safe to say that marrying an American was not one of them. She wanted to show me off, my father's daughter. In effect, it seemed she was at least slightly proud of me. I wondered if he had shared her dream. I think not. It is a female thing, the dress, the flowers, the day of days. But I have a clear picture – my father's beaming face, his silvery beard, his morning suit, his affectionate pride, the paternal tilt of his head towards his daughter in satin swishing along beside him.

My mother relinquished the idea in seconds, buoyantly re-marking that we were now £250 in hand, a decent sum in those days. In January 1971, our family processed the entire length of St Giles's, Oxford, from the Randolph to the registry office, at that point in a tall terrace house nicely positioned between the Christian Science Reading Room and the Army Recruiting Of-fice. My mother wore a floor-length caftan of crimson crushed velvet, my bridesmaid Diana, Di the Finger, was in a trouser suit of purple crushed velvet, my brother wore a green suit and bright yellow patent shoes, and my father a monocle that popped every few yards and made him frown hideously. I was in pink, with a white felt hat which today would do perfectly for line-dancing. Terrell and two friends fell out of the Eagle and Child a minute before we passed. I've always been glad there were no photos. We used my father's underwater camera, and that day, in true Golding fashion, it declined to work. The subsequent lunch went on till six. Two weeks later, my father gave me a cheque for five thousand pounds, with a letter for the tax people.

Later that year I got a real job, and was supporting not only my-self but Terrell as well. That was a shock, strangely almost a griev-ous one, to my father. By September I had bought a house with part of the five thousand. A few months later, Anthony Barber took the lid off housing loans, and house prices doubled. Through luck rather than judgment, I had doubled my investment.

These were good days for me. I still thought Oxford the most beautiful place in the world. Moreover, I now had a husband and would never have to worry about a date for Saturday night. I had a little house with a little garden. I worried about money, but gradually realised I always would. I worked as a copy-editor at the Clarendon Press, starting out on Helen Gardner's new ver-sion of *The Oxford Book of English Verse*. It was a dream job. Every morning I would cycle up St Aldate's, along Walton Street past the Scala cinema, and plunge in through the pillared portico of the Press.

There, accompanied by two immensely learned young

classicists and a woman who really knew her Anglo-Saxon, I spent all day happily reading scholarly typescripts, thinking up abstruse queries. One of these was put to Helen Gardner, and I'm glad to remember it astonished her. Since copy-editing is meant to be undetectable, its main consolation is shocking the author into humility, and this is surprisingly easy to do. We would all lunch in the Duke of Cambridge in Little Clarendon Street, where Terrell would come and add his quota to the general abstruseness – perhaps about the numbering of the volumes of the works of Marx and Engels, or the finer points of Russian transliteration. When we moved as a group around the building, we would sort ourselves, for some deep reason of the copy-editing unconscious, into alphabetical order (Allen, Carver, Dod and Speake), and sometimes people would come out of their hutches and watch. We thought we were a legend, but actually we were barely continuing the tradition. The previous head of the copy-editing department, a chap from Cambridge, used to watch cowboy films with Wittgenstein.

As for my thesis, my examiners had quite understandably referred it back, an Oxford term meaning that I had to do it again. Most evenings I would cycle straight from the Press to the Bodleian Library to work on it. Then I would race breezily home down the hill with Christ Church's Great Tom booming out for nine or even ten o'clock. To our surprise, my father told us that our house in Grandpont, the area below Folly Bridge, was a street away from his first digs at Oxford, where he had hired a piano.

When, after his death, I transcribed his journal, I was shocked at the contrast between what I remembered of him in the 1970s, and what I now learnt. I was typing out sentences like these:

I find it difficult to decide when the crisis began. You could say that it was intense during 70/71; but you could also say that it began in 60/61; and then again in '54 – or in 1911, come to that. But by 71 it was unendurable.

That was part of his account, written in November 1971, of his terrible difficulties, his wretchedness, his experiences with drink – 'the old, old anodyne' – and the misery of not being able to write. He called the account 'History of a Crisis'.

I had realised for several years that he got drunk occasionally. We were all alert to the signs. There would be restless discontent, rudeness, sometimes cruel words. He would consume drink in a particular way, swigging it down as if the taste was unpleasant. His conversation would still be precise, but repetitive and with an edge of menace. Bizarrely, he would have huge sneezing fits, which we learnt as an infallible sign.

At that point, Terrell would get up and go into the kitchen. A few minutes later he would return with a mug of hot milk. He would put it down beside my father without a word. The silence was vital, as he knew. Usually the situation was saved.

Sometimes, however, nothing helped. He would stay up most of the night. There would be distant crashes of bottles, and occasionally thunderous playing on the piano. The next day he would surface at about eleven, and walk about the house deathly pale, carrying a glass of dissolved Disprin or Alka-Seltzer. Sometimes he would have a hair of the dog at lunch, and the whole thing would begin again. Sometimes my mother and I would try for hours – till one or two in the morning – to persuade him to go to bed. He would tease us, lumbering up the stairs, even perhaps getting into pyjamas. Then, at the last minute, he would sidle past, shoot downstairs again quite agilely, and resume drinking. It was exhausting. He was as much a victim, I believe, as those around him, more if anything. It was so clear he hated himself at those times, and needed to make himself into a fit object for that hatred.

I don't know where the hatred came from, but it was very deep. Nor do I believe it was caused by the drink, as a kind of allergic reaction or substance intolerance. The drink allowed something to be shown to the world, but that something was there already.

Very occasionally, it did emerge without the drink. Over

August Bank Holiday in 1973, Terrell and I went to stay at Bowerchalke together with our friend John Harris and his then girlfriend Vicky Taggart. Adam Bittleston, an old friend of my father's from his time at Oxford, who was a priest in the Anthroposophist community, was there too. Soon, I realised that the mood was unusual. My father was sober but energised with a cold, practised fury. This was partly – and ludicrously – the result of their being landed with some kittens. A semi-feral cat had been run over, leaving these four mewling creatures in their hedge. No one suggested we should ignore the problem – that was not a possibility. But my father hated cats, and for some reason saw Terrell and me as entirely responsible for their presence. Apart from some jokes ('First prize one kitten; second prize two kittens'), they were a disaster. But this was only part of the business. At every meal, where I could not escape without a scene, my father managed both to ignore me and shovel contempt over me. His behaviour was monstrous and would have been so if directed against anybody. Against his supposedly much-loved daughter, it was simply extraordinary.

By the end of lunch on Sunday, I had had enough. I went upstairs and Terrell came to find me. I was crying. He said my father was now in a good mood. Things would be fine. I washed my face and went downstairs. But it didn't stop. Either Terrell had been mistaken or the sight of me reawakened all my father's anger. It went on and on relentlessly, fuelled apparently by a single-minded dislike of his daughter.

John and Vicky were due to drive back to Oxford that afternoon. Adam would stay on, and so would we. John came upstairs to my attic bedroom to say goodbye. I had cried so much I could not bear to face him.

Terrell explained. 'Judy's not getting on very well with her father.'

Off they went. I heard their polite and genial farewells, my parents' hospitable jokes. I began packing.

Within half an hour we were ready to return to Oxford. My

parents showed surprise, and my father's was, I think, genuine. Until we drove out of the gate, I was frightened that I might be talked into staying. It was a beautiful evening, and we went on impulse to Silbury Hill, and walked up it, as you could in those days. We looked out over Wiltshire – we were about four miles from Martinsell, a huge curve of downland where my father used to take me for walks as a child. The ground rose gradually towards it, an expanse of green, luscious country, like the landscape Shakespeare describes as King Lear's gift to his daughter – wide-skirted meads, champaigns rich. It was beautiful. I felt I must be especially, uniquely annoying, and stupid, and ugly, to call forth such feelings from my own father.

Later that night, prompted by my mother, he apologised. She, who had some idea of the score, phoned first and asked if I would speak to him. Even then he didn't admit to the worst, the ignoring, the evil looks, the cold, deliberate turning of his shoulder, part of that wide frame which had sheltered me so often in the past. He merely said he was sorry that he had been rude about my political ideas. And it is true that he had said, in a rather picturesque formula, that I was a political slot machine. You put your penny in, he said, and out came a cliché. Perhaps my mother had enlightened him about the sexual nature of such imagery. That would have shocked him dreadfully, far more than any idea that he was a bully. But I did not challenge him on those grounds. I said that I thought Adam brought out the best in him, and so he had to express the bad as well. Meekly, mildly, he agreed that it might well be so, though even then I thought I could hear the resonance of anger in his voice. (How dare she analyse *me*?) We never, ever, spoke about it again.

Now, thinking of my own children and the idea of treating them like that, I am simply at a loss. Perhaps he chose to hate my not very radical politics because I refused to conform on such matters. In most other respects I was a dutiful, quiet, well-behaved daughter. But, about my own watery socialism (I still hesitate to use that word, fearing his anger), he had not managed to mould me to suit his tastes. Was that the explanation? It seems a meagre one for such a piece of savagery. After more than thirty years of pondering this, I have come to the conclusion that he picked on politics merely because he needed an excuse to feel rage about me. But that just pushes the question further back. Why did he need to feel rage at all?

It seemed to me at the time to be an inherited ceremony between parents and children. The story of Abraham and Isaac is carefully placed at the beginning of *The Spire*, in picture form, perhaps a child's-eye view. A window bursting with colour – a brief acknowledgement of my father's lifelong love of stained glass. But the subject, too, was a preoccupation. He was fond of saying how close human sacrifice is to so-called civilisation. He would be at once triumphant and disgusted ('You *see*?') at any examples. He observed how close it lay to the surface of Greek mythology (Iphigenia sacrificed by her father) and was certainly there, large as life, in the Old Testament (as well as Abraham and his son, there is Jephthah and his daughter). Maybe such stories lay behind his understanding – one hopes, misunderstanding – of the relations between fathers and sons. Sometimes, gazing affectionately at a robin in the garden, he would murmur

> He sings because the other night
> He killed his father in a fight.

He mythologised such relations as a struggle to the death, despite his own love for his father. But they had fought when he was younger, and I believe he saw Alec as wanting in part, despite all his generosity, to deprive him of things – money, sex, poetry, music, and even perhaps, at some level, life itself. Small children in all his books seem unbearably fragile, weak, susceptible, a sacrifice waiting to happen, especially if like Simon, Liku, Sammy Mountjoy, they have – ideas. These portraits in his books were created while his own children were small. And the weaknesses of those real children were not always protected. Was that because he could not endure looking at the reality, the painful vulnerability of the children he knew best, versions no doubt of himself? This is my interpretation, and it is to say the least subjective. Do I believe it was the same for fathers and daughters as it was for fathers and sons? I suspect it wasn't supposed to be the same, simply because daughters, if they were daughterly, would not need to rebel against their fathers. Jephthah's daughter assents to her sacrifice.

Poor old Dad. I know he loved me, or at least the version of me he chose to see. I loved him intensely, and was appallingly eager to please him. I thought that his minimalist apology to me about the political slot machine was both miserly and self-serving. Even so, in my reply, I hoped he would think I was clever. Do I also hope he suffered agonies of self-reproach? I am fairly sure he didn't. Apart from his drunken sessions of self-hate, he was robust, funny, capable of self-defence, or even of forgetting the whole thing. In his journal, the whole miserable weekend is recounted in a couple of lines:

[August 1973: the actual date is not given]
For a long time now writing has been in abeyance. We had a whole week in David's canal boat Sans Souci which was very pleasant. We went from Saul to within a mile of Stratford on Avon and back. I forgot both my diary and camera. Then, last long weekend, Judy, Terrell, Vicki Taggart and John Harris, and Adam Bittleston were here, which was pleasant but exhausting.

How confusing it is. About a year later, in September 1974, I was living in London on my own, because Terrell had just started his first job at Liverpool University. In my lunch hour I was walking along New Oxford Street, near Jonathan Cape where I then worked. To my great surprise I saw my father walking towards me. He swept off his tweed trilby and kissed me.

'Hello, darling. On the loose?'
'Hello, Daddy. I've just been burgled!'
He turned white.

*

Two years later, in early September 1976, my father was up in London, reading the whole of *Lord of the Flies* on to tape, an exhausting and for him curiously dispiriting process. Making his way home on the evening of the 10th, he stopped at Waterloo station to phone my mother.

'Hello, Grandpa,' she said.

Our first son Nick had been born that morning. Egotistically, I see the role of grandfather as defining the remaining years of my father's life. The poet and critic Craig Raine was astounded to find, when he and his family were coming to lunch at Tullimaar in 1985, that the distinguished novelist and Nobel Prize winner knew all about buying fish fingers and spaghetti hoops. My father also knew about Duplo, Lego, Brio, the Mister Men books and a whole collection of children's TV programmes, diligently recorded by him for his grandsons. As the boys' taste matured, so did his. He was always particularly fond of the Mos Eisley bar scene in *Star Wars*.

For my parents, apart from the excited expectation of their first grandchild, 1976 had been grim. In June, my mother had a mastectomy, something I believe she never came to terms with. Later that month my father's much-loved friend John Milne died suddenly of a heart attack. Tony Brown was also beginning to be very ill. He died the following April. Their world was eroding.

A few weeks after the birth, I took my very small baby to stay with my parents. Nick was a beautiful, lively child, intelligent and tremendously responsive, delighting in contact with people. He didn't see the point of sleep, and had to be fooled into it by food or exhaustion or both. When he awoke from such slumber, he did so with howls of grief and anger, which perhaps fancifully I took to be a memory of his difficult and protracted birth, his painful emergence into light. At six weeks old, he was growing tremendously and doing very well.

But I was exhausted, as desperate for sleep as a desert traveller is for water. I was also, I now realise, rather depressed. I had given up my wonderful job at Jonathan Cape and moved to Liverpool, where I had no friends. I had felt gorgeous while pregnant. After the birth I found that nature had completely dropped me, calculatingly, like an acquaintance whose usefulness is past. Masses of my hair fell out and plugged the shower, and naturally I bled, something people tend not to warn you about. Sitting was painful, still, six weeks later. I was a shambolic saggy shape, wearing what seemed like a bizarre medieval bra from which I intermittently dripped milk. And there had been personal troubles, which had demoralised me greatly. I was at a low ebb, worried that I was not a good mother, desperate to give my child all the love he needed, yet fearful that I was not capable of such a task. I was also struggling to work as a freelance copy-editor. Lots of work appeared just as Nick was born.

In October, Terrell delivered Nick and me to my parents' house in Wiltshire. At once the place was transformed into a house with a new baby, and that is a very particular thing. Conversation centred on him. Activity sprang from him. The house was silent or noisy, depending on whether he was asleep or not. His small, volatile body, his clothes, his nappies, his carrycot, became the essential things. All else was in the background.

Nick and I slept, in so far as we slept at all, at the front of the house. I put him in the pram, which I would park in the bathroom next to the bedroom. Generously, my parents had given me the proper spare room, rather than my attic, and I would push the pram back and forth along its bathroom floor, to get him to sleep. One night I was doing this at about two in the morning, when the door creaked open and my pale, bearded father appeared in his pyjamas. He looked rather like Banquo's Ghost.

'Push him for a bit if you like –'

He took the handle of the pram and moved it adeptly, with a rocking rhythm, along the pink carpet of the now luxurious bathroom, transformed from its earlier spartan state where long ago I had rescued spiders, another of my father's dark terrors. I went back to bed and slept gratefully for an hour or so, waking to hear Nick's cry and his agitated movements. Once more I fed him – it must have been about five. He and I then slept till nine or ten, the house obediently silent around us. I have no idea if my father slept. I never thought to ask him.

Later in the week, my father records:

> I got carried away at our (non-alcoholic) lunch because Ann said how Judy was begotten in one go before I left for Walcheren and she wondered when she heard on the news how tough it had been who would believe her possible baby was legitimate. This led me into a sudden and astonishingly sombre bit of recounting – my poor little midshipman hanging onto the side of the sinking ship and saying 'My legs are gone.' Judy burst into floods of tears as well she might. I am a fool all over again.

To me, he said ruefully, 'I'm sorry, ducks. I was doing a bit of all chaps together stuff, how manly we were, how tough.'

We were back to the war, The War of my childhood. Nothing could erase it, certainly not a grandchild. Rather, Nick's presence increased the intensity. My father's painfully sharp sensibility about children somehow linked itself with his identity as a perpetrator of war. I don't know why this link is so close – perhaps because he was a child in the First World War, and a very new father in the Second. And *Lord of the Flies*, with its cast of pitiable children, set on an idyllic coral island, is framed by a global atomic war, a world catastrophe. In January 1991, my father writes,

> Well, we have had the first day – or most of it – of Operation Desert Storm . . . War is an indescribable activity. It is scaring, terrifying, boring, depressing, exciting, obsessively absorbing, fascinating, exhilarating, mournful, tragic, comic, melodramatic, dull, infuriating, cruel and nearer to the human appetite than anything else, bar sex.

The little midshipman ('Mr Midshipman Fisher' in my father's contemporary account) haunts me still. With my six-week-old baby, in all his perfection, I at last understood that heavy phrase, 'every mother's son'. As for my father, he thought of Fisher, and his mother, as a kind of touchstone of grief. 'I am sure my midshipman's mother still mourns him in a sad way,' he wrote on Armistice Day in 1974. Would it have affected him so intensely if Fisher had not been a mere boy, nineteen or so? He always had an appalled if distant tenderness for the young, especially young men. All combatants have such memories – how could they not?

But there was more. Walcheren is a smallish diamond-shaped Dutch piece of land. It used to be an island before the Dutch got going on it. But, in an adaptation of the famous Chinese curse, Walcheren, island or not, lives unluckily in an interesting place, controlling the mouth of the southern outlet of the River Scheldt, which gives access to the Rhine as well as to the Belgian port of Antwerp.

In 1944, the Allies had taken Antwerp by land. Antwerp's enormous docks were intact, but its seaward approach, vital for landing supplies – food, fuel and men – had yet to be conquered. If they were to make it to Berlin – and before the Russians – Antwerp had to be available. So, in October 1944, the Allies launched an attack on Walcheren in order to clear the seaway to Antwerp. My father's task, as commander of a so-called rocket ship, a landing craft adapted to fire a thousand or so shells, was to demolish the enemy's coastal defences by bombarding them.

After the Walcheren operation, fearsome in its loss of life, my father went ashore at Ostend to visit his injured commanding officer. There, he found the hospital full of Dutch civilians, terribly injured in the attack on Westkapelle, the small town which had been the focus for the seaborne operation. More than two hundred of the villagers had been killed. My father's briefing had told him that the civilian population had been evacuated. The very efficiency and bravery of his own actions would now haunt him. In military terms, he had done well. But his rockets formed a significant share of the fire that had killed so many of Westkapelle's inhabitants.

The situation was tragic for the Dutch. Their homes were flooded, their farmland poisoned with sea water, many people dead, many more injured. I don't know how they acted at the time, but their later response has always seemed to treat what happened as an unavoidable necessity. When we were sailing in the waterways of Holland in 1960, the Dutch people we met were all emphatic that the invasion had been right and necessary – the heavy cost had not been unreasonable.

I visited Westkapelle in 2004, and saw then that the attack on the place was still seen in those terms. As soon as we got off the bus in the main square we encountered a plaque, in English and Dutch, prominently displayed there since 1954. 'In 1944 Westkapelle suffered inevitable destruction in the battle for freedom.' On the sea wall, as it rounds the westernmost point of the diamond, there is a Sherman tank, and another plaque 'in commemoration of the landing of No. 4 Commando Brigade' by the Royal Marines on 1 November 1944. Children were playing on the tank.

I looked out at the grey sea. I felt a mixture of pride and tears, both of which I distrust greatly. The sea wall was an impressive sight, and the stony beach shelved down through the mud to the sea. I could picture the landing craft approaching it, the muddy troops and vehicles, the frantic explosions, the wide, smoke-cluttered vista of war, and the bitterly individual deaths and drownings.

In 1944, as part of the offensive, the Allies blew a hole in the sea wall. Most of Walcheren is below sea level, so it filled up like a saucer of milk. To the east, we could see the former gap. Now, behind the repaired wall there is a small inland lake, brackish, surrounded by trees and dune-grass, and haunted by the crying of sea birds. It is used for fishing, for recreation. When the resourceful Dutch rebuilt the dykes and pumped out the water, they left the lake as a silent witness – *als stille getuige*, says the guidebook.

Of course, there was a visitors' centre. It had an orderly queue.

In front of me was a middle-aged German applying for a fishing permit, probably for the inland lake. The Dutch girl behind the counter – I should think she was about twenty-three – spoke to him in fluent German, very friendly, very helpful. Then she turned to me. Inescapably, I thought of Fawlty Towers. *Don't mention the war.* The blood rushing to my cheeks, I mumbled that we had come to look at the site of the 1944 invasion. The man with the fishing permit stood there, politely listening, deferentially unembarrassed. Behind me was another German, in hiking boots. Absolutely everyone seemed to speak English. I felt like a tearful child surrounded by puzzled adults.

My companion, bolder than I, said, 'Her father was in the British Navy attacking force. He fired rockets at the town.'

The effect of these words was not what you might have predicted. The Dutch girl became personal and enthusiastic. We could see it was for her a familiar story, a legend – heroic – and a part of her life, despite being as long ago to her as the First World War was to me. But she was vocal, interested, even emotional, pressing leaflets on us, wishing us luck and smiling dazzlingly as we left. As we went out of the door, she was beginning to talk in German to the person behind us.

Yet for my father the matter was never so settled. He could not say that the price was worth it; he could not do that calculation. He knew that the Walcheren invasion, though appallingly costly in lives, had been a success. As planned, it opened Antwerp up to the sea, allowing vital fuel, stores and troops to be landed there by the Allies rather than over the beachheads in Normandy, hundreds of miles to the west. It was just in time to oppose the final German offensive. Without this, the war would probably have gone on longer, and progress to Berlin would have been far slower.

My father often said the struggle against Hitler was 'a just war if there ever was one'. He was not a conscientious objector, although I must say he seems to have thought that such a position was not only tenable but courageous. And for him it did not make everything all right if you were the victor, even if you were the victor *and* fighting a just war. I believe he never resolved the rights and wrongs of that complex knot of ideas.

You can see from his novels that the war affected him profoundly. It was not only the horror, not only the imagined loss of individuals. It was not even the bitter realisation of what ordinary people were really quite ready to put their hands to, if given the slightest encouragement. For more than five years, he had not been able to determine his own life. His will – a very strong one – was at the command of the navy and the country's leaders. His was a strong, competitive personality and he liked to succeed. This drive could – and did – serve the war effort very well. His qualities were useful in the great task of killing the enemy. He used his initiative at Walcheren, taking a calculated risk about his own life and those of his crew. He was successful *and* returned safely. But his imagination was very powerful, and I suspect it got a great deal of practice during the war.

The years before the war had given him another experience. He had a wife and son, both, he says, very dear to him. He makes this clear in his unpublished writings. But he could not avoid the realisation that among the people he had killed there would have been families – wives, children, Dutch and French, as well as soldiers and sailors as precious to a German family as he was to my mother and brother, my grandparents. And he had seen people die, had seen death and mutilation right next to him. He had lost people he knew. Perhaps even more powerfully for him – I don't know – he had imagined terrible things he had not seen – the death of Midshipman Fisher, for example.

In his account of how he began to compose *Rites of Passage* he says, 'It became necessary for me to understand . . .' In that case, he needed to understand how a man could die of shame. After the war he needed to understand how ordinary people could do all these things, with energy, with efficiency, and sometimes with satisfaction.

He didn't believe that the Germans he was fighting were especially wicked people. He considered that to be a comforting fantasy. He said many times that he knew he could easily have been a Nazi – that if he had been born in a different place he too would have followed Hitler. The enemy was to be defeated, but the enemy included hundreds of thousands of young men like him, young men obeying orders, as he obeyed the order to bombard Westkapelle.

Would I think this if he hadn't become a novelist concerned above all with the darkness of man's heart? I don't know. I am sure, however, that the war not only taught him – as he says in his essay 'Fable' – that 'man produces evil as a bee produces honey'. It also showed him that he too – the yellow-haired boy in the sailor suit, the musician, the would-be poet, the lover, the teacher, the father – he could kill, could be rather good at it, could even feel a certain zest for it.

16

Grandchildren

In 1978, when Nick was two, and still an only child, my parents took us to France on the first of a series of summer holidays. The last was in 1992. The only year missed was 1985, and that was because we were away in Virginia. The holidays usually lasted a month, and my father paid for most of the accommodation and all the ferries. We tried, rather feebly, to pay for some of the food, but it was still a great expense for them. And there were other costs as well. He started worrying gently about it all in October, soon after our return from the previous holiday. The worry would increase until he was beset by monster anxieties, and above all faced with the terrifying challenge of Phoning France. On one of these occasions, when his colonel-like voice had reverberated throughout the house, my mother said mildly, 'Next time, why not use the telephone?'

Soon after this, I took over the phoning, and once we were actually abroad Terrell did the cooking. But that was really all. The rest was down to them and it was immensely generous. It continued unflinchingly as more grandchildren appeared, and demands on time and pocket increased.

That first year we stayed in central France, in the converted stables of the Château du Méage, a small, exquisite castle with turrets and moats. It was surrounded by tall pine trees, and under them was a carpet of cyclamen, casually in full bloom. I left in tears. Nick learnt some French, including 'baguette', which he shouted joyfully back home at a mystified Liverpudlian on a motorbike, who happened to have his fishing kit across the back, as a Frenchman carries the bread home for lunch. The following year we went almost to the Pyrenees, and a couple of years later, when Laurie was still a baby, we went to Léchiagat, a village in Finisterre. We stayed in a modern white Breton house with a slate roof. The beach was just down the road.

Laurie was particularly sleepless that summer. We found out why a couple of years later, but at the time we just thought he yelled a lot, especially in the evenings. This took a great deal of our attention, and my father worried about Nick's feelings.

Poor Laurie, suffering more than we realised, developed a special piercing shriek, and in a moment of expansiveness my father said one evening to Nick, 'He sounds just like a parrot. Shall we paint him green and stick feathers on him?'

Nick's response was enthusiastic. For some time afterwards, he would sidle up to my father and whisper hopefully.

To distract him, my father started telling him the story of the *Odyssey*. I saw then, with envy, his practical understanding of what a story needs, of the economy to be employed. I saw how he placed necessary details carefully but unobtrusively in the listener's mind. I saw the way he kept description to a minimum, making it serve the narrative. Poetry, if there at all, was carefully disguised by vigour.

Night after night, my father would point away into the distance, and Nick's eyes would follow, seeing not the white walls of the dining room, nor the sideboard with photos of old ladies in Breton costume, but the pink-tipped fingers of the dawn, the dark sea with oil holding the rough waves in a snood to calm them, the fights, the mysterious islands on the horizon, the tired, intelligent face of Odysseus at the helm of his boat. Nausicaa turned into a kind of Godolphin girl, very well brought up. Athene and the other gods were matter-of-fact, ruthless beings, no magic about them. They just walked in and out of the action at will, charismatic but daylight figures. There was a judicious amount of bloodshed. My father's practical sense – about boats, forging metal, about the way people lived, what they ate, what they wore – set the story in a completely believable world. Many years before, he had told me with scorn about one translator of

Homer who had used the phrase, 'a twi-handled chalice'. What the chap really meant, for God's sake, said my father, was a cup with two handles. That was the way he told the story to Nick. At the end of each evening's instalment, Nick would look around like someone emerging from the cinema. None of the books we brought could touch it.

So, as my father said about Alec, I find myself recognising that he mellowed. I have a grandchild myself, Nick's son, with his perfect little face and bright, round eyes. No doubt I am mellowing too. I wonder if Nick sees, with a flicker of jealousy, my capacity for loving his son. And then I think, Oh but of course we were far more patient, loving, focused on our children, than my parents were on theirs. I expect my father believed the same.

From 1967 onwards, the year of *Tenace*, it was difficult for him to find a novel to write. Between 1954 and 1967 he had published six, besides dozens of reviews and essays, and several plays, most for radio. Between 1967 and the late 1970s, the nearest he got to a novel was *The Scorpion God*, which was a collection of three short stories, one of which had already appeared in 1956. Finally, in 1979, after many years of doubt and misery, he published *Darkness Visible*, an enigmatic, colourful book about which he would say nothing.

My mother, that super-rational person, had a surprising gift. She would predict the future, but absent-mindedly, as if it had slipped her mind for a while and then turned up again like a lost dog. When *Darkness Visible* won the James Tait Black award, my father reacted superstitiously, refusing to show pleasure or pride in case they presaged a fall, as my grandmother might have hinted. My mother was dishing up the supper.

'Come on,' she said. 'This year the James Tait Black. Next year the Booker. Then the Nobel Prize.'

We all shushed her, shocked.

David had ostensibly recovered from his breakdown, or so we all wanted to believe. Psychoanalysis by a Freudian agnostic had been followed by his embracing the Catholic Church, my father not being the only contrary person in our family. In many ways religion was a helpful development for him, giving him a framework, a sense of belonging, and a belief in a loving father, albeit one in heaven. During the 1970s he gave away his Marxist books and took instruction from a priest, who told him – as no one else had done – that he really should have an occupation. 'Laborare est orare,' my father and I quoted to each other cheerily.

In August 1976, a few weeks before Nick's birth, David was christened and thus formally received into the Church. On the day of the service, my father drove morosely into Salisbury and bought him a sterling silver goblet. Later that morning my mother and I were discussing the situation over coffee. I was complacently aware of my status as the sceptical sibling – definitely the flavour of the month.

'After all,' I said, stirring my coffee, 'There has to be something rather odd about a religion whose chief symbol is an instrument of torture.'

My mother nodded thoughtfully.

We went to the service that evening. A bunch of resolutely Anglican agnostics, we were mystified by the Catholic custom of starting the hymn at first go, instead of waiting for the C. of E. two-line run-up. But we learnt quickly and gave it our best shot.

Later that evening, when my father and I were alone, he suddenly said to me, 'All this business of David's has finished religion for me, you know.'

Then he added, casually, 'When you come to think of it, there has to be something rather strange about a religion whose central emblem is an instrument of torture.'

I nodded silently. I was afraid I'd laugh if I said anything. It was a small insight into how careless he could be, not fearing in the least that I might pass this judgement on to my mother, from whom he'd appropriated it. Clearly, it had never occurred to him that it came from me. Rather flattering, really. At least no one said it to David.

But my father's journal shows that religion wasn't finished for him at all – his ideas on the subject had never been formalised, and that characteristic no doubt became more pronounced. His remark shows how his relationship with David made it hard for the two of them to think of themselves on the same side. It was like politics – when David was left-wing, my father posed as a re-actionary. They were perpetually at odds, even if this took some personal rearranging.

Over the next few years, as my own children grew, I had the chance to see behaviour in my father that offered me some un-derstanding of him. I saw his anxiety, and I realised how much tenderness he hid with his practised understatement. But David did not have the same chance.

When Nick was about two, we had announced to both sets of grandparents that our children would not be christened – at least not by us. My parents-in-law, whose unspoken hope had been that we would call our first son after his father and grandfather, charitably said nothing. My parents' reaction was characteristic as well. They went off and bought Nick a silver christening mug. But my father, embarrassed at the traditionalism of this gesture, added a saving touch of frivolity, much as he had advised me to put my wedding gift of five thousand pounds on a horse. He drew on the family passion for Georgette Heyer, telling me that I could think of the mug as having belonged to the first-born son of Judith Taverner and Lord Worth, from the novels *Regency Buck* and *An Infamous Army*. It was a good way of warning me that it was Regency silver, and not to be taken – as he said – to playgroup. But it also showed that her novels had created a world he enjoyed. He admired her language, and I strongly suspect that some of it went into the Sea Trilogy.

In May 1979, before the General Election, he and I managed to achieve an unusual, calm discussion about politics.

'Who do you think will win?' I asked.

'Labour,' my father said heavily.

I was thrilled. Hope surged back, despite all I knew.

'Why?'

He looked at me over his reading spectacles. Then he said, 'Because I think it'll be Mrs Thatcher, and I'm always wrong.'

Were we on the same side?

Later that year, a few months before Laurie's birth, Terrell got a job at the University of Bristol, and we moved into a nice Victorian semi in Redland, a prosperous suburb. My parents generously helped us with a bridging loan. We were happily settled, far away from Liverpool and my miseries there. All seemed set fair. Then, one day in May 1982, at ten o'clock in the morning, Laurie aged two and a half lay down on the kitchen floor and went to sleep. This would be unusual for most children. For mine, who fought sleep as if it was the end of the world, it was a symptom of catastrophe. I took him to our doctor, only to be surrounded by that sort of kindness that tells you something is dreadfully wrong. We were told to take him straight to the hospital for a blood test. At the hospital they told us, 'We don't do blood tests just before a bank holiday.' Then they looked more carefully at the piece of paper from the doctor. 'Oh,' they said. 'We'll do this one.'

All of a sudden I couldn't stop noticing things. His little legs were so thin; he was so pale. My Greek told me that leukaemia meant white blood. I was sure they would tell me this was their fear. But they gave no diagnosis. They said we could go away for the weekend. But we should check his breathing every few hours. If it speeded up we were to go to the nearest hospital.

Nick was already staying with my parents in Bowerchalke. I took Laurie down to Temple Meads to catch the train to Wiltshire. We got off at Warminster and my father met us. He took Laurie out of my arms and marched over the footbridge. Halfway across, he stopped. A train was coming. Laurie was beside himself with excitement and waved hysterically. At the barrier, I explained Laurie was too young to need a ticket. The guard, a young man, looked at him and gently tugged his foot.

'You're just trying to pretend he's under five,' he said.

My father smiled gratefully.

'Big for his age,' he said.

They were co-conspirators – my father, bored to tears by trains, none the less making sure Laurie had his share of them; the nice young man pretending he was well grown.

We got through the weekend somehow. When we rang up on the Tuesday, the hospital doctor hardly waited to hear Laurie's name. 'It's all right,' she said. 'I mean,' she added, 'it's not completely all right but we can fix it. He'll be OK.' He turned out to be suffering from an inflamed hiatus hernia, which – besides being very painful – made his stomach bleed. No wonder he had been so fretful. No wonder he was painfully thin.

If anyone else besides me burst into tears I never saw. In fact we all became slightly irritable, the reaction I suppose to being the best of ourselves for a whole weekend. Four months later, in early August, Laurie had a three-hour operation to repair his hernia.

My parents took David and Nick to France with them for the whole of that month, to stay in a beautiful old Breton house, la Ferme du Créac'h, where we had all spent the previous year's holiday. They made it a sort of finishing school for a five-year-old: painting, stories, archery, cricket, swimming. My father took charge of the swimming – heroically, since it was rather a cold summer. My mother told me he set Nick an unimpeachable example, dashing into the cold grey sea and stifling his gasps of pain. They took Nick shopping, they read the *Ladybird Book of Henry V* (chosen by Nick especially for its French interest), and they understood and coped with his occasional tempestuous outburst. Intermittently he slept but it was an exhausting time for them, and sterling work. We were supposed to join them when Laurie recovered, but he finished up in intensive care, a fact we did our best to hide from them, successfully I thought at the time.

Since my parents were quite unable to operate the French public telephones, they used to go into the hotel in Rosporden a few miles away, and ask them to phone us. When our landlady, Madame Lahuec, heard on the grapevine that her *locataires* had a grandchild in hospital, she turned up at the farm with an old carrier bag. Out of it she pulled a telephone, which she plugged into the wall.

'Faîtes comme chez vous,' she said and disappeared.

So my mother phoned me twice a day and I then phoned her back. Once she phoned me on the ward phone, and I had to get her off it without explaining that we were tying up the only line into intensive care.

They arrived back in Bristol one sunny day in early September. By then, Laurie was out of hospital but still pale and shocked, and still distressingly thin. When we told them how ill he had been, my father hardly turned a hair. He had guessed. My mother, uncharacteristically, asked for a glass of brandy. She was taken completely by surprise. I feel now they were both heroic, my mother concentrating on Nick so much that she never suspected the truth, my father hiding his suspicions from her, his confidante and usual source of reassurance.

My children called my father Bill. This was his choice – homage, I think, to Alec – but it's also true that granddad, grandpa and so on do not trip off the tongue as easily as grandma or granny. My children liked using his name, and I would sometimes hear them explaining to other children about their great-grandfather, about Alec.

One day Nick came back from playgroup looking worried, and said, 'Bill, are you my real grandfather?'

There must have been talk, perhaps suggesting he was some kind of step-relation. It was nothing to do with my father being a novelist – few people knew. In such situations, my father would reply politely to polite enquiries that he was a retired schoolteacher. But he recognised Nick's anxiety.

He looked at Nick, smiled, and said, 'Yes, Nick. I'm your real grandfather. You can tell anyone that straight from me.'

*

In April 1985, my parents moved house. They left the village they had known since 1940. They left their cottage, where they had made a happy return in 1958. Bowerchalke had changed. It became less and less a working village with farms and farm workers. It was no longer possible for young couples to buy a house in their own village unless they had extremely wealthy parents. Even renting was difficult. This changed the demographic. And economics changed the day's shape. In the 1960s, every morning at about seven thirty, when I was getting myself ready for school, we used to hear a long deep rumble as a farm tractor drove past our house. At some point in the 1980s this simply stopped. Things that had been useful became ornamental or disappeared. The village school closed, no doubt for sound educational reasons. The pub was sold and turned into a private house.

Some changes were long overdue. My mother used to look uncomfortably at the women knee-deep in the river, cutting the watercress with bare hands. For those of us who just looked, it was lovely – the water had to be kept clean and clear, and the winter sunlight sparkled on its coldness between the vivid green plants. Gradually, such picturesque, uncomfortable occupations disappeared, along with much of the harsh labouring on the land. Other crafts revived. Thatching came back in, along with the people with well-paid jobs in Salisbury or further afield, who liked the ruralness of a Norfolk-reed roof. The few young people of the village also had more comfortable and better-paid jobs, with homes no longer tied to their employment. But such change gave a dream-like quality to the place, as if everyone was in heaven. Besides, many of their Bowerchalke friends had died; others, like the extraordinary scientist James Lovelock, had decided to move away as well.

In 1976, the year before Tony Brown's death, my father gives a flavour of their life in the village:

At about one o'clock I rang Tony to thank him for helping us out with the Goodes, when he interrupted courteously as he was ringing the fire brigade to put out their chimney. We seized our fire extinguisher and rushed up to help: but already David Laity the thatcher was on the roof, and Roy and Iona were running round. So we stood on the lawn with the extinguisher at the ready until two fire engines with many flashing blue lights and firemen in huge helmets roared up (bell clanging) and parked outside the house. Then we sneaked away but had to drive right round via Ebbesbourne Wake because they filled the road. Exciting . . .

After Tony's death, life grew duller for many reasons. They had known each other since 1938, they played chess almost every day, and they talked music and philosophy. It was a rich friendship and its absence was a daily loss. My father said to me, 'the heart has gone out of Bowerchalke'.

A more mundane source of discomfort was the nearness of Bowerchalke to London. There were forays by journalists and others seeking a sight of my father. One year we were getting ready to go on holiday to France, loading the cars for the night ferry and running the children round the garden to tire them out. I noticed a young woman by the gate at the end of the drive. I assumed she wanted to know the way, or perhaps the time of the next bus.

She turned out to be a charming Spanish girl called Lourdes, writing a thesis on my distinguished father. She was very likeable, but I hardened my heart, pointing out that we were very busy and he was, in any case, indoors. At this unfortunate moment he appeared, shabbily dressed and wearing an old trilby in case he hit his head. He walked down the drive carrying several pairs of my mother's shoes and some masks and snorkels. Seeing someone whom he did not recognise but assumed to be a neighbour, he moved everything to one hand, and with the other raised his hat in a carefully graded gesture, courtly but generalised.

'Good evening.'

He dropped some shoes and I went to help him.

'Who's that?'

'Her name's Lourdes. She's a fan.'

'Oh God.'

I carefully didn't add that she was rather pretty, but in fairness I doubt that this would have made much difference. He took off at speed for the car, threw the stuff in, straightened up, hit his head and set off back to the house. I wandered back to the gate.

'Who was that?' said Lourdes in her fabulous intriguing accent.

'That was him,' I said ruthlessly.

To my irritation she turned pale. I resolved not to tell my father about that either. I had thought for quite some time that all this adulation, especially female adulation, was bad for him – and for his writing. I believed it was my job to keep his feet on the ground, to keep him in touch with his own frailty. Now I have read his journals, I understand I need not have tried so hard.

But this sort of incursion began to happen more often. Increasingly, those who arrived were less persuadable and far less likeable than Lourdes. They often had back-up. Sometimes photographers would arrive, often at the weekend, claiming that there had been an arrangement. My father, unable to phone Faber for confirmation, grumpily acquiesced. This gave the resulting photographs a brooding cosmic gloom that made them highly saleable. Some talented photographers, in cases where the appointment was acknowledged, had the wit to create that ambience themselves. Lord Snowdon told my father he had much enjoyed his novel *The Lord of the Rings*. The resultant portrait was a smasher.

His best revenge on such people would have been to assume an expression of pixieish glee, but this was beyond him unless he was actually happy. Some of the Nobel photos, for example, make him look tremendously cheerful, partly because he initially thought the prize money was only about twenty thousand. He was quite shocked when he found out the actual amount.

The money encouraged their plans to move, and they soon settled on Cornwall, spending some happy months driving round, half-believing they might buy things. One brilliant summer evening they drove across the heathland of North Cornwall, listening to *Così fan tutte* on the car radio. Newquay, Penzance, all the old, troubled associations, horrid grandmothers, encroaching bungalows, sea miseries – even their own personal shipwrecks – vanished. Eventually they bought the ravishing Tullimaar, a house about as different from 29 The Green as could be. They sold their Wiltshire cottage without a pang.

Before the move in 1985, I spent a day and a half helping them sort out the Bowerchalke cottage, with its heaped accretions from family life. We ordered skip after skip. We threw out masses of stuff. I felt pleased to kill the past, the house I'd never liked. But there, among my old dolls, some abandoned tents, old coat hangers, and piles of copies of the *Radio Times*, was Alec's dressing gown. I brought it down from the attic. It was full of moth, shredded and useless. I took it into the big room, the one that they had built to replace the old study and music room. It was also known as the new room – after all, it had been there only fifteen years. They were sitting looking at the soon-to-be forsaken view, a much-changed version (minus several elm trees, for example), of the prospect they had known since 1940. I suggested to them that it was time to throw the dressing gown away. They resisted, but I was uncharacteristically firm and they gave in. I put it in the skip. Later, I regretted my zeal, as I do still. I wish we had buried it, as we did not bury Alec.

I understood, then, that my parents' house would never become the new 29 The Green, with its forgotten treasures and hidden mysteries. No child of the future would riffle through their home, coming to an understanding of them bit by bit.

Besides, my father was too famous. It was hard to know – were we saving things for us, or for his archive?

On the Saturday night before I left, the three of us watched a television documentary about Antonio Stradivari. It described the way his violins had labels inside them, and how later makers painstakingly forged them, it being easier to fake the label than the violin. The next morning my father and I decided, for fun, to have a look at the old instruments up in the attic – Alec's three-quarter-size child's violin, my grandmother's viola and Alec's own violin, a good one which I know he loved. My grandmother had given it to him before they were married, when he was a paying guest in her mother's boarding house. I'd love to know how the Curnoes, with their boarding house and their tin mining, acquired such a fine instrument.

So my father and I went up to the attic, which had been my bedroom since the mid 1960s. I realised after some time that he had not sat down, because he was waiting as my guest to be asked. He sat, then, on the end of my bed, self-consciously. I opened the sliding cupboard door. In the early days birds had got in under the thatch. You could hear them bustling about. Sometimes there were more sinister leapings and thumps that Terrell said were mice or even rats. But now all was quiet. I took out the old cases, dusty but nothing worse.

We considered them. The years of silence about Alec were over, but there was still reserve. I took out his violin and laid it on the bed. Then I squinted through one of the f-holes. On the inside of the back of the instrument I could see a piece of paper. I could read it. *Faciebat*. It was as the programme had said – and it even had a handwritten date.

We collapsed with laughter. What would the Browns think? No more *Taté-Lylé* now. More soberly, we agreed it must be a fake, a good fake but a fake. Later that day I took the Sunday train back to Bristol, Alec's three-quarter-size fiddle on my knee. I was going to get it restored in case one of the children liked the idea of playing it. But I left the full-size one behind. The matter was too complex, and my father's feelings had been harder to read even than usual. He did not seem as excited as I had been, though he had laughed, possibly more than I had.

A year or so after his death I took the various instruments to be valued at a local violin shop in Bristol. When I went back, I half expected to be told we were all now millionaires. But they only *quite* liked the three-quarter-size, and not its earlier restoration at all, done by the competitor across the road. They hated my grandfather's ancient cello (it was not even *Taté-Lylé*, it was another dreadful instrument). The shop owner said it looked as if the village carpenter had knocked it up by copying a violin. They more or less ignored the poor old orange viola. Then the chap took up Alec's old fiddle, given him in Newquay nearly a century earlier. He held it solicitously. This was not accidental. He felt sorry for it.

'I thought I'd really found something with this. Look at the back and the sides. And the varnish.'

He gently tapped it with the soft part of a fingertip. I knew this was too good.

'But look at the front. Not the same wood, inferior work, hopeless. Someone's botched it, repaired it and botched it. Poor old thing.'

I looked up at him, and then at the dark, unshiny, coarse-grained wood of the violin's belly. Now I noticed that the lip at the edge wasn't smooth like the one on the back. It had ridges where the broad grain had been ineptly chosen.

'But it's only a fake, isn't it?'

He smiled and said nothing. I paid him his modest fee in cash. He offered to buy the three-quarter, but I felt we should keep all of them now I knew they weren't valuable. Except for the cello, they are in a cellar, away from the central heating. The cello is in my father's room at Tullimaar, as it was in his lifetime.

Then I read two things. I read the section in *The Pyramid* where Oliver smashes the family piano with his fist, right between the candle-holders. And I read a cryptic announcement in my father's adolescent diary. It has lines of space before and after.

'The fact that the violin has been broken has been discovered.'

My father, aged sixteen, had put his fist through the front of my grandfather's cherished violin. Maybe a Stradivarius, maybe not. But he had apparently been forgiven.

17

Yesterday

My father was forty in 1951. I was six. I asked him, apparently, if he was going to die soon. His reply, to my sorrow, does not survive. A little later, he told me carefully that he had got happier and happier throughout his life, and was now happier than he had ever been.

Later, when I was an adult, he sometimes said to me that he would be happy to die. It would make room, he said, and he meant it, for somebody else.

One day in 1982, he was driving my mother and me back from shopping in Salisbury. The car by then was a large Jaguar lined with beige leather. It felt like a hovercraft, as if something big and soft lay between you and the outside world, a cushion not of air but money.

I was making conversation, one of the duties and accomplishments of a Godolphin girl, even one in her thirties. I looked out of the window for inspiration. I had already commented on the weather, the architecture, the buses. Then I noticed the hedgerows, whitened with the silky seed-heads of wild clematis.

'The old man's beard is very fine this year.'

'Thank you,' he replied.

A year or so after the move to Tullimaar, in 1985, it stopped being a joke.

First, my mother slowed up drastically. She had put on weight, and since her mastectomy in 1976 had given up taking any real exercise. My father found it hard even to get her to walk with him round the garden. She gave up driving. She asked people to fetch things for her, everywhere, not just from upstairs. My father brought her breakfast in bed every morning. When we stayed at Tullimaar, I would find that he had put out two sets of breakfast things by about nine o'clock at night.

In their Cornish house, David once again acquired a room of his own. But by that time Terrell and I had three children and a wagonload of luggage. So our arrival was rarer and came with suitable advance warning. We had the status of proper, adult visitors, and were given the guest room (south- and east-facing with two large Georgian windows), complete with ensuite bathroom, a small brass plaque commemorating Eisenhower's stay there before D-Day, and (in winter) the view through the trees towards Restronguet Creek, described by Francis Kilvert the diarist, who stayed in the house in 1870. The first time I was there I developed flu and assumed my memory of the house's beauties was the result of fever. Next time I visited, in perfect health, I found it was just the same.

I can see now from my father's journal that our arrival at Tullimaar was described as a blessing, but mingled in truth with a sense of impending fatigue, and a need to treat the whole thing like a military operation, especially feeding the troops.

While I was unpacking in our room, with its white cornice and folding shutters, my father would knock gently on the door and bring me a freshly poured flute of champagne. Ironically, it was a drink we both disliked, thinking the bubbles a silly distraction from the serious business of consuming wine. But it was the mark of the occasion and his hospitality. I look at that door nowadays, half expecting the sound of his knock and the entry of that figure, white beard, cardigan, smile of welcome. It still pushes through me a familiar jolt of loss.

He was still lively, light-footed and agile. He climbed up and down ladders. He bought a small scaffolding tower, which he used to strip ivy off the yards and yards of stone walls, some ten feet high, around the garden. And he shot around the house as he had always done.

In 1987 we were all at Tullimaar for the summer half-term. Friends of ours turned up with their two sons. The day turned into cricket out on the meadow, the big sloping expanse of grass to the west of the house. We were all playing, even – miraculously – my mother, which shows how seriously she took cricket. My youngest son Roger, three and a half, got bored and wandered off. I kept him in sight as the cricket continued, my father bowling, the four elder boys taking it in turns to bat, and the rest of us fielding, trying to prevent the precious leather cricket ball being lost among the rhododendrons.

But Roger was suddenly right at the edge of the meadow. I walked towards him. Then, unbelievably, I saw him start to sink into the ground, in the shrubbery. I ran. And out of the corner of my eye I saw my father break into a fantastic sprint. In less than half a minute he reached my small son and grabbed him, as the ground continued to crumble. Roger just had time to be frightened. But what he remembers most is the feeling of my father's arms pulling him, lifting him, out of the hole. My father was not even out of breath. He was seventy-five.

He had always walked fast. It was a challenge – not, perhaps, on the way to Old Sarum or Martinsell, when I was still very young. But from the age of about eight I became used to forcing my short legs to keep up with him, three then two steps to his one. Then, during those last years – he was seventy-nine perhaps, or eighty – we were in Truro, walking through one of the little granite-walled passages off River Street, doing some shopping. I accelerated as I usually did with him. After a while he stopped, and of course I did too.

'I'm sorry, darling. I can't keep up with you.'

So we arrive at June 1993.

There is a handsome room, a hall with a Regency staircase. A party is in progress. The room is crowded and people are drinking champagne. Although it is after nine at night the room is still full of daylight. Sun strikes down from the westerly windows. A group of four people stand and talk. One of them, a pretty, light-voiced woman, is talking to a white-haired, bearded man. He is courtly, hostly. He wears a grey suit and a brilliant red silk bow tie. She wants him to have a typing contest with her husband. Another in the group, a younger woman, ill at ease, says with sudden, sharp laughter, 'Yes, you could see how long it took you to write Shakespeare's Sonnets.' 'Thank you,' says the bearded man to his daughter, getting the joke and not at all grateful.

The group drifts in the current of people, but keeps together. The light is going, and the old glass in the windows no longer shows the folds and faults and strange colours of its age. Once, when my father was in bed with a cold, he told me he had just watched an aeroplane slide *backwards*, in one of these faults, across a pane in his window. There will be time later, I think, to say I'm sorry about my stupid joke. The other man observes, silently. They drift again, into another room. The light-voiced woman and the bearded man sit down to supper. I think to myself, I can talk to him any time. I mustn't ask for his attention now.

Eventually, the party almost over, and the house emptying its crowd into the June midnight, a few of us stay in the dining room. My mother has gone to bed, as have my parents-in-law, guests for the weekend. We sit, my brother, my father and I, with the silent, observing man, now quite talkative. Someone mentions Dido's lament. Don Thomas sings it, accurately and quietly. 'Is it in G minor?' I ask, making conversation but also showing off. 'I don't know,' says he. Still in party mode, I tell everyone that when we went to Santiago di Compostela and arrived in the huge square in front of the cathedral, the loudspeakers were playing 'Yesterday', by the Beatles.

'I have never heard "Yesterday",' says my dad.

David, my brother, begins to sing. He has a nice light tenor voice when he relaxes enough. Don Thomas joins in with his lovely voice. I add my much lesser one, and we sing until the tune moves too high and sadly but predictably my voice cracks. There is a tactful pause.

My father recites a poem by Ronsard about the soul – a translation of 'Animula, vagula, blandula' by the emperor Hadrian. There are more pauses as we sip some Rioja. Then, Don asks, 'What would you say to each other if you knew you would never meet again?' I say, still thinking of my stupid crack about the sonnets, that I had always wanted to be like my father, but I never could because I was a girl.

'Nonsense,' says my father and Don, both of them rather briskly. David doesn't say anything. He probably agrees with me.

Then, Don turns to my father.

'What would you say to Judy?' he asks.

Daddy looks at me, and puts his large, warm hand on the back of my neck and rubs it as if he knew there was a pain there. 'Love,' he says. 'Just love.'

A perfect ending – for me, at any rate. There was no word for David, though I failed to notice that at the time. But it was not the end. My father drank too much of the Rioja I had stupidly opened. Don left. My mother emerged from her bedroom, angry with my father for drinking. We walked him up the stairs, and halfway up he stumbled. He swung dangerously against the banisters. They seem a robust barrier when you look at them but actually they are fragile – he could have broken through them and fallen ten or twelve feet to the floor below. And apparently I cried out to someone to help me – I wasn't strong enough to hold him. David came and we got him safely up the stairs. I know I cried out because Laurie, my son, remembers it. He was in bed on the other side of the wall, and heard everything. Next morning, he was the only one of us not surprised. He believed my father had died then.

Daddy went into the bathroom and we waited outside, uneasily. After a while I decided to go in. He was kneeling on the floor, a look of great surprise on his face. David asked him something and my father responded angrily. David pursed his lips and turned away. My mother once more showed her irritation. My father, quick as a flash, got in the bath, lay down and folded his arms so that he looked like a tomb effigy. My mother, more furious still, and foreseeing a long, troubled night – it was already gone two – turned on the tap. I turned it off again.

Then Terrell said, 'You go to bed. And your mother. I'll put him to bed next door in David's room, and David can sleep in the room at the back.'

I looked at him.

'Go on. He'll carry on like this while the two of you are around.'

So I went to bed. About half an hour later Terrell came to bed and went to sleep. But I couldn't sleep. For some reason I was troubled. I read David Cecil's *Early Victorian Novelists*, the section about the Brontës, and eventually at about four I too went to sleep.

I had an extraordinary dream. I dreamt that I could write, now, about anything. At last my mind, my imagination, could roam wherever it wanted. All the fetters were gone. Curiously, my dream took me back to the Victorian streets of Liverpool, where Terrell and I had lived fifteen years earlier. There were lines of terrace houses, small, impoverished, and opening straight on to the street. There was an old corner shop on the street, built at the same time as the rest, of the same dullish red stone, like you get in Cheshire. But the windows of the shop were a strange bluey-purple. I could see the colour vividly. I knew with dream logic that I could write, daringly, even about that.

The next morning Terrell was up early as usual. Searching for a task, he took our free glass tokens along to the petrol station, returning with a dozen highball glasses. Later, at about ten, my mother said to Terrell, 'You'd better take him up a cup of tea.'

I went upstairs as well, to make the bed. After a few minutes Terrell appeared. He looked puzzled.

'It's very strange. He's on the floor.'

I said (what made me say this?), 'Is he alive?'

Terrell replied, 'I think so.'

I went to look. As soon as I saw him, I knew. The blood had sunk down and was left in great whorls under the skin, surrounded by white flesh. I touched his thigh and it was utterly cold, cold like a joint of meat.

Terrell stayed there in case my mother or the children wandered in. I went to get Terrell's father, a doctor. I could see in his face that even he was not used to death. Perhaps one never is. But he braced himself, professionally, ready to deal with it.

He and Terrell were going to lift the body on to the bed, and Terrell said to his father, 'I'm not sure if I can do this.'

Terrell's father was a man of extraordinarily few words. When he did speak, he sounded rather like John Wayne.

'Oh yes, you can,' he replied.

And they did.

The duty doctor arrived, and then, later in the day, the coroner's constable, because the death was sudden and there would have to be a post mortem. I had cried so much that I was sick, and I was lying on the floor outside the kitchen, with a pudding basin beside me, just like the one years ago in *Wild Rose*. I saw the policeman's serge trousers, the large and shiny shoes. I scrambled to my feet. Then my mother arrived.

'Mummy,' I said, while I read his name tag.

My voice flew like a homing pigeon to Godolphin.

'This is Sergeant Pascoe, the coroner's constable.'

Then I turned to him.

'This is my mother, Lady Golding.'

They shook hands, and she ushered him hospitably into the drawing room. You could see him thinking, Say what you like about the gentry, they pull themselves together. My father would have been pleased.

They took his body away in a specially adapted hearse with an invisible compartment. To the innocent eye, it looked empty. As it disappeared down the drive and turned out of sight, I thought, Well, at least he never had to leave Tullimaar. I think even then I guessed my mother would have to.

Within the family, we debated what had happened during those hours of the early morning. Soon, I was fairly sure. He slept heavily for a few hours because of the wine, and woke about four o'clock, a little sobered. He got up to go to the loo next door, and when he came back, his attention was caught by the view from the window, opposite the door. It faces east, a seven-foot space of glass, twelve panes from floor to ceiling.

It was midsummer. He had never slept in that room before, never seen the dawn come up behind those beeches, trees as big and green, as grey and gold, as the ones in Savernake Forest near Marlborough, where he walked as a child. He sat on the sofa facing the window, and he died there, perhaps quietly, I don't know. Then his hands slipped down into his lap, and his enormous head nodded on to his unmoving chest. Eventually, the weight of that head pulled him over, and we found him there, on the floor, knees bent, head on the carpet, hands underneath him. But, before that, he must have sat upright, dead, immobile, silent, for so long that the blood sank to those fingertips. They were bluey-purple, the colour of the older window panes at Tullimaar, the colour of the windows in my strange dream.

Life became different. There was a mass of accounting stuff that I didn't understand. There was a constant need for food, though one disliked it. A daily trial was that not one single, solitary ballpoint pen in the entire house would work. Eventually I stopped screaming at them or jumping up and down on them. I went and bought a hundred more. Years before, I had given my father a similar pack – perilously, since it was in the 'silent' period. I remember him laughing. I had carelessly thought that he would like some pens, and – as he did – I adored buying stationery. But I had made a faux pas, a dreadful thing in our family, something that had to be repaired with much effort. He pulled himself together, generously.

'Actually,' he said, 'this house has a biro-shaped hole . . .'

Two days after the death, my mother had a stroke. When we

wheeled her, slumped and grief-laden, into the church at Bower-chalke, a gasp of horror rose from the congregation.

Afterwards, we gathered around the deep trench in the church-yard. I saw two things. First, there was a small brass plaque on the top of the coffin and it said William Golding. I understood, then, that the large warm figure, sober, drunk, laughing, frightening, in the grey raincoat, the oilskin, the suit, the rather unwashed sweater, the silk dressing gown – he was gone, his pathetic remains unimaginable. Second, I had just become the head of the family. It was up to me to take a handful of Wiltshire soil, and throw it down on the wooden shape my father had feared and loathed all his life.

Soon after the funeral, Terrell went back to Bristol. I stayed at Tullimaar.

A few days later, David came up to me. I was busy, and took care that I should seem so.

'Have you seen my grey trousers?'

I replied that I had not.

'Oh.'

I created for myself a voice of exasperated patience.

'Where did you have them last?'

'I put them in my room. On the back of the little chair with the green seat.'

He had moved back into that room quite soon, untroubled by the thought of death in it. I went to look. There were no grey trousers. The remaining pair had been put away by the house-keeper, Mrs Humphries, with appropriate reverence. I went to check. Yes, it was clear they were his and not David's.

'I don't remember seeing your trousers. Just the two pairs belonging to Daddy.'

David thought for a moment. Then he said, 'Are you sure he had two pairs?'

I was too angry to reply. I went straight into my mother's room, ruthlessly interrupting her misery.

'Didn't Daddy have two pairs of grey trousers to go with his suit? The one he was wearing at the party?'

My mother looked at me drearily, with familial dislike, rather I expect as I had looked at David.

'No.'

We had buried my father in David's trousers.

Months later, my mother and I were sitting together in the library, while the rain of that autumn – the first season without him – rattled on the windows and drenched the garden.

She suddenly said to me, 'I know you always thought Daddy loved you more than I did. But I *did* love you. I just couldn't show it.'

Acknowledgements

One of the attractions for me in writing this memoir has been the tantalising prospect of bringing my father to life again. That may be why it has taken so long. I have tried to be honest, telling the good and the bad and not choosing between them. And I have tried to be disciplined about the material to be included. I could have written three times as much. Mainly, I sought answers to two questions: first, why did my father become a writer, and, I believe, such a good one? And, second, to what extent do parents shape their children, and their children's lives? Unsurprisingly, my answers to both are incomplete.

I have incurred many debts, and I am sorry that so many of those who have helped me are no longer alive to receive my thanks. John Bodley of Faber and Faber first suggested to me, in 1993, that I might write this book. The current staff at Faber have been patient, supportive and encouraging, particularly Stephen Page, Julian Loose, Rachel Alexander and Angus Cargill. In addition, Julian has been a gifted and imaginative editor. I am grateful to him and to Kate Murray-Browne for their suggestions. I am much indebted as well to Trevor Horwood for his thorough and knowledgeable care of my text.

Many other professionals, especially librarians and archivists, have helped me. My thanks for help are due to Stuart Bailey, Archivist at the University of Oxford, and Elizabeth Boardman, Archivist of Brasenose College, Oxford. I am grateful to Suzanne Mainzer and the Anthroposophical Society of Great Britain, the staff of the BBC Written Archive, the staff of Bristol Central Library, the staff of the Library of the University of Bristol, Anna Manthorpe and the East Sussex County Record Office, Vic Gray, formerly of Faber and Faber, and Robert Brown, his successor as archivist, Christian Maclean and Floris Books, Rick Gekoski, the staff at Kent County Library, Robert Machesney and the Macmillan Archives, the head teacher and staff of Maidstone Grammar School as well as many former pupils, the head teacher and staff of St

John's Comprehensive School, Marlborough (formerly Marlborough Grammar School), the headmaster and staff, in particular John Cox, of Bishop Wordsworth's School, Salisbury, Penelope Bulloch, Librarian of Balliol College, Oxford, Georgina Ferry and *Oxford Today*, Andrew Whitmarsh and the D-Day Museum, Portsmouth, the Naval Records Branch of the Public Record Office, Tanya Tilbury and the *Salisbury Journal*, Trowbridge Reference Library, Rosemary Tweddle and the Savile Club, London, the staff at Sydney House, 21 Bourne Avenue, Salisbury, the staff at Truro Public Library, and the staff at Wiltshire County Record Office. Thanks are due to the staff at Barclay's Bank in Truro and Clifton, Bristol. I am very glad also to thank Anne Hardy and her assistants and Sally Rees for transcribing my father's huge journal, and Roger Clements for photocopying it. Malcolm Manwaring found me vital books. Tim Kendall helped me with a question concerning my father's poem quoted in Chapter 14, and he and Camille Fort have encouraged me by their scholarly interest in William Golding. Anna Keeling has been a calm and clear-sighted ally.

The headmistress of Godolphin School, Salisbury, has given me permission to quote from the Godolphin School prayer.

Extracts from William Golding's unpublished writings, including his journal, appear by permission of William Golding Limited.

The following people answered my queries and/or gave me help: Cecily Beeching, Arthur and Joyce Bowden, Françoise Bowyer, David and Gillian Bromige, Fiona Brown, Tim Brown, Julia Burcombe, Nancy Butler, Hugh Cecil, Glenn Collett, Linda Coombs, Ron Teague Curnoe and Olga Curnoe, Brian Curnoe, Caroline Dawnay, Cyril Eyre, Pamela Gravett, Sally Hallam, John Harries, Norman Hidden, Doreen Humphries, Jill King, Stephen Medcalf, Hamish Milne, Betty Morris, Dr Michael Moss, Peter Mosse, Sue Mullaly, Peter de Paris, J. A. C. Pearce, Denis Price, Gordon Purdy, Craig Raine, Alistair Ross, Lilian Ross, Gill and Dom Shirley, David Stedman, Ken Stiles, Jim (Mike) Thorrowgood, Virginia Tiger, Michael Tillett, Kenneth and Ann Walsh, Tim Warren, Lyn Weeks, Caroline Wynburne, and Liz and Wayland Young.

Mrs Vivien Clark and her husband Nigel made me welcome at 29 The Green, Marlborough. Mrs Stella Hornby gave me the freedom of my parents' former garden at Bowerchalke. Vicky and Robert Payne of the Blenheim Hotel, 47 Mount Wise, Newquay, my father's birthplace, have always been welcoming. Mr and Mrs R. Naas, of May Street, Kingswood, Bristol, hospitably allowed me to see the house in Bristol where my grandfather lived as a young man. Their neighbour Grace Manners was helpful as well. My aunt Joan Crisp, with charm and determination, managed to get us into the former Brookfield family home in Maidstone. Tony Davies, Doreen Humphries, Dave Kemp, Noel Kingsbury, Andrea Nias, Tim Price, David Reed and Birgit Wiedwald have helped to preserve Tullimaar and its memories.

My parents' siblings and their wives and husbands – Eileen Hogben, Theo Golding, Richard and Joy Brookfield, Marion Brookfield, Joan Crisp, Betty and Maurice Chesner, and Stuart Brookfield – have helped me with information and encouragement. I should like to thank my cousins, pre-eminently Ann Harrison and Elizabeth Hogben, for their companionship and encouragement. Also Adrian Harrison, Judith and Julian Wardlaw, Suzanne Segal, Alison and Robert Abbey, Ralph and Moira Brookfield, Alison Golding, John Golding, and Ian and Mary Chesner. My thanks are also due to Mary Chesner for a crucial reminder.

Many friends have listened patiently and encouraged me, particularly Sheila and Mike Shevlin, Zuzana and Martin Crouch, Valerie Jones, Diana and James Wetz, Bonnie Hurren and Rob Meech, and Judith and Martin Rieser. Belinda Wingfield Digby has optimistically believed this book would emerge. Davina Williams gave me excellent advice. Jessica Mann and Charles Thomas, Maggie Weber, Gilbert and Maryke Horobin, and Perle Besserman all made me feel that the book was worth writing, as did several members of the Bristol Phoenix Choir. Donald Shell gave me important encouragement in 1993. Vernon Hewitt drew my attention to various works on memoir and autobiography. Geoffrey Pridham and John Forester shared with me their own stories. Paulette Anderson, Diana Bulman and Anne Clune were good friends during our years at Sussex and afterwards as well. Roger Clements helped with my research, and with my father's journal, and has consistently encouraged me about this book. Dinah Cannell discussed many of the book's themes with me, and in addition shed light on my father's ideas through her examination of the French translation of his first novel. Terrell Carver read the typescript at a late stage and made many helpful suggestions based on his long intimacy with the Golding family. Peter Green helped me with his knowledge of my father's life and also with his affection and respect for my father. Laurie Carver gave me excellent advice on how to structure the book.

John Carey, in writing such a brilliant biography of my father, gave me the freedom to write my own book. He and his wife Gill have been encouraging and generous in our joint pursuit of Golding. In particular, I should like to thank them and Wendy Holmes, the niece of Mollie Evans, for an account of Mollie's later life.

My thanks are due to Ellen Hart for her help. Glenys James has provided the circumstances in which I could at last complete this book. Ane Christensen has been amused by our family stories, and showed me they were worth telling. I am grateful to my three sons Nick, Laurie and Roger Carver for their love, and their enjoyment of life. My brother David has generously allowed me the freedom to describe our lives together. For many years Pamela Trevithick has helped me look clearly at the past. She has been joined in this uphill task by her partner Charlotte Paterson, and I thank them both.

Finally, turning towards the future, I should like to dedicate this book to Viggo, with love from his grandmother.

Illustrations

Photos without attribution are from the Golding family archive